# COMMUNITY LISTENING: STORIES, HAUNTINGS, POSSIBILITIES

# PERSPECTIVES ON WRITING

Series Editors: Rich Rice and J. Michael Rifenburg
Consulting Editor: Susan H. McLeod
Associate Editors: Johanna Phelps, Jonathan M. Marine, and Qingyang Sun

The Perspectives on Writing series addresses writing studies in a broad sense. Consistent with the wide ranging approaches characteristic of teaching and scholarship in writing across the curriculum, the series presents works that take divergent perspectives on working as a writer, teaching writing, administering writing programs, and studying writing in its various forms.

The WAC Clearinghouse and University Press of Colorado are collaborating so that these books will be widely available through free digital distribution and low-cost print editions. The publishers and the series editors are committed to the principle that knowledge should freely circulate and have embraced the use of technology to support open access to scholarly work.

## Recent Books in the Series

Steven J. Corbett (Ed.), *If at First You Don't Succeed? Writing, Rhetoric, and the Question of Failure* (2024)

Ryan J. Dippre and Talinn Phillips (Eds.), *Improvisations: Methods and Methodologies in Lifespan Writing Research* (2024)

Ashley J. Holmes and Elise Verzosa Hurley (Eds.), *Learning from the Mess: Method/ological Praxis in Rhetoric and Writing Studies* (2024)

Diane Kelly-Riley, Ti Macklin, and Carl Whithaus (Eds.), *Considering Students, Teachers, and Writing Assessment: Volumes 1 and 2* (2024)

Amy Cicchino and Troy Hicks (Eds.), *Better Practices: Exploring the Teaching of Writing in Online and Hybrid Spaces* (2024)

Genesea M. Carter and Aurora Matzke (Eds.), *Systems Shift: Creating and Navigating Change in Rhetoric and Composition Administration* (2023)

Michael J. Michaud, *A Writer Reforms (the Teaching of) Writing: Donald Murray and the Writing Process Movement, 1963–1987* (2023)

Michelle LaFrance and Melissa Nicolas (Eds.), *Institutional Ethnography as Writing Studies Practice* (2023)

Phoebe Jackson and Christopher Weaver (Eds.), *Rethinking Peer Review: Critical Reflections on a Pedagogical Practice* (2023)

Megan J. Kelly, Heather M. Falconer, Caleb L. González, and Jill Dahlman (Eds.), *Adapting the Past to Reimagine Possible Futures: Celebrating and Critiquing WAC at 50* (2023)

# COMMUNITY LISTENING: STORIES, HAUNTINGS, POSSIBILITIES

Edited by Jenn Fishman, Romeo García, and Lauren Rosenberg

The WAC Clearinghouse
wac.colostate.edu
Fort Collins, Colorado

University Press of Colorado
upcolorado.com
Denver, Colorado

The WAC Clearinghouse, Fort Collins, Colorado 80524

University Press of Colorado, Denver, Colorado 80203

© 2025 by Jenn Fishman, Romeo García, and Lauren Rosenberg. This work is licensed under a Creative Commons Attribution-NonCommercial-NoDerivatives 4.0 International license.

ISBN 978-1-64215-253-1 (PDF) 978-1-64215-254-8 (ePub) 978-1-64642-737-6 (pbk.)

DOI 10.37514/PER-B.2025.2531

Library of Congress Cataloging-in-Publication Data

Names: Fishman, Jenn, editor. | García, Romeo, 1987– editor. | Rosenberg, Lauren, 1987– editor.
Title: Community listening : stories, hauntings, possibilities / edited by Jenn Fishman, Romeo García, and Lauren Rosenberg.
Description: Fort Collins, Colorado : The WAC Clearinghouse, [2025] | Series: Perspectives on writing | Includes bibliographical references and index.
Identifiers: LCCN 2025002774 (print) | LCCN 2025002775 (ebook) | ISBN 9781646427376 (paperback) | ISBN 9781642152531 (adobe pdf) | ISBN 9781642152548 (epub)
Subjects: LCSH: Storytelling—Social aspects—Case studies. | Listening—Social aspects—Case studies. | Communities—Case studies.
Classification: LCC PN4193.I5 C66 2025  (print) | LCC PN4193.I5  (ebook) | DDC 302.2— dc23/eng/20250527
LC record available at https://lccn.loc.gov/2025002774
LC ebook record available at https://lccn.loc.gov/2025002775

Copyeditor: Caitlin Kahihikolo
Designer: Mike Palmquist
Cover Photo: "You Talk Too Much," monoprint (2018) by Ella Hepner.Used with permission.
Series Editors: Rich Rice and J. Michael Rifenburg
Consulting Editor: Susan H. McLeod
Associate Editors: Johanna Phelps, Jonathan M. Marine, and Qingyang Sun

The WAC Clearinghouse supports teachers of writing across the disciplines. Hosted by Colorado State University, it brings together scholarly journals and book series as well as resources for teachers who use writing in their courses. This book is available in digital formats for free download at wac.colostate.edu.

Founded in 1965, the University Press of Colorado is a nonprofit cooperative publishing enterprise supported, in part, by Adams State University, Colorado School of Mines, Colorado State University, Fort Lewis College, Metropolitan State University of Denver, University of Alaska Fairbanks, University of Colorado, University of Denver, University of Northern Colorado, University of Wyoming, Utah State University, and Western Colorado University. For more information, visit upcolorado.com.

**Citation Information:** Fishman, Jenn, Romeo García & Lauren Rosenberg (Eds.). (2025). *Community Listening: Stories, Hauntings, Possibilities.* The WAC Clearinghouse; University Press of Colorado. https://doi.org/1010.37514/PER-B.2025.2531

**Land Acknowledgment.** The Colorado State University Land Acknowledgment can be found at landacknowledgment.colostate.edu.

# CONTENTS

Acknowledgments . . . . . . . . . . . . . . . . . . . . . . . . . . . . . . . . . . . . . . . vii

Editors' Introduction . . . . . . . . . . . . . . . . . . . . . . . . . . . . . . . . . . . . . .3
    *Jenn Fishman, Romeo García, and Lauren Rosenberg*

PART 1. HAUNTINGS AND POSSIBILITIES . . . . . . . . . . . . . . . . . . . . 27

Chapter 1. Getting Closer to Mass Incarceration: Proximate Listening
as Community Activism . . . . . . . . . . . . . . . . . . . . . . . . . . . . . . . . . . .29
    *Sally F. Benson*

Chapter 2. Crafting Crip Space through Disabled Political Advocacy:
#CripTheVote as Community Listening . . . . . . . . . . . . . . . . . . . . . .47
    *Ada Hubrig*

Chapter 3. Keeping Bad Company: "Listening" to Aryan Nations
in the Archives . . . . . . . . . . . . . . . . . . . . . . . . . . . . . . . . . . . . . . . . . .69
    *Patty Wilde, Mitzi Ceballos, and Wyn Andrews Richards*

PART 2. STORIES OF SUSTAINING COMMUNITY . . . . . . . . . . . . . . . 91

Chapter 4. The Public Art of Listening: Relational Accountability
and The Painted Desert Project . . . . . . . . . . . . . . . . . . . . . . . . . . . .93
    *Kyle Boggs*

Chapter 5. The DJ as Relational Listener and Creator of an Ethos
of Community Listening . . . . . . . . . . . . . . . . . . . . . . . . . . . . . . . . . 117
    *Karen R. Tellez-Trujillo*

Chapter 6. Listening In: Letter Writing and Rhetorical Resilience
Behind Bars . . . . . . . . . . . . . . . . . . . . . . . . . . . . . . . . . . . . . . . . . . . 135
    *Alexandra J. Cavallaro, Wendy Hinshaw, and Tobi Jacobi*

PART 3. NEGOTIATING SELF AND COMMUNITY . . . . . . . . . . . . . . 153

Chapter 7. Civic Community Listening: The Nexus of Storytelling
and Listening within Civic Communities . . . . . . . . . . . . . . . . . . . . 155
    *Bailey M. Oliver-Blackburn, April Chatham-Carpenter,*
    *and Carol L. Thompson*

v

Contents

Chapter 8. Community Listening In, With, and Against Whiteness
at a PWI. . . . . . . . . . . . . . . . . . . . . . . . . . . . . . . . . . . . . . . . . . . . . . . . . . 177
  *Mary P. Sheridan, Cate Fosl, Kelly Kinahan, Carrie Mott,*
  *Angela Storey, and Shelley Thomas*

Chapter 9. On Being In It . . . . . . . . . . . . . . . . . . . . . . . . . . . . . . . . . . . 199
  *Katie W. Powell*

Chapter 10. Daunting Community Listening: Designing and
Implementing a Community Listening Framework and Accountability
Group for Undergraduate Students . . . . . . . . . . . . . . . . . . . . . . . . . . . . 217
  *Keri Epps and Rowie Kirby-Straker with Casey Beiswenger,*
  *Zoe Chamberlin, Hannah Hill, Lauren Robertson, and*
  *Kaitlyn Taylor*

Contributors . . . . . . . . . . . . . . . . . . . . . . . . . . . . . . . . . . . . . . . . . . . . . . 249

Index . . . . . . . . . . . . . . . . . . . . . . . . . . . . . . . . . . . . . . . . . . . . . . . . . . . . 255

# ACKNOWLEDGMENTS

This book has many beginnings. One of them dates back to Tuesday, October 29th, 2019, at 4:17 p.m. Mountain/5:17 p.m. Central. That's when Romeo emailed Lauren and Jenn:

> Hi Lauren and Jenn,
>
> Hope all is well. Thank you for reading my short piece.
>
> I was thinking about the importance of community listening the other day and began wondering whether an edited collection is in the works already for it. If not, would both or one of you be interested in chatting about such a collection?
>
> rg

The "short piece" Romeo refers to is "Creating Presence from Absence and Sound from Silence," which appeared in *Community Writing, Community Listening*, the special issue of *Community Literacy Journal* that Jenn and Lauren co-edited.

The seed for that publication, and thus a seed for this book, was planted more than two years earlier, on April 30th, 2017, when Jenn wrote to Lauren somewhat out of the blue with "a wild hair of an idea." She was following up on a brief conversation they had that spring during the Community Writing Mentoring Workshop at the Conference on College Composition and Communication annual convention; she was also responding to a call for proposals that Veronica House had circulated. The latter invited colleagues planning to attend the fall 2017 Conference on Community Writing to put forward ideas for a related issue of *Community Literacy Journal*, which House had just begun co-editing with Paul Feigenbaum.

On May 25th of that year, Jenn and Lauren met online to talk and listen. They didn't really know one another at the time and had mainly interacted through a few conference events; however, there was much to discuss, especially when they began brainstorming special issue possibilities. Their wide-ranging conversation spanned longitudinal writing research, their appreciation of the mission and legacy of the Highlander Research and Education Center, and *We Make the Road by Walking: Conversations on Education and Social Change*, the book that Highlander founder Myles Horton and Paolo Freire "talked" together about shared aspects of their work. No matter the topic Jenn and Lauren considered, the conversation kept pointing toward community listening: listening as way-of-knowing, as praxis, as community building, and so on. By August

vii

Acknowledgments

2017, the concept of community listening was in circulation along with the call for what would become *Community Writing, Community Listening*. What started then with six articles has now grown into a veritable carnival: a rich and complex ecosystem of new ideas, new voices, and new work that extends beyond any single example.

We have many other beginnings to acknowledge. Our list includes August 2020, when we three began circulating the call for proposals for this volume. It also includes February 2021, when we emailed the authors we have come to know with invitations to contribute. It was March 2021 when we first approached Heather Falconer, Rich Rice, and Michael Rifenberg about placing this work with the Perspectives on Writing series at the WAC Clearinghouse. So much has happened—so many conversations and revisions have taken place—between then and 2024, when we shared the complete manuscript with Rich and Michael, as well as Qingyang Sun, Jonathan Marine, and Johanna Phelps. As we think about the final stages of our work together, we are grateful foremost to the contributors to this volume and the many people and communities with whom they collaborate. We are also grateful to everyone involved in the WAC Clearinghouse, especially Mike Palmquist. And last, we are grateful to our readers and listeners. We look forward to ongoing conversations with you.

**From Romeo**: I am grateful to my co-editors, Jenn Fishman and Lauren Rosenberg, whose work on community listening in the *Community Literacy Journal* inspired many invigorating conversations, some of which are now represented in the pages of this collection. Both their eye for detail in the process of writing and thoughtfulness during the feedback stages were truly encouraging for me. Many thanks to my colleagues in the Department of Writing & Rhetoric Studies at the University of Utah, who have always shown me an unwavering amount of support. Lastly, I am deeply grateful to my family for their care, support, and patience with me.

**From Lauren**: Many thanks to the adult literacy learners who have spoken with me, participated in my research over the years, and taught me to listen differently. They showed me how to pay deep attention to the voices of ordinary people interacting in their communities for self and social change. I am grateful for the many communities that shape me as a listener, including my students and colleagues in Rhetoric and Writing Studies at the University of Texas at El Paso. Thanks especially to Jenn Fishman, who invited me to propose a special issue of *Community Literacy Journal* with her back in 2017, and for the opportunity to work with the authors of that issue on the articles that first defined community listening. Thanks to Romeo García for approaching Jenn and me with the idea for this book. As always, I am most grateful for my daughters Bess and Ella Hepner, wise women and community listeners.

Acknowledgments

**From Jenn:** The prospect of acknowledging, let alone thanking, the people who constitute my lineage of listening is a daunting one. How to begin? I think about the interauditors I associate with the end of a coiled harvest gold phone cord, all those handwritten letters, and their digital counterparts. I think of the earliest circles and rows where I learned more formally about the triangulation of community, listening, and literacy, and I think about the most recent sites of my continuing education, including Marquette University. Too, I think of places that are so much more than an address: Cascade Drive, Wonderful Town, the 'bier, ClearFish Pond and Manor, 315 E. Wisconsin Ave. There is Charlie among all the more-than-human interauditors. And, certainly, I am grateful to Lauren and Romeo as well as all Ada, Alexandra, Angela, April, Bailey, Carol, Carrie, Casey, Hannah, Kaitlyn, Karen, Katie, Kelly, Keri, Kyle, Lauren, Mary P, Mitzi, Patty, Rowie, Sally, Shelley, Tobi, Wendy, Wyn, and Zoe for the listening entailed in and hopefully also conveyed—even inspired—by this book.

# COMMUNITY LISTENING: STORIES, HAUNTINGS, POSSIBILITIES

# EDITORS' INTRODUCTION

**Jenn Fishman**
Marquette University

**Romeo García**
University of Utah

**Lauren Rosenberg**
University of Texas at El Paso

Stories and storytelling praxes play a significant role across space-time and provide the foundation for this book. Judy Rohrer offers one perspective in *Staking Claim: Settler Colonialism and Racialization in Hawai'i*. "[W]e are," she claims, "the set of stories we tell ourselves, the stories that tell us, the stories others tell about us, and the possibilities of new stories" (189). At the micro level, stories attune all individuals to an inheritance, our historical bodies inseparable and determined by historical, social, and cultural forces of the world. Though we are all heirs to what is passed down to us, this inheritance un/settles individuals differently. Some are settled in/to that inheritance, benefiting from certain privileges (broadly conceived). Others are unsettled and haunted by it: *thrown* into a world of haunted/ing inheritances and dwellings; *forced* to return to and learn how to address oneself to hauntings; imperiled to carefully reckon with how to cultivate *situated knowledges* (Haraway) and *theories in the flesh* (Moraga and Anzaldúa) out of haunting situations. Stories and hauntings both un/settle and help individuals know themselves.

Stories also work at the meso level. They can attune individuals to what is collectively inherited: collective memories, cultural histories, and political economies. This inheritance, too, constitutes communities differently. Some are settled in/to wounded/ing spaces and places (Till), benefiting from the privilege of not having to know its histories of settler displacement, de-territorialization, and re-territorialization. Others are unable to separate their identity from, and thus are more attuned to, its effects and consequences: *thrown* into its generational cycle of hauntings; *forced* to contend with the specificities and particularities in which hauntings haunt; *imperiled* to hold hope and struggle as two paradoxical realities within their stories-so-far. In *For Space*, cultural geographer Doreen Massey presents the concept of stories-so-far to reflect what is struggled over and what can be hoped for with-others (9). That is to say, though hauntings and haunting

DOI: https://doi.org/10.37514/PER-B.2025.2531.1.3

situations demand returns and careful reckonings, even though meaning is to be gained out of both, there is a hope and struggle for a being-and-becoming otherwise (Kirsch and García). Stories-so-far are communal relations that provide insight into the historical struggles of and for new beginnings and futures.

Stories function at the macro level, too. They attune individuals and communities to societal inheritances: co-histories, trajectories, interrelations, and futures. This inheritance, however, is unlike other inheritances mentioned in that it unsettles singular versions or interpretations of what it means to be haunted or even who can be haunted. Humanity and society's story is a palimpsest narrative of constellated hauntings and wounded/ing spaces and places whether made visible and audible or not. Hauntings live deep in the bones and are not just derived from inheritances but are themselves *structures of feelings*—a force felt every day in Society. Raymond Williams and Avery Gordon might say hauntings are initially inaudible and lifeless. Both attribute this to difference and the choice to readjust the senses. The difference that constitutes humanity has been accounted for above, but it is the latter that situates all on a demand. Haunted/ing stories can help all of humanity come to terms with the demand for something else: to hear, to see, and to recognize and acknowledge the demands of hauntings and ghosts themselves.

The listening conceived in this volume is part of the everyday. It does not belong to the disciplines of the university any more than it belongs to others who inform its contents, terms, and meaning within a given community. Yet, readers might find that the listening advanced in this collection invites a rhetorical standpoint insofar that meaning is exchanged; a materialist framework considering bodily and historical happenings occur; and a decolonial perspective seeing that "community" and "listening" have been typically defined in books, at the detriment of others, by those who engage in certain rhetorical activities. Like hauntings, community listening is a shared structure of feeling and thought that attunes: *I am where I do and think*. It may be imperceptible and yet its everyday language, grammar, and meaning are embodied, experienced, and practiced. To have stories, hauntings, and community listening as a point-of-reference is to situate oneself at the nexus of stories-so-far and the possibilities of new stories *otherwise*.

Readers might find in this collection that community listening is like absence and/or a textual trace. It has many stories, forms of rhetoricity, and recipients spanning space-time. Community listening has set precedents, confirmed conventions, informed human projects, and compelled consensus. It has seeded, materialized, and circulated precarious stories-so-far and unknown possibilities of new stories to be told, retold, remembered, and reimagined. Community listening is rife with hauntings. What would it mean for all of humanity to begin a listening-with community from the point-of-reference of hauntings?

Community listening is not an attempt to reconcile differences under the same contents and terms but rather is an invitation to engage in what María Lugones refers to as playful world-traveling, a mutual determination, or what Nelson Maldonado-Torres calls a generous reciprocity towards *being-with* others *otherwise*. It is the hope of this collection to extend an invitation to all to listen, deeply and slowly, so as to travel into other worlds presented by contributors not because ethics or morals say so but because a choice has been made to begin elsewhere and otherwise on the principle of relation-ing and reciprocity.

Community listening generates more questions than answers. It makes intelligible the "so-far" in stories-so-far and yet makes illegible a singular direction. This volume animates stories of community listening across personal stories, family stories, and workplace stories: a classroom, a campus reading circle, or a university archive to a prison, a community center, a cemetery, or anywhere it's possible to catch a particular radio broadcast. It is less about foreclosing on definitions of community listening and more about an invitation to become enmeshed in the patterns of its praxis and the kinds of labor it entails: somatic, affective, intellectual, and otherwise. Stories-so-far and possibilities of new stories form an essential focus of this collection on, about, being-with, and thinking from community listening.

## COMMUNITY LISTENING IN ACADEMIC CONTEXTS

While community listening does not belong to the academy or originate in its classrooms and labs, this volume is part of ongoing work to surface community listening in academic contexts, including research and scholarship, teaching, and community-engaged work. As editors, we three—Jenn, Lauren, and Romeo—see great value in amplifying the questions that community listening raises: about communicative praxes and relations; about human (and nonhuman) endeavors to listen in community; about the technical and ethical aspects of engaging in, with, and from community listening, whatever our roles (e.g., practitioners, students, teachers). We especially appreciate that such work has only just begun.

The first concerted effort to collect academic accounts of community listening was a special issue of *Community Literacy Journal* published in 2018. An outgrowth of the 2017 Conference on Community Writing, this issue introduced community listening to readers in relation to a cadre of feminist scholars, drawing attention to its resonances with several other listening praxes (Fishman and Rosenberg). Issue 13.1 of *Community Literacy Journal* also framed and reframed community listening as a combined invitation and dare. Instead of prescribing a single approach to the study of community listening, the issue asked: ¿donde comenzamos? (García). Through a series of specific, specifically located examples, contributors offered possible starts, hoping to improve the ability of teachers, scholars, and activists to enact it together (Stone). They identified the work before the work (Rowan and Cavallaro), including empathic listening(Lohr and Lindenman); they linked writing-to-listen with the rhetorical labor involved in community partnerships that cross boundaries (Hinshaw); and they showcased how community listening lends itself to enduring stories as well as the endurance of storytellers and their audiences (Jackson with DeLaune). Together, these examples answer the question of where to begin, encouraging readers to do the work wherever and whenever they can.

Continuing and expanding these conversations, this volume does more than offer additional examples. In the pages that follow contributors confirm the interrelationship of listening and storytelling, and they complicate our knowledge of these activities as entangled means of seeing, being, and doing. Rather than asking "Where do we start this time?" this volume queries: "What has been done? What is being done? And what might be done next?" While each chapter explores different answers, together they strike familiar chords. Among rhetorical arts, speaking and writing may have prominence, but listening, like reading, taste, and silence, has powerful cultural presence. Since the early twentieth century, it has garnered attention from scholars and teachers committed to intervening in critical and pedagogical praxes. Community listening, in many ways then, serves as a locus of and for the iterative work of starting and restarting, while storytelling is the vessel through which community listening is (re)made.

## Cosmologies of Listening

As an object of inquiry, listening eludes easy capture. An embodied act, it can look like the turn of a head or the twitch of an ear. Some bodies crouch on high alert when they are listening; others relax into sound. Plants engage in sonic call and response, while animals, including the symbol-using and -misusing kind, add gestures for aid and emphasis. Picture a curved hand cupped to the side of the head. Idiomatically, listening is transactional: Lend me your ear. Pay attention. Take heed! As auditors, we listen up, we listen in, and we listen to all kinds of things: the wind, the radio, the tone of voice of an interlocutor. More metaphorically, we encourage listening to reason, experience, authority, our hearts, our bodies, our better angels, and the true meaning behind what someone else is saying. Like other communicative acts, listening is social and it is relational. Listening is also mediated, and not just by tech. Fraught with imperfections, listening is enmeshed in lived experience, and as such it is inflected by individual quirks, available resources, and systemic arrangements of power. Rife with here and now, listening is as attuned to then and there as it is replete with possibilities, intended and otherwise.

Across disciplines, when teachers and scholars make listening their focus, enriching instruction or advancing knowledge is often the aim. A brief survey of named types of listening suggests the scope of activity. Appropriately enough, there is academic listening (Richards; Powers), and there is attentive or active listening (Rogers and Farson; Zelko). It extends to critical and cooperative listening, which can be found in a variety of artistic, educational, and professional settings. There is also civic listening, understood as both a facet of organizational listening (Capizo and Feinman) and a reciprocal means of circulating civic knowledge (Schmoll). The arts invite us to engage in deep listening (Oliveros) along with close and distant listening. The former extends attention, for example, from a published version of a poem to "the poet's own performances" of it and, thus, the "total" sound of the work, and the relation of sound to semantics" (Bernstein 4); the latter uses digital tools to turn noise into configurations that are open to interpretation (Clement). While language learners work on extensive and intensive listening, and educators strive to create optimal scaffolding, people across sectors work on empathic listening. Popularized in the early 90s as one of seven habits of "highly effective people" (Covey), empathic listening has been identified since the mid-2010s as not just a constructive civic response to political division and divisiveness but also a solution to it, whether a means of becoming more resilient (Scudder) or building connection and trust across differences (Andolina and Conklin).

In rhetorical studies, listening is omnipresent even if it is not always privileged or prominent at all levels (i.e., micro, meso, macro). Historically, listening and other forms of reception, such as reading and taste, are often actively distrusted or downplayed, while speaking and writing are associated with social and political agency and regarded as expressions of power as well as authority and domination. Even more fundamentally, speaking and writing are aligned, even elided, with thinking and, thus, with being human and having related rights. Histories of literacies and literate cultures show us how knowledge of speaking and writing is valued. Both are markers of genius, expertise, and professional acumen; individually and together, they signal talent, training, and hard work. On a broader scale, the intensity of conflicts that arise—clashes over free speech, freedom of the press, and access to information—offers yet another measure of the power attributed to speech and the recorded word. Of course, speaking and writing are nothing without uptake, and that makes listening a *sine qua non* of the *ars rhetoricae*. To gain a greater sense, in future projects we might turn to big data analyses. Whether scholars mine primary or secondary texts, we anticipate the resulting visualizations of the language we have used to evoke, describe, and analyze listening will give us a "network sense" of how, so far, listening has shaped the "maturing discipline" of rhetoric and composition (Mueller 159).

Browsing back issues of the *International Journal of Listening* (*IJL*) offers further perspectives. Founded in 1987 as *The Journal of the International Listening Association*, this publication was established not only "to share . . . knowledge," but also to encourage "new understanding, new discovery, and new application of information about listening," and to promote participation by providing "an active, moving force that, through its contribution toward communication effectiveness, will ultimately lead to better relationships among people everywhere" (Smith 1). Issue 1.1 leads with a trio of articles by senior scholars from across rhetorical studies. The first, "Listening–Ubiquitous Yet Obscure" by James I. Brown, opens with a timeline of previous firsts: the first published article on listening in a modern or "familiar" sense, 1912; the first major study of listening, a 1926 dissertation; the first national professional committee on listening, 1952; and so on (Brown 3). Together with "Manipulation versus Persuasion" by Ralph G. Nichols and "Someone Should Do Something About That (A Comment about Listening Research)" by Carl H. Weaver, the journal sounds a call for interventions that subsequent work answers mainly through empirical research plus occasional scholarship on listening aesthetics, histories, and theories. Nearly four decades later, the *IJL* continues in a similar vein. Now a genuinely international publication, it almost exclusively features empirical work that aims to improve how listening is understood as cognitive activity, as teachable (and testable) skills, and as socially and culturally situated behavior with discernible impacts.

There is also a great deal of listening scholarship that lies beyond the scope of the *IJL*. In particular, since the late 1990s scholars in rhetoric and adjacent fields have been interested in how listening and action connect (or can be connected), especially in response to signal imperatives: survival, reconciliation, peace. Rather than a single corpus, scholarship in this category might be better pictured as a night sky filled with celestial bodies, some blinking like fires lit at a great distance, others shining steadily as if close by. We recognize the academic impulse to at least try to catalog or index this vast work; we also imagine making selections from it, as if preparing a table of contents for a proposed volume in the Landmark Essays Series. Here, however, in this volume, we encourage readers to join us in considering some of the many groupings it is possible to create among scholarship on listening and action. As Andrea Riley-Mukavetz explains in "Our Story Begins Here: Constellating Cultural Rhetorics," "It's through listening to decolonial scholars that we've come to understand the making of cultures and the practices that call them into being as *relational* and *constellated*" (Act I, Scene 2). She adds, "The practice of constellating gives us a visual metaphor for those relationships that honors all possible realities," noting with her coauthors: "It also allows for different ways of seeing any single configuration within that constellation, based on positionality and culture." Listening and action are always already in constellation.

In this spirit, we turn our focus below to some of the constellations we see within turn-of-the-millennium and more recent listening scholarship. Guiding our practice is our abiding interest in identifying and exploring some of the interrelations among extant listening scholarship and emergent work.

## LISTENING ATTUNEMENTS

When we look into the night sky, depending on where we stand and with whom, we see outlines of humans and animals, ghosts and gods. By naming and storying such constellations, we make meaning both of and with them. Some stories persist, while their formats and meanings multiply. Other stories live in briefer moments, their timelines not always a measure of their impact. When we consider scholarship on listening in our discipline, work on rhetorical listening is one of the most prominent and complex configurations. Even before the publication of *Rhetorical Listening: Identification, Gender, Whiteness* by Krista Ratcliffe, there was considerable engagement with her key terms (e.g., rhetorical listening, rhetorical eavesdropping), and subsequent publications steadily followed, including *Silence and Listening as Rhetorical Arts*, which Ratcliffe edited with Cheryl Glenn; *Rhetorics of Whiteness: Postracial Hauntings in Popular Culture, Social Media, and Education*, which Ratcliffe edited with Tammy Kennedy and Joyce Irene Middleton; and *Rhetorical Listening in Action*, which Ratcliffe authored with Kyle Jensen.

In outer space, through mass and gravity, stars enable communication among planets through gravitational lensing, a phenomenon that allows for the transmission (and reception) of messages across timespace. In rhetorical scholarship on listening, communiqués travel across constellations at different frequencies, and sometimes they overlap or converge. In "Rhetorical Listening: A Trope for Interpretive Invention and a 'Code of Cross-Cultural Conduct,'" for example, Ratcliffe introduces rhetorical listening in conversation with Jacqueline Jones Royster's scholarship. Their relations, forged through inspiration on the part of Ratcliffe (103) and through intertextual exchanges between Ratcliffe and Royster, point to additional constellations that center Royster's work along with African American women writers and their ancestors; their literacy practices, including listening; and the worlds they strive to create through the texts they circulate. By contrast, there seems to be very little direct messaging among constellations that center rhetorical listening and those that center Linda Flower's scholarship and praxes. Consistently collaborative and rooted in both

9

literacy and rhetorical studies, Flower's work is, nonetheless, key to contextualizing community listening and understanding its affinity for community writing and community-engaged academic work more broadly.

Throughout her career's work, Flower brings steady attention to listening as not only a consequential practice that can be learned but also an essential aspect of effective inclusive communication. The importance of listening is consistently apparent in her collaborations with students, colleagues, and community members through initiatives like the Community Think Tank and the Community Literacy Center. In addition, in "Drawing on the Local: Collaboration and Community Expertise," Flower and Shirley Brice Heath report on a project that focused on listening and, specifically, listening to community partners. Working with nearly two hundred university and community stakeholders, Flower and Heath sought mainly to teach faculty and students "not simply how to hear" local experts but also how to listen to them and, in doing so, "construct a transformative understanding" (44). Fundamentally, what Flower and Heath taught was rivaling, which Flower, Lorraine Higgins, and Elenore Long describe as a means for "people [to] explore open questions through an analysis of multiple perspectives and evidence" (4). Rivaling is both a stance and a set of activities. It involves inquiry, which is a very concrete form of uptake, and it involves listening, which is an embodied critical and intellectual act. Thus, rivaling "takes one beyond merely considering available alternative understandings to actively seeking them out"; it also entails "eliciting rivals that might remain silent," "striving to comprehend them," and "embracing the difficulty of talking across difference" to gain a sense of "a more multi-faceted reality" ("Intercultural" 257).

When such brief but representative examples from Flower's work are constellated with community listening, key aspects of both are cast in relief. For Flower, community literacy names the transformative public force that university and community members co-create when they work together on problem-driven, solution-seeking intercultural inquiry. Rivaling, the practice of "seeking rival hypotheses" that drives such collaborations, is an academic invention informed by scientific method and pragmatism (cf. Dewey, West). However, as Flower makes clear in *Learning to Rival, Community Literacy*, and elsewhere, rivaling can be taught, and through instruction, it can become an everyday activity that helps people identify and articulate the complexity of their own and others' experiences along with issues and circumstances that contribute to problems they wish to solve. As such, rivaling is an antecedent to other teachable listening stances and tactics. Indeed, listening is the means by which rivals empathetically attune to differences, including those voiced by direct participants and those sounded by available texts (*Community Literacy* 57). Like all literacy activities, both rivaling and community listening reflect cultural contexts and social frameworks; both are also closely calibrated to the discursive and immediate, lived contexts of their practitioners. Yet there are differences. Distinct from community literacy, community listening is rooted in (or elemental to) community settings rather than imported into them from rhetoric, literacy studies, or other academic disciplines. Community listening and literacy also differ in their orientation toward action. The latter, through rivaling, compels practitioners toward specifically democratic ends; thus, rivals pursue solutions to shared problems (e.g., disruptions, explanations) that are collective, ameliorative, and egalitarian. By contrast, community listening arcs toward acknowledgment, which is a social act that involves simultaneously asserting independence (i.e., self and other) while broaching both dependence and interdependence.

Listening is also a powerful force throughout the career contribution of Jacqueline Jones Royster. For her, listening is integrated into reading, writing, and speaking, and as such it is fundamental to the world-building and world-sustaining literacy traditions of the African American women writers whose rhetorics she amplifies across timespace, texts, and situations. Always fiercely invitational, Royster asks us, her reader-listeners, to join her in recognizing the profound importance of both listening and being listened to, which she juxtaposes against the harm of forced listening and being silenced. For example, scene one of "When the First Voice You Hear Is Not Your Own" opens with this recollection:

> I have been compelled on too many occasions to count to sit
> as a well-mannered Other, silently, in a state of tolerance that
> requires me to be as expressionless as I can manage, while
> colleagues who occupy a place of entitlement different from
> my own talk about the history and achievements of people
> from my ethnic group, or even about their perceptions of our
> struggles. I have been compelled to listen as they have com-
> fortably claimed the authority to engage in the construction
> of knowledge and meaning about me and mine. (30)

Observing that "subject position is everything" (31), Royster goes on to demonstrate how listening is essential: first, to recognizing "cross-cultural misconduct" as such (32); and second, to redressing it by repositioning interlocutors (who are always also interauditors) in reciprocal relations. In the classroom, these ideas undergird a multisensory pedagogy of listening. Looking back on more than a decade of teaching at Spelman, Royster writes: "What unfolds for me from observing and listening is questioning and engaging in dialogue with students to see what their issues are and what problems there are. We then reflect together and figure out how best to act" ("Looking" 23). Almost fifteen years later, the same principles inform the listening stance she encourages everyone to take at the 2014 Watson Conference. "Linking listening to ethical codes of rhetorical behavior" (287), Royster advocates speaking and listening in ways that demonstrate care and respect in the form of responsivity (i.e., talking or not talking back) and "its dialectical counterparts, responsibility and accountability" (288).

Constellating community listening with Royster's work raises a series of provocative questions, including several that Royster poses directly—*When do we listen? How do we listen? How do we demonstrate respect as listeners? How do we transform listening into action* ("First Voice" 38)—and many that can be found in the spaces made legible by her work. Importantly, though Royster offers numerous scholarly examples, her understanding of listening is not simply academic. In *Traces of a Stream*, she demonstrates how listening and storytelling are concomitant in African American women writers' literacy traditions, where they constitute a joint means of agency that extends from the power to imagine what is possible to the courage and strength to strive toward it. Like teaching and learning, listening is "a people-centered human enterprise" (5), both in her estimate and in ours. Thus, between the lines and wavelengths, Royster encourages us to examine how we name the various roles that practitioners of community listening play. Are they rivals in Flower's sense? Are they negotiators, people "who can cross boundaries and serve as guide and translator for Others," as Royster names herself ("First Voice" 34)? Or, when we examine the specific activities of radio DJs, muralists, community educators, and others (as contributors to this volume do), would we term them something else? Whatever the case, Royster encourages us to pay close attention to listening and to the interconnectedness of listening and telling stories.

Readers attuned to listening will already be aware of the numerous ways in which Royster's and Ratcliffe's work on listening aligns. Both "encourage speakers to listen rhetorically," in Royster's words, emphasizing not only "the need to be highly skilled in both listening and speaking" and "develop the habit of paying attention to context, stakeholders, and the stakes of an interaction" but also "to take into account the multiple discourses that are embedded in and surround our conversations" and "develop a sense of personal and professional accountability for reasonable action" ("Responsivity" 287–288). There are also important differences. While for Royster subject position is everything, for Ratcliffe it is cultural position, and she locates rhetorical listening firmly in modern American culture, a "then-that-is-now" where listeners continuously must reckon with white supremacy and related tropes (e.g., racism, whiteness) (*Rhetorical Listening* 107–120). Rooted in literary examples and the Greco-Roman rhetorical tradition, rhetorical listening is itself a trope, specifically "a trope for interpretive invention" that involves four moves: "understanding of self and other" (27), operating within "a logic of accountability" that is cognizant of the past while prioritizing the present (and future) (31–32), identifying (in a Burkean sense) with both commonalities and differences (32–33), and analyzing both argumentative claims made in any situation and their cultural logics (33).

A powerful means of sense-making, rhetorical listening emerges from Ratcliffe's oeuvre as an omnibus method, a rhetorical device ready for application in response to any text or situation. As a "code of cross-cultural conduct," rhetorical listening is also Ratcliffe's powerful and personal response to the gauntlet Royster threw down at the inaugural Feminisms and Rhetorics Conference in 1997. As Ratcliffe recalls, Royster "challenged attendees to construct . . . rhetorical tactics for fostering cross-cultural communication," including mechanisms for the kind of "gender/race work" that rhetorical listening is designed to enable (3–4). Specifically, rhetorical listening gives rhetors ways of doing more than just listening and really trying to hear what others have to say (e.g., paying close attention, responding empathetically). Rhetorical listening is a means of "listening in" and responding productively, especially when one is not directly addressed, whether the context is public discourse, an unfamiliar text, or a conversation overheard. The latter, rhetorical eavesdropping, is an important example, not least because idiomatically it raises specters of actual and discursive violence (e.g., trespassing, invasion of privacy, romanticizing marginalization). Ratcliffe addresses these concerns directly, and in doing so, she distinguishes the context in which rhetorical listeners, including eavesdroppers, operate. While "the common definition" of eavesdropping may consign "listening in" to problematic situations, Ratcliffe assures: "Within my reworked definition, this claim is groundless" because "rhetorical eavesdropping entails positioning oneself to overhear both oneself and others, listening to learn, and, most importantly, being *careful* (i.e., full of care) not to overstep another's boundaries or interrupt the agency of another's discourse" (106, original emphasis). This idea strongly carries over into the enumerated tactics that Ratcliffe and Jensen offer in *Rhetorical Listening in Action*, where they present (1) building cultural logics, (2) eavesdropping, (3) listening metonymically, and (4) listening pedagogically as samples or models that "listening writers who possess the capacity to develop their own tactics" might evolve (33–34).

When we constellate community listening and rhetorical listening, we see the various ways they correspond, overlap, and diverge. Practitioners of both are motivated by their interest in others, and that relational pull generates momentum for action inflected by curiosity, concern, and a sense of responsibility or care, broadly understood. Both community listeners and their rhetorical counterparts grapple with the limits and possibilities of agency, however it may be construed, and both are sensitive to hauntings, the absent presence of the past in the present, which calls for and calls forward historical knowledge. Notably, Ratcliffe formulates rhetorical listening in terms of tactics. In fact, in *Rhetorical Listening*, she deliberately rewrites de Certeau when she vests the tactics of rhetorical listening (e.g., listening metonymically, eavesdropping, listening pedagogically) with discursive power (16, 189n15). This is a bold move of critical performativity: first, because it mainstreams rhetorical means (i.e., tactics) that are usually considered the critical provenance of the margins; second, because it accepts the great risk of cooptation that comes with mainstreaming, buoyed by what readers might recognize as the signature, stubborn hope of rhetorical feminism (Glenn 341). By contrast, in this volume and elsewhere, we tell stories to represent community listening *in situ*, as praxes embedded in the everyday knowledge of specific communities. As such, community listening is akin to walking, talking, and storytelling: it is local repertoires of prosaic acts whose efficacy is not keyed to general standards or external measures so much as it helps make and is made by the confluence of circumstances that occasion it, host it, and receive it.

Like all forms of knowing-through-doing, community listening may be best revealed through a combination of lived activity and recorded stories. The latter encourage a range of affective and intellectual responses that complement the phenomenology and range of experiential learning that action and participation enable. We see similarities in the stories about listening told by Flower, Royster, and Ratcliffe. We also observe a shared commitment to responsivity across the examples we singled out of the starry sky, which represents the scholarly horizon of possibility for this volume. Royster discusses this concept in her role as moderator of the 2014 Thomas R. Watson Conference. Organized by Mary P. Sheridan, a contributor to this volume, the conference centered on responsivity as a framework for forward-thinking attuned to "desired and emerging trends in the ways we research and teach, partner, and mentor" (12). In Royster's words, responsivity "functions critically as part and parcel of a values construct, shaped, informed, and exercised amid the complex interactions and relationships of our sense-making assets" ("Responsivity" 283). Responsivity also names the impulse to avoid "lockstep, paint-by-numbers" applications of listening (Ratcliffe 189n15), as if listeners could simply skill and drill. Instead, the collective aim of all of us working to define and describe listening praxes is most basic: to ensure they are discernible, distinguishable from one another, and available for ongoing consideration and use.

## INTERVENTIONS IN RHETORICAL INTERACTIVITY THROUGH COMMUNITY LISTENING

For the good rhetor committed to listening as well as speaking, writing, and reading well, invention is not the romantic poet's fantasy of ingenious solo origination, nor is intervention the stuff of swashbuckling hero narratives. Instead, the latter entails dwelling within and working efficaciously with commonplaces. Certainly, this is the spirit in which the contributors to this volume offer insight into community listening as it is enacted across diverse contexts. If we were to map the sites of community listening represented in the chapters below, we might start with pinpoints across the continental U.S., including the Pacific Northwest, the South, and the Western states, as well as the Borderland. Next, we might map some of the currents of media circulation that occasion community listening: public art, hashtag activism, radio broadcasts, and letters sent from incarcerated writers to both public and private recipients.

Through stories about community listening set in these analog and digital locations, the contributors to this volume showcase some of the many ways community listening enables practitioners to make space, to come between established ideas, expectations, and relations—sometimes for just a flash, a moment of insight; sometimes for an interval long enough to make change, whether to policy, a legacy, or someone's mind. In earlier pages, we differentiated community listening from various established theories and emergent methodologies. Now, we look at the contributions of the individual chapters to get an understanding of when and how the authors see community listening at play and what they believe community listening is doing to intervene in the ways we understand rhetorical interactivity. We consider how the chapters function as interventions when their authors probe the social, rhetorical, and political relations they work through in the act of defining community listening. While we, as editors, can identify various interventions in how we understand listening inter- and intra-actions emerging in the contexts described within the chapters of this book, we expect that readers will recognize many other connections and disruptions.

Here we note that authors often coin an original version of community listening that suits their project or names their vision, such as community-centered listening, civic community listening, proximate listening, storied community listening, and daunting community listening. In articulating their own terms, each chapter advances our understanding of what community listening can mean and achieve. We see these acts of customizing the term as opening possibilities for community listening when it is put into practice rather than codifying it. Every author or author group extends community listening in ways that give the concept greater complexity as a means of identifying and understanding community practices, critiques, disruptions, and means of creating knowledge. Beyond customizing terms that extend our understanding of community listening, we also acknowledge that the chapters challenge readers to pay attention differently to the ways we think of listening inter- and intra-actions. We observe authors disrupting existing practices, changing their actions when they are community listeners themselves, handling ethical conflicts, taking responsibility, and assuming new positions in response to what they discover through community listening. Listening occurs in retrospect and as an entanglement with other concepts.

In the chapters that follow, readers will recognize various other disruptions expanding their understanding of community listening and begin to consider the possibilities they offer for change in the ways community members (academic and nonacademic) relate to one another guided by community knowledge. The work included in this volume challenges what we can know by listening to and in carceral spaces as well as archives. It offers listening as more than one kind of ethical stance, and it shows how listening stances can open listeners to new kinds of understanding, whether online or on-site. Taken together, the chapters push readers to consider what it means to listen to, through, and with, communities and how we can learn from community ways of knowing to act differently.

## PART 1. HAUNTINGS AND POSSIBILITIES

In the opening chapter, "Getting Closer to Mass Incarceration: Proximate Listening as Community Activism," Sally F. Benson, coins *proximate listening*, a form of community listening that depends on relationality and responsibility. Proximate listening refers broadly to the many listening moments that occur within the prison complex; specifically, it is about the author learning to listen and understand from the community as Benson explains: "I identify *proximate listening* as an active means of listening toward members of our communities from a stance of both nearness and radical uncertainty." Through Benson's compelling narrative of her ongoing experience as a prison educator in New Mexico, we watch her find her way as a proximate listener who is always in a state of moving toward; that is, she remains hopeful even when her incarcerated students' situations seem dire. Though the chapter is about Benson's work as a prison educator in a maximum-security men's prison, and the community she writes about is the prison itself (a kind of non-community according to Benson's descriptions of individual cells and the isolation in which the men exist), the primary listener in this piece is herself, the non-incarcerated teacher-author-woman. "Proximity engages ways of listening beyond what we tell ourselves we hear. Leaning toward understanding, but not assuming understanding, allows listeners to remain open to new, plural, or unattainable meanings." Benson shows us how she works to listen more deeply, to understand the educational and personal needs expressed by her study as a way of also understanding the prison system, the injustices of and attempted reforms to that institution, and for her as an educator to have some degree of impact. By coming near to this incarcerated population as a community listener, Benson is transformed: "Listening toward others without appropriating meaning has invoked me to change, to position myself to advocate, or to move closer to do more proximate listening."

Hauntings and possibilities for change through activism and identifying differently are threaded through Chapter 2, Ada Hubrig's "Crafting Crip Space Through Disabled Political Advocacy: #CripTheVote as Community Listening." Unlike some authors who build upon community listening by contributing an original way of using the term, Hubrig is interested in the entanglement of concepts, that is, how disability advocacy is shaped by community listening, as well as how listening practices can be better defined and enacted through disability perspectives. Focusing on the social media hashtag #CripTheVote, Hubrig looks at the activist site *as* community listening, explaining that "#CripTheVote employs community listening practices—carefully attending to issues by directly and deliberately engaging those most impacted—to build community, counter ableism and oppression, and exercise political agency." In this way, "#CripTheVote lets us see community listening when it is used and modified for purposes defined by a virtual activist community." Hubrig's argument that sites of disability activism like #CripTheVote create spaces for new ways of listening across disabilities, across bodies, and across differences can help us better understand that community listening can be directed toward "challenging the ableism and other forms of oppression that dismiss the forms of engagement used by disabled and otherwise marginalized rhetors." In this sense, community listening becomes a vehicle for the changes we might hope to see enacted within communities of practice and, more broadly, as sites interacting in the world.

For Patty Wilde, Mitzi Ceballos, and Wyn Andrews Richards, authors of Chapter 3, "Keeping Bad Company: Listening to Aryan Nations in the Archives," the decision to take on the Aryan Nations texts collected in Washington State University's archives and library shelves marked an intervention in and of itself. Intended initially as a class project on archival research, studying their university's collection of local Aryan Nations publications disturbed them as readers and researchers to the point that they were propelled into becoming active community listeners. Haunted by both the periodicals and their presence as a collection shelved within and sanctioned by their university's library, the authors had to listen to absorb and believe the actions that had been taken by their university community when it acquired manuscripts from the Aryan Nations and archived them. The form of listening the authors undertook was a complex openness to the difficult, troubling actions taken by the library's archivists as a vehicle for paying attention to their own listening when they encountered texts they found offensive. Similar to other author groups in this volume who attempted to reconcile university positions they found objectionable, Wilde, Ceballos, and Richards interrogated their own positions and practices of listening within the university community as they confronted the documents in the archives, and as they tried to come to terms with the librarians' choices in regard to the Aryan Nations' texts. Community listening for Wilde, Ceballos, and Richards is about handling an ethical conflict. They write, "Though the Aryan Nations documents are abhorrent and detestable, we must listen to these sources to confront the racist legacy that continues to haunt the Pacific Northwest and avoid the kind of white supremacy propagation that occurs when such ugly voices are routinely ignored" (13–14). For them, community listening means taking responsibility in situations in which they believe others have been irresponsible. "The story that we tell, then," they explain, "is also about our attempt to use community listening to encourage the archivists to further contextualize this collection and, more broadly, adopt antiracist archival practices."

## PART 2. STORIES OF SUSTAINING COMMUNITY

In Chapter 4, Kyle Boggs brings public art into the discussion of community listening, arguing that art can be a vehicle for change when it makes a deliberate intervention into the ways communities are portrayed and how they portray themselves. "The Public Art of Listening: Relational Accountability and The Painted Desert Project" takes readers on a tour of mural artist Chip Thomas' large paintings that are displayed on sides of highways and in towns in the Navajo nation of Arizona, bridging the visual, auditory, and sociopolitical. For Boggs, looking becomes a form of listening: "Public art has also been established as a valid form of community writing, but it also constitutes a particular kind of community listening that is expressed uniquely through the medium of art that reflects community values, goals, and lived experiences, histories, identities, and needs." Boggs makes a case for the importance of listening to art, especially when the goal of the work is to showcase community experiences: "If community listening is to be understood through relationality, which I argue it should, then it precedes not just reading, writing, and speaking, but all forms of community engagement, including art." Chip Thomas, the artist Boggs studies, is also a community listener, someone who inhabits a listening role so that he may take in the perspectives of community members before creating his work. Boggs interprets Thomas' art as an intervention because of the way it interrupts the landscape, injecting human images on billboard-sized displays and demanding that viewers pay attention. The attention paid by the artist, and the call for viewers to attend to the work comprise listening acts, as Boggs has us understand them: "When it is rooted in building trust, reflecting a relational process that establishes structures of accountability, community listening becomes a mode of perceiving, reflecting, and responding that is personal and situational."

In Chapter 5, Karen R. Tellez-Trujillo considers community listening from a different angle as she explores nostalgia and memories of home in "The DJ as Relational Listener and Creator of an Ethos of Community Listening." In Tellez-Trujillo's work, which focuses on a Sunday afternoon oldies program in a mostly Latinx southwest U.S. location, listening to the radio is treated literally as an activity that binds and sustains. The author explains: "For me, community listening means coming together to honor people, places, and memories through music. I think I have been listening in this way my whole life. I have listened with the purpose of connecting with fellow listeners through their stories and recollections surrounding the music that is the soundtrack of their lives while simultaneously creating my own soundtrack." Family members relate to one another as they dance at home; faraway travelers listen remotely to connect with memories of community; the DJ relates when he engages callers and when he responds to their music requests as a means of creating new memories. Listening to music is an action that moves through the body, Tellez-Trujillo writes, "As I listen, I access people that are out of reach, listening through my body, moving my body, and being emotionally moved as acts of remembrance of my past, my family, and my culture." Tellez-Trujillo characterizes a loyal community of listeners across three generations, as they participate in a practice she calls *relational listening* that is oriented around the idea of multiple forms of relationship. Relational listening is not only about relationships with family and the practices of a close-knit community; it is also a means of looking at situations relative to one another and acting in response. Much of the chapter focuses on "Mike, el DJ," who enacts and models the listening stance that Tellez-Trujillo attributes to The Fox Jukebox, a Sunday radio show, noting through one story after another how a local way of being is created through music and family. Mike carries the responsibility of keeping it all happening. Tellez-Trujillo's treatment of the radio show leaves readers with a sense of possibility: There is something about the way that Mike creates the show through relational listening that has a hold on listeners, keeping them tuned in week after week, year after year. This is the possibility for continued identification through moves and songs as a way to keep on listening. This is what keeps the community functioning.

Through their study of prison letter writing programs, "Listening In: Letter Writing and Rhetorical Resistance Behind Bars," Alexandra J. Cavallaro, Wendy Hinshaw, and Tobi Jacobi identify a unique form of community listening in Chapter 6 that they call *community-centered listening*. The authors explain, "We carve out a specific space for what we are calling community-centered listening to letter-writers behind bars to recognize the ways in which writers form community—however fragmented or partial—and enact practices of rhetorical and material resilience through listening." Differentiating this term from the more general community listening, they argue that "community-centered listening helps us navigate our relationship to the incarcerated writers we read and the writing we help to amplify, as well as the limits of what we can know through this writing." The term serves various functions. On the one hand, it names actions performed by incarcerated writers to connect out and within the space of the prison, demonstrating the kind of inter- and intra-activity that we witness in many of the chapters as authors peer in at community ways of being and out to acknowledge the impact of those ways of being in the world. The acts of communicating and writing press up against the boundaries of the prison. On the other hand, we see Cavallaro, Hinshaw, and Jacobi applying the term to themselves as community-engaged scholars who have been involved in prison writing projects and who are also researchers studying archives of letters and published letters. Community-centered listening thus serves as an umbrella for many actions, connecting them into a network of community-centeredness. The authors observe that they are "identifying listening relationships" as they study the letters individually in their research and together as a group of authors working through these interconnections in composing their chapter. In addition to making an argument for the multiplicity of listening relationships, they are also concerned with the disruption such connections can make in carceral spaces as they challenge a colonizing culture of punishment.

## Part 3. Negotiating Self and Community

The intersections between self, community, and listening are apparent in this volume too. Communication scholars Bailey M. Oliver-Blackburn, April Chatham-Carpenter, and Carol L. Thompson employ community listening as a means of negotiating self and community. In Chapter 7, "Civic Community Listening: The Nexus of Storytelling and Listening Within Civic Communities," the researcher-authors study the storytelling and listening practices cultivated by members of a nonprofit community organization whose goal is to talk across differences: "The key in these contexts is for the participants to learn to engage in 'civic community listening,' which we define as listening that operates in a civic context in which individuals openly share their diverse perspectives and listen to others with the goal of understanding, as they work across their political differences." By observing and analyzing the listening interactions among community members in the Braver Angels organization, they examine the concept of *civic community listening* as it is put into practice to speculate about the possibility of bringing this approach to other civic contexts. It also provides them with a means of evaluating community listening by applying the concept as methodology and method: "Indeed, when members of a group share stories and employ listening practices to actively engage together with and across their differences in the context of a community, they are participating in community listening. Put simply, storytelling and listening become an entrée or an invitation for others to enter into community with each other." Oliver-Blackburn, Chapham-Carpenter, and Thompson center the role of storytelling in civic community listening by demonstrating through examples of interactions between Braver Angels members how storytelling is the medium that encourages talking and listening across perspectives and viewpoints: "We found that civic community listening, as observed in the settings of this community, occurred in specific moments in workshops, but also happened where there were multiple sequences of exchanges between individuals in a group, with time allotted for both parties to be listening and telling stories."

Community listening as methodology is developed further in Chapter 8 by Cate Fosl, Kelly Kinahan, Carrie Mott, Mary P. Sheridan, Angela Storey, and Shelley Thomas in "Community Listening in, with, and against Whiteness at a PWI." This cross-disciplinary group of colleagues reflect on their experiences as facilitators of antiracist reading circles sponsored by the University of Louisville's Anne Braden Institute. Their reflections are informed by their attention to positionality, including their status as white women scholars at a PWI, and their desire for accountability, as they contemplate how their university has addressed, and simultaneously failed to address, structural racism. In their quest to confront and contemplate their own whiteness as well as the racism within their city and campus, the authors incorporate community listening as the framework guiding this work. Mary P. Sheridan explains: "To me, community listening is a practice of defamiliarization meant to expose majoritarian biases (including our own) and to foreground community knowledge." Community listening is engaged as a means of critiquing, analyzing, and restorying community stories and knowledge. It aids the reading circle facilitator-authors in challenging notions of community that have circulated historically and culturally; it also provides them with a central concept for evaluating the reading circles. For the facilitators, the online reading circles become sites for learning to practice community listening. Shelley Thomas reflects that the facilitators "learned substantive counterstories that challenged the cultural logics I had learned."

Similarly, in Chapter 9, "On Being in It," Katie W. Powell brings together community stories and personal experience through the process of studying a historic event in her community in Fayetteville, Arkansas, as it has been renegotiated in the present. *Storied community listening*, a term Powell invents, is best understood in retrospect as she looks back at the ways that story was used to re-narrate a racist historical event and its effects. She explains, "Critical to our group's mission and directly in line with the goal and intention of storied community listening is prioritizing and unearthing the ways of knowing and pieces of the story that have not been prioritized or centered. In this spirit of storied community listening, the group heard the need to bring to light these competing narratives." Thus, storied community listening becomes a method for employing counterstory. Powell witnesses and participates as the community chooses to alter, and thereby correct, its own stories. Reflecting on the dynamics that occurred as community members learned to listen to one another's responses to a troubled, raced history taught Powell a unique way of understanding what can happen when one listens and then listens again. By learning to trust the process of storied community listening, Powell finds a way of entering and contributing to a conversation on racial reconciliation.

In the final chapter by Keri Epps and Rowie Kirby-Straker with Casey Beiswenger, Zoe Chamberlin, Hannah Hill, Lauren Robertson, and Kaitlyn Taylor, we witness community listening employed as a method for critical analysis and action. The authors, along with a group of their undergraduate students, engaged with a community organization, Authoring Action (A2). "The A2 pedagogy," they explain, "is grounded in deep listening." Epps and Kirby-Straker's engagement with A2 reminds us that community listening has been happening in nonacademic and academic settings all along, prior to our study of it in this collection and other scholarly work. A2 offered Epps and Kirby-Straker and their students an important model that their partner termed *daunting community listening*. This spin on community listening acknowledges the discomfort and difficulty that may be associated with a deep listening engagement. The authors refer to the listening stance they learn to take as a "full-body listening practice." Initially, Epps and Kirby-Straker learned the process by training with the organization; they then applied it in an extracurricular Community Listening Accountability Group (CLAG) created with their students. It is through the activities of the pilot group that readers begin to see the challenges of applying daunting community listening as an intentional and ongoing process. Student participants reflect on their listening process as part of their training to work for A2. Through this "redefinition" practice, they learned to listen and connect in new ways that can continue to inform academic and community-based interactions.

In sum, the interventions that emerge throughout the chapters rise out of juxtapositions, interrelations, inter- and intra-actions, and even collisions. We see this, for example, when Wilde, Ceballos, and Richards struggle to reconcile their university library's acceptance of Aryan Nations texts on the shelves and in the archives, and in the chapter on the Braver Angels in which the researchers-authors seek to understand the efforts of a bipartisan community group to reach across political affiliations for better understanding. In these cases, community listening is taken up as a means of making sense from a collision of ideas and ways of being. That entangling action is something readers can witness occurring via the community listening practices explored in every chapter. Part of the intervention exhibited through each piece comes through the author's/s' contemplation of ways of knowing individually and collectively, past and present, and how those ways weave together and change through the listening practices explored in the individual chapters as well as the authors' representation of what listening means and how it can be used and understood, now and in the future.

## WORKS CITED

Andolina, Molly W., and Hilary G. Conklin. "Cultivating Empathic Listening in Democratic Education." *Theory and Research in Social Education*, vol. 49, no. 3, 2021, pp. 390–417.

Bernstein, Charles. *Close Listening: Poetry and the Performed Word*. Oxford UP, 1998.

Brown, James I. "Listening—Ubiquitous Yet Obscure." *The Journal of the International Listening Association*, vol. 1, no. 1, 1987, pp. 3–14.

Capizzo, Luke, and Meredith Feinman. "Extending Civic Values in Architectures of Listening: Arendt, Mouffe and the Pluralistic Imperative for Organizational Listening." *Journal of Public Relations Research*, vol. 34, no. 6, 2022, pp. 274–295.

Clement, Tanya. "Distant Listening or Playing Visualisations Pleasantly with the Eyes and Ears." *Digital Studies/le Champ Numérique*, vol. 3, no. 2, 2013.

Covey, Stephen R. *The Seven Habits of Highly Effective People*. Simon & Schuster, 1989.

Fishman, Jenn, and Lauren Rosenberg, editors. *Community Writing, Community Listening*, special issue of *Community Literacy Journal*, vol. 13, no. 1, 2018.

Fishman, Jenn, and Lauren Rosenberg. "Guest Editors' Introduction: Community Writing, Community Listening." Fishman and Rosenberg, pp. 1–6, https://doi.org/10.25148/clj.13.1.009085.

Flower, Linda. *Community Literacy and the Rhetoric of Public Engagement*. Southern Illinois UP, 2008.

———. "Intercultural Knowledge Building: The Literate Action of a Community Think Tank." *Writing Selves/Writing Societies: Research from Activity Perspectives*, edited by Charles Bazerman and David R. Russell, The WAC Clearinghouse/Mind, Culture, and Activity, 2003, pp. 239–279, https://doi.org/10.37514/PER-B.2003.2317.2.07.

Flower, Linda, and Shirley Brice Heath. "Drawing On the Local: Collaboration and Community Expertise." *Language and Learning across the Disciplines*, vol, 4, no. 3, 1999, pp. 43–55, https://doi.org/10.37514/LLD-J.2000.4.3.04.

Flower, Linda, Lorraine Higgins, and Elenore Long. "Preface: A Note on Intercultural Inquiry and Method." Flower, Long, and Higgins, pp. 3–26.

Flower, Linda, Elenore Long, and Lorraine Higgins, editors. *Learning to Rival: A Literate Practice for Intercultural Understanding*. Lawrence Erlbaum Associates, 2000.

García, Romeo. "Creating Presence from Absence and Sound from Silence." Fishman and Rosenberg, pp. 7–15, https://doi.org/10.25148/clj.13.1.009086.

García, Romeo, and Gesa E. Kirsch. "Deep Rhetoricity as Methodological Grounds for Unsettling the Settled." *College Composition and Communication*, vol. 74, no. 2, 2022, pp. 229–261.

Glenn, Cheryl. "The Language of Rhetorical Feminism, Anchored in Hope." *Open Linguistics*, no. 6, 2020, pp. 334–343.

Gordon, Avery. *Ghostly Matters: Haunting and the Sociological Imagination*. U of Minnesota P, 1997.

Haraway, Donna. "Situated Knowledges: The Science Question in Feminism and the Privileges of Partial Perspective." *Feminism Studies,* vol. 14, no. 2, 1988, pp. 575–599.

Hinshaw, Wendy. "Writing to Listen: Why I Write Across Prison Walls." Fishman and Rosenberg, pp. 55–70, https://doi.org/10.25148/clj.13.1.009090.

Jackson, Rachel C. with Dorothy Whitehorse DeLaune. "Decolonizing Community Writing with Community Listening: Story, Transrhetorical Resistance, and Indigenous Cultural Literacy Activism." Fishman and Rosenberg, pp. 37–54, https://doi.org/10.25148/clj.13.1.009089.

Lohr, Justin, and Heather Lindenman. "Challenging Audiences to Listen: The Performance of Self-Disclosure in Community Writing Projects." Fishman and Rosenberg, pp. 71–86, https://doi.org/10.25148/clj.13.1.009091.

Lugones, María. "Playfulness, World-Travelling, and Loving Perception." *Hypatia,* vol. 2, no. 2, 1987, pp. 3–19.

Maldonado-Torres, Nelson. "On the Coloniality of Being." *Cultural Studies,* vol. 21, no. 2, 2007, pp. 240–270.

Massey, Doreen. *For Space*. Sage Publications, 2005.

Moraga, Cherríe, and Gloria Anzaldúa. *This Bridge Called My Back: Writings by Radical Women of Color* (fourth edition). SUNY Press, 2015.

Mueller, Derek N. *Network Sense: Methods for Visualizing a Discipline*. The WAC Clearinghouse/UP of Colorado, 2017. https://doi.org/10.37514/WRI-B.2017.0124.

Nichols, Ralph G. "Manipulation versus Persuasion." *The Journal of the International Listening Association*, vol. 1, no. 1, 1987, pp. 15–28.

Oleksiak, Timothy, editor. *Queer Rhetorical Listening*, cluster in *Peitho*, vol. 23, no. 1, 2020.

Oliveros, Pauline. *Deep Listening: A Composer's Sound Practice*. Deep Listening Publications, 2005.

Powell, Malea, Daisy Levy, Andrea Riley-Mukavetz, Marilee Brooks-Gillies, Maria Novotny, Jenifer Fisch-Ferguson, and The Cultural Rhetorics Theory Lab. "Our Story Begins Here: Constellating Cultural Rhetorics." *Enculturation: A Journal of Rhetoric, Writing, and Culture*, vol. 25, 2014, n.p.

Powers, Donald E. "A Survey of Academic Demands Related to Listening Skills. Test of English as a Foreign Language Research." *ETS Research Report Series*, vol. 1985, no. 2, 1985, pp. i-63.

Ratcliffe, Krista. *Rhetorical Listening: Identification, Gender, Whiteness*. UP, 2005.

―――. "Rhetorical Listening: A Trope for Interpretive Invention and a 'Code of Cross-Cultural Conduct.'" *College Composition and Communication*, vol. 51, no. 2, 1999, pp. 195–224.

Ratcliffe, Krista, and Cheryl Glenn, editors. *Silence and Listening as Rhetorical Arts*. Southern Illinois UP, 2011.

Ratcliffe, Krista, Tammy Kennedy, and Joyce Irene Middleton, editors. *Rhetorics of Whiteness: Postracial Hauntings in Popular Culture, Social Media, and Education*. Southern Illinois UP, 2017.

Ratcliffe, Krista, and Kyle Jensen. *Rhetorical Listening in Action: A Concept-Tactic Approach*. Parlor Press, 2022.

Richards, Jack C. "Listening Comprehension: Approach, Design, Procedure." *TESOL Quarterly*, vol. 17, no. 2, 1983, pp. 219–40.

Rogers, Carl. R., and Richard E. Farson. *Active Listening*. Industrial Relations Center of the University of Chicago: 1957.

Rohrer, Judy. *Staking Claim: Settler Colonialism and Racialization in Hawai'i*. U of Arizona P, 2016.

Rowan, Karen, and Alexandra J. Cavallaro. "Toward a Model for Preparatory Community Listening." Fishman and Rosenberg, pp. 23–36, https://doi.org/10.25148/clj.13.1.009088.

Royster, Jacqueline Jones. "Looking from the Margins: A Tale of Curricular Reform." *Diversity and Writing within a Modern University*, edited by Jacqueline Jones Royster. The Center for Interdisciplinary Studies of Writing, University of Minnesota, 1990.

―――. "Responsivity: Thinking in the Company of Others." *JAC*, vol. 34, no. 1/2, 2014, pp. 279–292.

―――. Traces of a Stream: Literacy and Social Change among African American Women. Southern Illinois UP, 2000.

―――. "When the First Voice You Hear is Not Your Own." *College Composition and Communication*, vol. 47, no. 1, 1996, pp. 29–40.

Schmoll, Katharina. "Listening as a Citizenship Practice Post-Arab Spring: Mediated Civic Listening as a Struggle, Duty and Joy in Urban Morocco." *Media, Culture & Society*, vol. 43, no. 1, 2021, pp. 84–100.

Scudder, Mary F. *Beyond Empathy and Inclusion: The Challenge of Listening in Democratic Deliberation*. Oxford UP, 2020.

Sheridan, Mary P. "Responsivity: Defining, Cultivating, Enacting." *JAC*, vol. 34, no. 1/2, pp. 11–24.

Smith, Voncile M. "A Beginning, and An Editor Anticipates." *International Listening Association Journal*, vol. 1, no. 1, 1987, pp. 1–2.

Stone, Erica M. "The Story of Sound Off: A Community Writing/Community Listening Experiment." Fishman and Rosenberg, pp. 16–22, https://doi.org/10.1353/clj.2018.0018.

Till, Karen. "Wounded Cities: Memory-Work and a Place-Based Ethics of Care." *Political Geography*, vol. 31, no. 1, 2012, pp. 3–14.

Weaver, Carl H. "Someone Should Do Something about That (A Comment about Listening Research)." *The Journal of the International Listening Association*, vol. 1, no. 1, 1987, pp. 29–31.

Williams, Raymond. *Marxism and Literature*. Oxford UP, 1977.

Zelko, Harold P. "An Outline of the Role of Listening in Communication." *Journal of Communication (Pre-1986)*, vol. 4, no. 3, 1954, pp. 71–75.

# PART 1. HAUNTINGS AND POSSIBILITIES

This section opens the book with hauntings and possibilities, that is, resonances from the past and potentiality for something else, whether it is a change of focus or digital activism. Community listening provides the means for naming, acting, responding, and enacting differently. Through the individual and the collective, the chapters in this section introduce us to the scope of community listening spread across three contexts. Sally F. Benson opens the collection by introducing the concept of *proximate listening*, a praxis for engagement with prison inmates as she learns to listen to and with her incarcerated students. How can one be an educator of any relevance? How can education matter under the conditions Benson brings to life in this chapter, in which the educator must lean sideways at a barred cell door to interact with students? What can the author—and readers—learn from this learning with the inmates who take in math exercises while putting out their life lessons and stories? Benson can get closer to knowing, but she can never fully know. The hauntings that shape the inmate-students' stories and the ways those narratives are accompanied by notes flying along wires or flooded spaces become part of our experience of listening *to*—of listening *with*—Benson.

What are the possibilities for such listening? Chapter 2 moves us toward action by exploring disability advocacy as the work of community listening. The haunted experiences that drove Benson and her students to become proximate listeners yields to the energy of contemporary disabled political advocacy, as Ada Hubrig traces #CripTheVote, a form of community listening rooted in digital action and hashtag activism. Here, community listening is deliberate, concentrated on activism, always with a social justice purpose. Crip voices demand to be expressed and heeded, reaching for and toward possibilities for voice, for change, for current and future action. While hauntings linger in bones, bodies propel into action by using the power to vote—to bend and queer and crip—as forms of community listening that call uniquely for a response.

These three chapters provoke readers to linger with hauntings and possibilities as a way of being awash in community listening, as a sensation as much as a call. Patty Wilde, Mitzi Ceballos, and Wyn Andrews Richards' chapter, "Keeping Bad Company: 'Listening' to Aryan Nations in the Archives," calls in another way, demanding a reach into the past to question the ethical responsibilities held by universities and their libraries. What are the limits of our commitments? How does the presence of offensive historical texts, publications by the regional

Part 1

Aryan nation chapter, continue to haunt? And how can we listen differently as witnesses to such occurrences? What are the responsibilities of community listeners? Readers take in what the authors have put out, the display of pain and potentiality, that provokes our reading through this section.

CHAPTER 1.

# GETTING CLOSER TO MASS INCARCERATION: PROXIMATE LISTENING AS COMMUNITY ACTIVISM

**Sally F. Benson**

Penitentiary of New Mexico

*This chapter is about an author's attempt to listen and understand from a community as an educator in a men's maximum-security prison, an environment fraught with shifting power dynamics. The author explores where she stands in her own narrative about incarceration and education and engages personal reflection to explore concepts of proximity and interrogate ways of listening. As a result, she questions how to ethically produce scholarship based on others' narratives, particularly those of people inside prisons. Acknowledging that personal hauntings or histories distort or haunt the stories we tell ourselves about others, the author theorizes proximate listening as a praxis of listening toward others from a stance of both nearness and radical uncertainty.*

"We tell ourselves stories to live."

– Joan Didion, *The White Album*

## 2009. WHEN LISTENING CALLS

*In 2009, I work for the state of New Mexico's Income Support Division of Health and Human Services, screening applications for public assistance. I conduct intake interviews during the day while taking classes toward state teaching certification at night. Income Support operates in crisis mode, expressed by lines of people in the waiting room each morning. Paper files spill off shelves, along hallways, onto floors. Intergenerational files for families occupy entire shelves. Others' narratives unsettle my own, and the distance from where I sit behind the counter to a client's location can feel uncomfortably narrow. A woman my age, educated and never married, lost her business and lives in*

DOI: https://doi.org/10.37514/PER-B.2025.2531.2.01

*her car; an unforeseen health condition sets us apart. I learn that people coming out of prison need more resources than are available, and the lack of support positions them by default for imminent failure. These narratives haunt me, live inside of me. Some trigger a deep-seated fear of financial insecurity, and others call me closer. To help.*

*The calling pulls my attention toward the state penitentiary, a couple of miles down Highway 14 from Income Support. Upon release from prison, men walk along the highway to our office to stand in line. Interviews expand into stories. No driver's license. No job. Criminal record. No money. The mother of his child reported him for back child pay. He asks me to read the application to him. I type in information while having an internal dialogue: "Let me understand, sir. You just got out of prison. You cannot get a driver's license until you complete your parole. You need a job, but you cannot drive there. If you do get a job with your criminal record, your wages will be garnished, and you cannot keep the money." In my head, I emphasize, "And, you do not read." My supervisor praises my case narratives for their detailed clarity. I listen to people's stories.*

Obstacles for individuals coming out of incarceration unfolded toward me during these interviews, telling a story of injustices and brokenness long before a conviction. Poverty, racism, drug abuse, limited access to education, lack of role models, violence, retaliation—the list expands into a minefield of social inequities and missteps leading to incarceration. The tasks for those released from prison create more obstacles. Not knowing how to read suggests a broken relationship with formal education and further narrows the scope of possibility by limiting job searches. At Income Support, listening to the men who left prison and who did not read required me to leave the comfort of my own narrative around literacy and lean in to listen toward a broader and uncomfortable narrative about incarceration.

In this chapter, I explore a type of community listening that demands responsibility from the listener. Rhetoric frequently concerns speaking and being heard on one's own terms. We less frequently look to listening as critical agency toward speech. By exploring concepts of proximity while interrogating ways of listening, I identify *proximate listening* as an active means of listening toward members of our communities from a stance of both nearness and radical uncertainty. Proximity engages ways of listening beyond what we tell ourselves we hear. Leaning toward understanding but not assuming understanding allows listeners to remain open to new, plural, or unattainable meanings. I argue that leaning toward understanding, and listening proximately, actively precedes hearing-as-understanding and requires our willingness to acknowledge the other and embrace that which we cannot know.

My interest in proximity as a listening concept starts with Bryan Stevenson. Stevenson, attorney and award-winning author of *Just Mercy: A Story of Justice and Redemption*, begins his story with an admission. When tasked as a legal intern to visit an incarcerated man on death row, Stevenson admits he "wasn't prepared to meet a condemned man" (3). Stevenson writes about "proximity to the condemned" and "getting closer to mass incarceration," arguing that we, as a country, have allowed "fear, anger, and distance to shape the way we treat the most vulnerable among us" (14). Stevenson's proximity to the condemned brought him physically and purposefully closer to mass incarceration. The 1983 meeting changed Stevenson's life. He went on to establish the Equal Justice Initiative legal practice and has devoted his career to criminal justice reform. Stevenson shares his grandmother's advice with us—*get closer to what is most important to understand it.*

Prisons, by design, distance incarcerated individuals from people outside of prison, keeping those inside recessed beyond sight and behind layers of surveillance. As Stevenson argues, one must get closer to mass incarceration to understand it. Here, I explore ways of being proximate while situating listening as an active stance of being in relation to others in carceral spaces. I engage proximate listening as an intentional leaning toward understanding. I borrow *listening being* from communication theorist Lisbeth Lipari, who describes listening as an "ethical act" prior to understanding ("Listening" 348–49). Lipari introduces listening being as the dwelling place that "begins not from a speaking, but from the emptiness of awareness itself," or a transcendental place of both being and becoming (348). Listening is the empty inner silence we offer and receive when making space, which Lipari describes as "inside us where we are not" (349).

When we make space to be fully present, relinquishing our need to conclude or lay claim to meaning, we allow for new possibilities. In "Argument as Emergence, Rhetoric as Love," Jim Corder suggests that when we release the convictions of our own narratives, we may "lose our plot, and our convictions as well" (19). Only then can others' speech approach. Until I listened toward the men who came from the prison to Income Support, whose stories speak of impossibility, I did not spend my days wondering whether incarcerated people receive education in prison or what role literacy may have in relation to their incarceration. Corder would say that my narrative "was wanting all along" (19). The wanting is a lack, a missing-ness.

Our personal narratives, while we may not be intending, can brush up against those of others—strangers whom we unconsciously relegate to the sidelines of our main stories. For example, the tangle of problems around incarceration and literacy was not central to my own story until I leaned closer to engage members of my community previously absent from my narrative. Corder suggests that when "contending" narratives bump up against ours and ask us to leave the history and comfort of one narrative to enter the present and discomfort of another, we have options. We can turn away from contending narratives, pretending to ignore them, or we can learn to change (19).

My concern in this chapter is with the teacher-researcher-author practicing community listening. In introducing a 2018 special issue of *Community Literacy Journal* (*CLJ*), Jenn Fishman and Lauren Rosenberg define community listening as a feminist rhetorical practice and intervention (2). Fishman and Rosenberg embed community listening in community literacy work (2), wherein the listener is "in a position of generous openness" (3). By maintaining a stance of generous openness, listeners sustain attention to identity dynamics and challenge their and others' biases (3). Community listening, "an active, layered, intentional practice," requires us to suspend judgment and notice what we do not always see or hear outside of our community interactions (1). Ascribing an element of risk to community listening, Fishman and Rosenberg argue that practitioners must be willing to change to ethically respond (1). Contributors to their issue of *CLJ* practice community listening in spaces of storytelling and memory (García; Jackson with DeLaune), in writing's embodied meaning (Hinshaw), in performative vulnerability and disclosure in public spaces (Stone; Lohr and Lindenman), and through precursory research for community literacy partnerships (Rowan and Cavallaro). Community listening assumes "none of us is ever outside of our communities," enabling us to "become better able to know each other, to find new levels of meaning, to challenge assumptions and biases as well as preconceptions" (Fishman and Rosenberg 3).

Other theorized forms of listening, such as rhetorical listening and hauntological listening, also bridge expanses between privilege and marginalization, across cultural differences, and through portals of time. For example, rhetorical listening has the potential for social justice by helping us hear that which we cannot see, allowing us to "invent, interpret, and ultimately judge differently" (Ratcliffe 203). Hauntological listening summons the dead to "walk amongst us—indeed, in us, as the living (un)dead," opening us to alternative or plural histories as narratives of possibility (Ballif 145–46). These examples of listening suggest the borders delineating *us* from *them* are permeable, fluid, kairotic, and generative.

Proximate listening also creates possibility but is intentionally practiced as radical unknowing and relational leaning toward the other. When attempting to frame listening in terms of reciprocal outcomes, we assume cross-boundary understanding of both our and others' experiences. When we listen to others, we silently tell ourselves what we hear. What is heard occurs when I take your words into me, into my narrative, making them mine (Lipari "Rhetoric's" 237). What I hear is thus my narrative. As a unique form of community listening, however, proximate listening precedes and anticipates the "I hear you" moment that implies we understand. Proximate means both being near and a rhetorical leaning toward that offers an inner emptiness, a blank slate, if you will, not unlike Fishman and Rosenberg's "generous openness." If we embrace listening toward others, we suspend our need to assign hierarchical meaning about others in our narratives. Listening toward others without appropriating meaning has invoked me to change, to position myself to advocate, or to move closer to do more proximate listening.

At Income Support, I had to lean in, suspend my inherited way of seeing things, and offer spacious listening toward others, whose stories are not mine, thus allowing for new meaning. When Lipari suggests we "listen persons to speech" ("Rhetoric's" 228), she assigns central agency to listening. Listening actively provides the object of speaking by offering a dwelling place for speech to sound or resonate. Through listening to the formerly incarcerated men's stories, I leaned toward understanding and made room. I changed. I started by volunteering for Literacy Volunteers of Santa Fe, teaching one evening a week. From there, I made more changes. In this chapter, I offer narratives of listening and proximity to incarceration by engaging identities across several communities. I write as a scholar of rhetoric while situating myself as a former state government employee, community volunteer, public school instructor, and full-time prison staff educator. Importantly, I write as someone who has not been incarcerated.

## LISTENING THAT RELOCATES

*After six months of working at Income Support while working toward my teaching licenses at night, I accept a position as a Special Education instructor at an elementary school. My morning commute along Highway 14 takes me past grazing buffalo and just beyond the entrance to the state penitentiary. I can now trace the walk from the prison to Income Support made by the men I interviewed. At the school, more contending narratives confront me. Students' parents struggle with their own literacy, impacting their children's reading development through limited modeling. Some students have incarcerated family members. I watch students cycle through excited anticipation and depressed withdrawal around prison visits. For three years, I witness meltdowns during enforced state testing. I wonder if some students will follow the paths of their parents. I have not forgotten about the men from the penitentiary who asked me to read for them, and again, I turn toward the prison. I am listening for an opening, a way to enter this story as an actor by mapping the connections. The understory about literacy—the men from the prison, the students at the school, the women I taught as a literacy volunteer—animates my own story with people in my community not seen or heard in prior versions. I write a letter to the New Mexico Corrections Department asking about teaching possibilities.*

Proximity, for Stevenson, means positioning oneself closer in relation to, confronting fear and prejudice of, and advocating for. Listening to stories of the near impossibility of post-incarceration success and witnessing the intergenerational pipeline from school to prison invoked me. I had to make room for new choices in my narrative, which meant finding literacy support, volunteering in that effort, teaching in my community, and eventually asking to teach at the penitentiary. Proximate listening unhinges our narratives about ourselves and others, creating the generous openness Fishman and Rosenberg encourage, thus moving us closer. Each decision moves me closer to prison.

## LISTENING TO ATTUNE

Dynamics of power shape our relationships, and our us-and-them locations create relational tension. Proximity both narrows and amplifies distance. Proximate listening requires being proximate to otherness and with alterity, a stance Lipari describes as attunement ("Rhetorics" 234). We attune ourselves to the speech and otherness of the other as a strategy for remaining present without assuming, which Jacqueline Jones Royster and Gesa E. Kirsch suggest enables a "broader view" (72). Royster and Kirsch's *critical imagination* engages reflexive listening to make room for "the possibility of seeing something not previously noticed or considered" by suspending assumptions (72). *Strategic contemplation* requires a stance of openness in our outward observations and in our inward meditations on how lived experience—embodied in ourselves, our research subjects, and surrounding contexts—shapes perspectives of both researcher and research subject (22). For example, Wendy Hinshaw describes listening to "tune to the material conditions of speaking and writing" in a prison writing exchange program ("Writing to Listen" 57). Undergraduate students exchange writing with incarcerated writers, exploring issues around incarceration and social justice. Participants then record themselves reading their own writing in their respective places of writing, juxtaposing privileged quiet with prison cacophony. Listening to participants reading in situ humanizes readers while emphasizing differences across privilege and oppression. Participants noticed previously unnoticed identifications and the power differentials that shaped them (59). Accordant with Lipari's listening to attune without assuming, Hinshaw's listening to recorded sounds of place actively situates listening in relation to difference yet closer in proximity.

As tools of inquiry, Lipari's attunement and Royster and Kirsch's critical imagination and strategic contemplation require us to put assumptions aside to listen responsibly to what may be possible. To listen *for*. Working closely with students who had incarcerated family members revealed prior absences within my narrative about incarceration and about my school's community. I had to continually learn not to assume. Once we claim to hear, the history that haunts our narratives threatens possibilities by shaping meaning. Our responsibility, then, is to acknowledge our role as agents in mapping our findings—what we tell ourselves we see/hear and how we enfold others' narratives into our own stories.

Romeo García asks scholars to first address their hauntings—the histories they inherit and the narratives they tell ("Haunt(ed/ing)" 239). We "bend and obey without question" as subjects of our hauntings (233). García cautions against peddling knowledge *of* the other as an act of responsibility *for* the other (234), another reminder that with listening comes responsibility. For example, García questions how white scholars, who can never sidestep privilege, practice community listening. They mine others' stories—"the kind of stories white academic 'scholars' tell themselves"—to take home and claim common ground within or "to traffic in the normative masquerading as gifts of responsibility" (240). I interpret García's claim as a one-way operation, in which well-meaning scholars take and carry what they hear, but their efforts do not necessarily reciprocate in kind. I understand this not as an accusation but as an invitation for scholars doing community literacy work to listen responsibly to respond ethically.

As listeners, we are responsible for the stories we tell. Can we assign meaning to others' experiences through our own narratives without making assumptions? When I suggest that identifying reciprocal outcomes assumes we understand others' experiences, I am questioning whether this is ethical or possible when listening in carceral spaces. Academic scholars doing community literacy work in prisons inevitably return to spaces of privilege with prison narratives in their own scholarship or through writings of incarcerated individuals. Curated prison narratives provide platforms for incarcerated voices and may help raise public awareness of prison while still functioning as scholarly currency. Incarcerated writers, whose narratives we escort out of prison and into scholarly spaces, remain behind. The tightrope between advocacy and "discursive imperialism" (Alcoff 17) becomes a "conversation of 'us' with 'us' about 'them'" (Minh-ha qtd. in Alcoff 6). We privilege ourselves, argues Linda Alcoff, when claiming expertise of others' situations or championing just causes and receiving praise (29). In attempting to understand, we often place meaning onto others' words and actions, translating listening into hearing. Proximate listening occurs before we translate. We offer space of unknowing and do not fill it with meaning.

## 2012. LISTENING AT THE SOUTH

*In 2012, I accept a position teaching adult education at the Penitentiary of New Mexico (PNM). Every morning, I turn into the prison complex off Highway 14, stop at the checkpoint, and show my badge. The gate patrol officer pokes his head far enough into the driver's side window to scan the backseat. "Hi there, young lady. Pop the trunk, please." He is young enough to be my son, yet he assumes the role of adult to mine as suspicious child. He slams the trunk hard. After a month, the taillight wire dislodges. I put a sign inside the trunk: "Please close the trunk gently. Thank you!" He slams it harder and motions me to drive on.*

*Open stretches of desert dirt delineate PNM. Everywhere I look, prairie dogs pop up from their mounds. Some consider prairie dogs well-deserved targets along their commute. At the end of the day, I weave my car through carcasses strewn along the two-mile drive exiting the prison complex. Coyotes, snakes, rabbits, hawks, and eagles also vie for dominance in the open landscape that separates the three facilities within the complex. The wildlife must negotiate territory and power like everyone else.*

*I am a foreigner in unfamiliar terrain. After completing forty hours of training, I have a three-inch stack of printed New Mexico Corrections Department policies, a gate key tag, and a radio. I am assigned to the maximum-security men's facility, or the "South." I do not know the paramilitary culture, the harsh physicality of the housing units, the deafening noise, the strong odors. Each feels like an assault. I take mental notes of the processes, the very exacting procedural way of moving through a maximum-security facility and in the dirty metal place of prison.*

Proximate listening demands that we move closer, practice active silence, and listen with generous spaciousness.

*I unlock and lock four consecutive outside gates on my walk toward the housing units. I announce into the intercom, "Education! Benson! K-pod!" K-pod is in Housing Unit Two. I hear only the piercing snap! of the entrance door electronically disengaging. The hallway door to K-pod roars open and immediately reverses direction, closing faster than I can write my name and time on the sign-in sheet. I lurch to get inside. "Woman in pod!" I call out. The housing roster on the wall tells me my student is upstairs on the far end. The echo chamber amplifies men's catcalling as I pass by cell doors. Facing a cell straight on affords me a view of an entire cell including the metal toilet immediately inside the door. I stand to the side and extend my arm to knock. "Education. Ms. Benson." A face appears at one side of the narrow window. I negotiate forms while carrying a bag over one shoulder and a clipboard in my other hand. I follow this routine for each new student on my roster. I learn subtle acknowledgments of respect. Never walk straight up to a cell door window. Slide papers through the air slot on the side of the door instead of on the dirty floor. Stand close to the air slot to hear or be heard. Stand back to see and be seen. Turn around and twist to one side to show your clipboard, making the yellow legal pad your whiteboard. This is my dance at the cell door.*

*An origami envelope on the end of a thread shoots past my foot toward another cell, where it can be reeled in. I step on the thread lightly, not wanting to break the "fishing line." I am supposed to report fishing, often used for inconspicuous exchanges of information or even weapons. I have eye contact with my student but say nothing.*

*I only acknowledge the envelope in a way that means stop. Respect me, and I will respect you.*

Before our hauntings inform our arguments, proximate listening asks us to take a leap of faith toward understanding by *not* understanding. We loosen the discursive lens that haunts our search for meaning and allow radical uncertainty. Envelopes also carry instant coffee.

*Soon, the fishing stops when I enter a pod. The catcalling stops when I pass cell doors. The shouting stops while I work with my student.*

In some narratives, I am being tested; in others, respected. The cell door stands between me and my student. I leave at the end of the day. Words and behavior, according to my world, my narrative, hold different meanings in others' spaces. Proximate listening creates room to transcend us-them assumptions. Is my student also listening proximately? I only know that within a larger system of power, where most relationships express complicated hierarchical dynamics, we carve out space to be in relation to one another. I navigate the shared spaces and find my way into my work.

## LISTENING AT THE CELL DOOR

Much of my teaching takes place when "pod walking," or entering housing unit pods and working with individual students at their cell doors. Our ongoing conversations occur in dynamic spaces between math problems, shared spaces in writing and feedback, or transitory spaces between exercise cages in the yard. A student asks if I read *Prison Legal News* (PLN), which he and others rely on for drafting legal documents (e.g., habeas corpus appeals). I subscribe and learn about some of the many legal issues incarcerated people face. Paul Wright, while serving time in Washington State, started PLN to provide incarcerated individuals information and resources related to prison labor, medical and mental health care in prison, juvenile justice, prison censorship, and more. Another student asks if I know about the hunger strikes at Pelican Bay and throughout California prisons. In 2013, 30,000 people incarcerated across California simultaneously stopped eating (Rideau A25). Like PLN, the hunger strikes respond to injustices and conditions in prisons.

My interest in understanding issues around incarceration leads me to journalism by people with direct experience such as Wilbert Rideau, former editor of the Louisiana prison newspaper, *The Angolite*, or John J. Lennon, a prison journalist incarcerated in New York. I seek out prison narratives in literature, memoirs, and blogs and listen for an opening. My search is pointed. I work with a volatile population entrenched in a social hierarchy of violence. I want to know how the writers risked walking away from prison's criminal ethic to work toward college degrees or how they managed to get out and stay out of prison and why they write. Where, in the complex web of problems, can intervention best occur?

*One of my students asks, "Ms. Benson, when you were a kid, you'd go to the kitchen on Saturday mornings and have breakfast with your family, right?" We're doing math at his cell door.*

*"Sometimes," I tell him. I don't tell him about my parents' constant yelling and fighting during meals and the subsequent eating problems I had.*

*"As a kid," he explains, "I'd go to the kitchen, and the table has scales and bags of dope on it. I'm told to run bags and bring back the money. I don't know any better. I'm eight."*

I try to see his kitchen table through his child eyes, but I know I cannot. I think about students I had taught at the elementary school, who had ties to incarceration, wondering how many others elude me.

*Same signs, add and keep,*
*Different signs, subtract.*
*Take the sign of the higher number, then you'll be exact!*

I teach my student a song to remember rules for adding and subtracting negative numbers. He is the first student on my roster to earn a GED.

*"I kept singing that song," he laughs.*

I imagine him hunched over a tiny prison desk reading Kierkegaard. This is my narrative bumping up against his, threatening to get in my way of being an effective teacher. I erroneously attempt to save through education. My idealizing higher education feeds my story about this student with my own hauntings about education. In my imaginary story's trajectory, he will stay under the disciplinary radar, work toward college courses, and embrace philosophy. Unlike mandatory adult basic education, college in prison is a privilege that requires good behavior. My own narrative has historically but falsely aligned higher education with promises of success. To embrace my student's narrative, Corder argues I must first lose my own plot. I cannot know what is at stake for my student or what risk participatory education, and its required clear conduct, might pose for him, and I cannot write his story. The more layers of assumed meaning we peel away, the closer we stand in relation to one another.

As much as I want students to develop skills to succeed and self-advocate, I cannot assume to know their choices and limitations. Lack of formal education is one of many obstacles incarcerated individuals face inside and outside of prison. I question the lack of quality post-secondary education available at PNM. When individuals choose to enroll in prison college classes, behavior dynamics in housing units can change and even produce a ripple effect, potentially interrupting patterns in families or communities beyond the prison. Students ask why there is no "real" college program at PNM in lieu of the limited correspondence courses offered. "It would give us something to do, keep us out of trouble," one tells me. Access to higher education in prison does not promise future employment outside of prison. Higher education and incarceration intersect with countless social inequities related to race, economics, class—a *wicked problem*, for which finding any one solution is nearly impossible.[1] Solving one problem requires solving many. I listen for openings to find a foothold for understanding.

## LISTENING IN LIMINAL SPACES

*Mr. C has a habit of showing up to his window without a shirt. He is covered in ink from the top of his shaved scalp, over his face in barbed-wire eyebrows, around his neck, on his chest and back, and down his arms. I ask him to put a shirt on.*

*"This is my house," he tells me.*

*"Yes, but this is our classroom," I say.*

*"Ms. Benson, if you can show me in policy where it says I have to wear a shirt to do education, I'll put a shirt on."*

*"Mr. C, I don't know if there is a policy that states that. I'm asking you to put a shirt on out of respect for me. You have stories written all over your body that distract me. This is school. I come to teach you math and writing." After that, Mr. C wears his shirt.*

Asking Mr. C to wear a shirt because his tattoos distract me responds to his need for respect with my own need for respect. His tattoos tell a history of gang affiliation through symbolism and monikers. We both know the rule: I cannot inquire about his gang commitment, and he is not supposed to glorify it. Knowing specifics about students' involvement with security threat groups implies "undue familiarity," which can cost me my job. Like stepping on a fishing line gently but saying nothing, we negotiate our mutual need for respect and exchange a moment of respectfully not knowing.

After Mr. C and I are done with our "class" at his cell door, I face the pod exit with twelve sets of eyes behind me and in clear view of the cameras and observation deck. I wait. Pushing the button or calling the officer upstairs prolongs the wait. I do not give in. My waiting is one of many spaces of resistance. Never ring the buzzer to get out of a closed space—hallway, stairwell, pod, housing unit— unless you want to wait longer. Like the respect I attempt to show my students, there is an unspoken rule about respect toward officers and other brass. Know the rank. Respect is currency. There are no doorknobs. You depend on others to allow you access, to open and close doors, and to keep you safe.

---

1    See Rittel and Webber's "Dilemmas in a General Theory of Planning;" unlike scientific problems with identifiable solutions, planners deal with societal problems, which are interconnected to broader social systems, making them unsolvable "wicked" problems (159–60).

Socialized hierarchies of power map dynamic borders in prison spaces. While working together, my student and I approach from different sides of the cell door to create a shared space of respect. We collaborate to preserve our working dynamic, which is in constant flux under surveillance. When we finish, and I move down the stairs to exit, the dynamic changes. Once I leave, that same physical location becomes yet another space of power.

*The exit door rolls open. "Thank you!" I call out.*

Like Stevenson's call to get closer to understand, Corder also argues for movement toward understanding: "[W]e have *to see* each other, *to know* each other, *to be present to* each other, *to embrace* each other" (23). My repeated visits with students over time help me see and hear what I cannot see and hear. Lipari describes listening being as a "utopian vision of listening" we aspire toward, which transcends the scope of language ("Listening" 348). Acknowledging that we cannot know surpasses suspending judgment. Stevenson writes that working closely with individuals caught in a criminal justice system riddled with injustices, suffering, death, and cruel punishment shows him that brokenness is "the source of our common humanity" in our mutual search for comfort and meaning (289). When owning "our weaknesses, our deficits, our biases, our fears," we seek mercy and are thus more compelled to offer it (290). Proximate listening is an invitation and a generous offering, which begins with trust and time spent being near.

Listening co-constructs a practice in understanding who and what we stand in relation to in a holistic narrative. By listening others to speech, Lipari claims we avoid "assimilat[ing] them into what we already know (or think we know) about their point of view" (*Listening* 203). Drawing from Emmanuel Levinas' ethics of relationality, our just relation to others, Lipari intertwines ethics and dialogue or "dialogic ethics" ("Rhetoric's" 228). Listening is no longer a strategy of reception, nor one of epistemological production of what we tell ourselves we hear. Listening and speaking interconnect, each existing in relation to the other (241). The co-constitutive relationship recasts speaker-listener binaries as inseparable parts of a whole. Proximate listening extends this relational dynamic through a relocation toward the other in a communicative collaboration. We move closer.

## LISTENING ACROSS THE FLOOD

*"This isn't a good time, Ms. Benson. Can you come another time?" Mr. F's voice comes from the back of his cell. They had moved him to the super max. I don't ask why. "Can I drop off some things for you to read?" I wait, standing to the side of his window. I have worked with Mr. F for a year in the college-readiness "bridge program." He enthusiastically participates in education, has a GED, and tells me he wants to take college correspondence courses. I hear sloshing, and he appears. "I had*

*to do it," he says. He has intentionally flooded his cell. When they find out, they will eliminate his eligibility for participatory education, which requires a year of clear conduct. We face one another in silence. I see his tears.*

Our exchange still haunts me, reminding me of what I cannot know and, therefore, cannot judge. Facing my student, my disappointment was clear. Again, my narrative interferes. I assumed Mr. F irresponsibly lost another chance at the very thing that could offer him more choices. He took the lower road. That is the explanation I told myself that made sense in my narrative about my student and about education. Yet, I cannot know. If I could retract this moment, I would relive it differently. Lipari argues that misunderstanding, both inescapable and valuable, is an ethical practice. Despite the agency language affords us, some aspects of our existence as humans are "ineffable," and our ethical response is "to listen more closely to others, to inquire more deeply into their differences, and to question our own already well-formed understandings of the world" (*Listening* 8). Proximate listening humbles us, demanding we actively practice generous spaciousness toward others, not despite misunderstanding but because of it.

Rather than assume my student's motivations and react as I did, standing at my student's cell door and not knowing offers space for possibility. I cannot know whether my student flooded his cell in solidarity or in fear, whether his transfer to the super max was protective or punitive, if my standing in front of his cell was ruining some plan, or what his tears meant. I can only lean toward understanding, unyoked from conclusions. If given another chance, this is the mercy I could offer and what I would hope for myself. Corder argues that we are all "fictionmakers/historians," authoring ourselves into our own narratives, seeing "only what our eyes will let us see at a given moment" (16). He motions us to relinquish what we imagine of others and "pursue the reality of things only partially knowable" (28). As García suggests, "not all knowledge can be archived" ("Creating" 9) but embracing others' truths creates a rhetorical movement toward. If I speculate about my student, I reappropriate his actions into my story, which is a story about me. Hosting the other by making space "where we are not" (Lipari "Listening" 350), we let go of our ideas about the other and about who we are to stay present (351). If listening and speaking become inseparable features of a whole, listening becomes a communicative practice to stand in relation to the other in a holistic narrative rather than as separate from the other.

## LISTENING TO THAT WHICH I CANNOT HEAR

*While navigating prison spaces and my duties, I listen to the world outside of myself and to my inner world. The world outside requires me to work under policy mandates, in harsh conditions, and within a hierarchy of power among participants. This world operates through surveillance and documentation. The inner world requires my constant alertness to listen through senses and intuition to stay present in a place of shifting dynamics that has high stakes, sometimes of life or death. This world exists in liminal spaces of nascent and evanescent moments constantly under revision.*

I carry trauma from my years at the prison. Memory replays fleeting exchanges, yet ascribing words to them dilutes the experience. A student tells me how he ended someone's life. His admittance bursts forth unsolicited. He is up for parole in two years, and he asks me how he could ever live a "normal" life, describing prison as "one hundred percent violent." What surprises me in this moment is that, rather than feel sorry for him or disappointed as I did with Mr. F, I feel only love. The "inner emptiness" Lipari ascribes to listening being (355) best characterizes how my student's words pass through me without fastening onto hooks of judgment. I continue to carry this spacious love, reminding me of its possibility.

We practice proximate listening to actively listen and follow the threads, the snippets that lead us into spaces where people comingle, invite, confide, and share. Like Lipari's listening being, Stevenson's proximity claims, "you see things you can't otherwise see; you hear things you can't otherwise hear. You begin to recognize the humanity that resides in each of us" (290). We follow and listen where people create space rather than resistance. This same generosity we offer in return. Soften the borders and listen without attempting to fill the space with certain meaning. We lean toward others responsibly, as they may choose to lean toward us as a result, and that asks something of us. When I embrace my student's admission, I do not understand him as an isolated act. I recognize a complex individual grappling with being human—like me.

## COMMUNITY LISTENING IN PRISON

So that others can gain a better understanding of incarceration, outside academics doing community literacy work in prisons share writing by incarcerated individuals (Hinshaw and Jacobi 2). Wendy Hinshaw's *Exchange for Change* prison writing program and Tobi Jacobi's *SpeakOut!* writing workshops in jails bring outside and inside writers together. Hinshaw and Jacobi point to prison writing's power to leverage public understanding, arguing that "writing by and with people in prison—has always been a primary agent in changing public perceptions and inspiring writing and movements for change on the outside on behalf of prisoners" (2). This type of listening through community writing aims to bring us closer to one another's stories.

While community-engaged prison writing strives to raise public awareness about prison, outsiders commingling with insiders to share writing acts involves risk, including increased surveillance. Incarcerated writers may be asked to participate or write in ways that make them vulnerable in other prison spaces, where they cannot share their reflections or commingle. Manifestations of prison, such as writing, artifacts, or reports, are shaped by layers of surveillance in terms of what is produced and why and for whom it is produced. García rightfully argues that scholars seeking to understand through community listening in prison are listening to those who cannot be seen or speak on their own terms ("Haunt(ed/ing)" 234). This is a partial listening. When we listen in prison spaces, what we hear may be highly curated and is informed by our limited access both materially and in our understanding as outside scholars.

Under surveillance by peers and academic institutions, however, scholars are expected to report their research findings. This is the dilemma. How we present our findings raises questions, particularly in how we measure success or reciprocal outcomes of our work. We must "interrogate the bearing of our location" on what we claim (Alcoff 25) and carefully consider whose experiences we report back. García asks if we can listen without attempting to extract knowledge-as-responsibility and "find solace" in accepting that we cannot necessarily conclude understanding ("Creating" 9). Can we ethically understand the impact of our work on anyone but ourselves? Even that becomes a curated story, and when we curate others' words and actions, we move dangerously close to authoring *our* stories about *them*. We carry something of the other back to our spaces to make it seen, but we carry only parts of a moving whole, some of which is beyond our reach.

We can investigate different ways of reporting. For example, do we ethically leverage public understanding of prison or garner support for prison reform by choosing narratives of only the incarcerated? Prisons host a network of individuals, all of whom shape narratives of incarceration. Community-engaged scholarship about prison, however, rarely includes narratives of individuals who spend countless hours inside prisons—prison staff educators, corrections officers, administrators—all members of prison communities who too easily fall into categories of them. Their absence from scholarship about prison, or generalized assumptions about these individuals, compromises prison narratives.

Community listening as proximate listening with more inclusive representation of prison communities opens up a broader site for inquiry. Many prison staff come from the same communities as their wards. Trauma in prison impacts individuals on both sides of the cell door in close proximity to one another.[2] Changing entrenched cycles of oppression begins with healing, which begins with healing ourselves. Stevenson claims that our own brokenness feeds our capacity for compassion (289). As Lipari argues, by setting our assumptions

---

2    For example, Kelsey Kauffman (*Prison Officers and Their World*) and Ted Conover (*New Jack: Guarding Sing Sing*) describe trauma experienced by corrections officers.

Benson

aside, providing space where we are not, we stay present and open to new meaning. When we foreground listening rather than speaking as a central concept of our rhetorical inquiry, listening toward understanding actively invokes the other. When we listen toward one another, we create community. We become.

## THE HEARD

Community listening seeks to center community voices. By engaging a broader prison community, we can expand on the ways we listen persons to speech. Rather than focus on our in/ability to speak for, why not question how we listen in relation to? García states that "[s]ome things are beyond the reaches of interpretation and certainty" ("Creating" 13) and asks us to create new stories and reminds us that the future is indebted to "people still denied presence and sound in the present" (10). Academic scholars practicing community listening in prison can lean toward understanding others' narratives of incarceration and share them without reappropriating them. Our leaning toward the other is ongoing, situating our own identities as works in progress. Thus, we overwrite old stories we carry in our narratives with new ones, and those stories are about us. The new possibilities are in our own thinking.

Proximate listening asks us to dwell near enough, long enough, silent enough to notice our relational differences, acknowledge our misunderstandings, and empty ourselves to make room for new ways of understanding. Proximate listening changes us. In this chapter, I have offered a pedagogy of critical listening that continues to reshape my stories and my mis/understanding. Rather than bridge, proximate listening respectfully acknowledges expanses between privilege and marginalization, across cultural differences, and through portals of time. By learning to recognize the expanses, we address our hauntings (García), hear that which we cannot see (Ratcliffe), find new levels of meaning and challenge our assumptions (Fishman and Rosenberg), and open ourselves to plural histories as narratives of possibility (Ballif).

Rather than listening to understand as a practice toward solving presumed problems, we might consider listening to interrogate the process of seeking to understand. We can move closer and lean in to listen without presuming solutions. Proximate listening, valuable for its own sake, engages unknowing spaciousness, uncertainty, and possibility for change and begins from a place of love. As a scholar, I still search for ways to communicate that.

## ACKNOWLEDGMENTS

I offer many thanks to Lauren Rosenberg, Jenn Fishman, and Romeo García for including me in this project and for their ongoing patience, support, and generous insight. I also owe thanks to the University of Arizona College of Social and Behavioral Sciences and the Bilinski Educational Foundation for supporting this work.

## WORKS CITED

Alcoff, Linda. "The Problem of Speaking for Others." *Cultural Critique*, no. 20, 1991, pp. 5–32. https://doi.org/10.2307/1354221.

Ballif, Michelle. "Historiography as Hauntology: Paranormal Investigations into the History of Rhetoric." *Theorizing Histories of Rhetoric*, edited by Michelle Ballif. Southern Illinois UP, 2013, pp. 139–53.

Conover, Ted. *New Jack: Guarding Sing Sing*. Random House, 2000.

Corder, Jim W. "Argument as Emergence, Rhetoric as Love." *Rhetoric Review*, vol. 4, no. 1, 1985, pp. 16–32. https://doi.org/10.1080/07350198509359100.

Fishman, Jenn, and Lauren Rosenberg, editors. *Community Writing, Community Listening*, special issue of *Community Literacy Journal*, vol. 13, no. 1, 2018.

Fishman, Jenn, and Lauren Rosenberg. "Guest Editors' Introduction: Community Writing, Community Listening." Fishman and Rosenberg, pp. 1–6, https://doi.org/10.25148/clj.13.1.009085.

García, Romeo. "Creating Presence from Absence and Sound from Silence." Fishman and Rosenberg, pp. 7–15, https://doi.org/10.25148/clj.13.1.009086.

———. "Haunt(ed/ing) Genealogies and Literacies." *Reflections: A Journal of Community-Engaged Writing and Rhetoric*, vol. 19, no. 1, 2019, pp. 230–52. https://reflectionsjournal.net.

Hinshaw, Wendy, and Tobi Jacobi. "Guest Editors' Introduction: Prison Writing, Literacies and Communities." *Reflections: A Journal of Community-Engaged Writing and Rhetoric*, vol. 19, no. 1, 2019, pp. 1–7. https://reflectionsjournal.net.

Hinshaw, Wendy. "Writing to Listen: Why I Write Across Prison Walls." Fishman and Rosenberg, pp. 55–70, https://doi.org/10.25148/clj.13.1.009090.

Jackson, Rachel C. with Dorothy Whitehorse DeLaune. "Decolonizing Community Writing with Community Listening: Story, Transrhetorical Resistance, and Indigenous Cultural Literacy Activism." Fishman and Rosenberg, pp. 37–54, https://doi.org/10.25148/clj.13.1.009089.

Kauffman, Kelsey. *Prison Officers and Their World*. Harvard UP, 1988.

Lipari, Lisbeth. "Listening, Thinking, Being." *Communication Theory*, vol. 20, no. 3, 2010, pp. 348–62. https://doi.org/10.1111/j.1468-2885.2010.01366.x.

———. *Listening, Thinking, Being: Toward an Ethics of Attunement*. Penn State UP, 2014.

———. "Rhetoric's Other: Levinas, Listening, and the Ethical Response." *Philosophy & Rhetoric*, vol. 45, no. 3, 2012, p. 227–245. *Project MUSE*, https://muse.jhu.edu/article/482891.

Lohr, Justin, and Heather Lindenman. "Challenging Audiences to Listen: The Performance of Self-Disclosure in Community Writing Projects." Fishman and Rosenberg, pp. 71–86, https://doi.org/10.25148/clj.13.1.009091.

Ratcliffe, Krista. "Rhetorical Listening: A Trope for Interpretive Invention and a 'Code of Cross-Cultural Conduct'." *College Composition and Communication*, vol. 51, no. 2, 1999, pp. 195–224, *JSTOR*, https://doi.org/10.2307/359039.

Rideau, Wilbert. "When Prisoners Protest." *The New York Times*, 16 July 2013, p. A25. https://www.nytimes.com/2013/07/17/opinion/when-prisoners-protest.html.

Rittel, Horst W. J., and Melvin M. Webber. "Dilemmas in a General Theory of Planning." *Policy Sciences*, vol. 4, no. 2, 1973, pp. 155–69, *JSTOR*, http://www.jstor.org/stable/4531523.

Rowan, Karen, and Alexandra J. Cavallaro. "Toward a Model for Preparatory Community Listening." Fishman and Rosenberg, pp. 23–36, https://doi.org/10.25148/clj.13.1.009088.

Royster, Jacqueline Jones, and Gesa E. Kirsch. *Feminist Rhetorical Practices: New Horizons for Rhetoric, Composition, and Literacy Studies*. Southern Illinois UP, 2012.

Stevenson, Bryan. *Just Mercy: A Story of Justice and Redemption*. Spiegel & Grau, 2015.

Stone, Erica M. "The Story of Sound Off: A Community Writing/Community Listening Experiment." Fishman and Rosenberg, pp. 16–22, https://doi.org/10.1353/clj.2018.0018.

CHAPTER 2.

# CRAFTING CRIP SPACE THROUGH DISABLED POLITICAL ADVOCACY: #CRIPTHEVOTE AS COMMUNITY LISTENING

**Ada Hubrig**
Sam Houston State University

*This chapter is about disability advocacy shaped by community listening in digital spaces. For the author, disability advocates uses of hashtag activism illustrate new ways of listening across disabilities, bodies, and differences all directed towards building community, countering ableism and various forms of oppression, and exercising political agency for change.*

"Discovering a community of disabled people and learning our stories gave me a sense of what is possible"

– Alice Wong, Disability Visibility

Too often, disabled people are considered arhetorical. We are expected to overcome our disabilities if we wish to participate in society (Hubrig "Fear"). As disability activist and badass Alice Wong put it, American political rhetoric and media depicts disabled people as "unmotivated and undeserving, passive consumers of taxpayer dollars who are out to 'game the system'" (27). Far from passive, disabled people put our collective crip genius to work not only to survive the ableist systems but also to organize and demand better ones, and I'm encouraged by the labor of fellow disabled people in creating community, resisting ableism, and demanding a better, more just future. Here I focus on the disability activist efforts of #CripTheVote, a social media hashtag (primarily on Twitter) as well as a blog space, where disabled people reclaim agency against interlocking ableist structures that ignore us, while proving new futures for disabled people are possible. As a disabled person personally invested and involved with the #CripTheVote community as well as a community literacy studies scholar, I am interested in reflecting on how #CripTheVote exemplifies

DOI: https://doi.org/10.37514/PER-B.2025.2531.2.02

47

community listening—and how community literacy studies more broadly can center disabled people and issues of disability.

In this chapter, I argue that for disabled communities, community listening[1]— "a literacy practice that involves deep, direct engagement with individuals and groups working to address urgent issues [ . . . ] anchored by long histories and complicated by competing interpretations as well as clashing modes of expression" (Fishman and Rosenberg 1)—is particularly important: Unlike some communities, that are established by living in a particular area or membership in a particular identity group, the disability community is formed of people who self-identify as disabled, a process of self-identification that usually happens in relationship with disabled community members. I refer to this space where disabled community can be formed and push back against ableism as well as find political agency as *crip space*, or a space created to affirm disabled identity *by* and *for* disabled people. It is described by disabled writer s.e. smith as "A place where disability is celebrated and embraced, something radical and taboo in many parts of the world, and sometimes even for people in those spaces." While smith focuses on physical spaces, I purposefully choose to center the creation of *rhetorical* crip space in this chapter, with the goal of better understanding the rhetorical choices that make crip space possible.

To better understand #CripTheVote's creation of rhetorical crip space through community listening practices, I first offer a brief—and most certainly incomplete—overview of the work of #CripTheVote. Then I describe three community listening practices #CripTheVote takes up. These are: building community through difference-driven inquiry and empathic listening, pushing back against ableism directed at disabled people and our ways of knowing/speaking through respectful listening, and finally, taking stock of the inadequacies of the present moment and creating better futures through hopeful listening. While I don't think #CripTheVote itself is a panacea that will end ableism and the connected systems of oppression that prop it up, I am inspired by the labor and brilliance of fellow disabled people in doing this work, and hope by

---

1    I pause to take up the trope of *listening* itself, concerned about the potential audism of equating *listening* with *hearing*. While many Deaf people do not consider themselves disabled but recognize the importance of Deaf culture (see Monts-Treviska in *Skin, Tooth, and Bone*), ableism and audism are related. In "D/dEAFNESS," Dany Ko points to ableism within Deaf communities and audism with disabled communities. This is another site of challenge in creating crip space, and Ko reminds us that "the beginning to a good alliance starts with sincere conversation" (92, in *Skin, Tooth, and Bone*), asking Deaf as well as disabled people to consider their own audism and archive (for more on this conversation, see Fink, et al., who take up audism in professional spaces in composition and rhetoric). I ask scholars doing writing about "listening" to think carefully about audism, and to be sure to avoid metaphors that uncritically invoke D/deafness as deficit.

better understanding the community listening practices of #CripTheVote, even more of this labor can be done.

## A BRIEF OVERVIEW OF #CRIPTHEVOTE

I offer a necessarily brief overview of #CripTheVote: The #CripTheVote hashtag and organizing efforts connected to it were created by Alice Wong (creator of the *Disability Visibility Project*), Andrew Pulrang (creator of *Disability Thinking*), and Gregg Beratan (the Director of Development at New York's Center for Disability Rights) during the 2016 presidential election, as they felt issues of disability policy were being fundamentally ignored (Barbarin).

Rather than the three founders setting #CripTheVote's agenda, #CripTheVote collaboratively identifies which political issues are most pressing to disabled people. While disability issues have frequently been ignored in mainstream politics (see Hirschman and Linker), #CripTheVote actively seeks feedback from disabled people about what policies are most important to them. Through Twitter, Wong, Pulrang, and Beratan frequently hold Disability Policy Chats, where a series of questions are posed about disability issues, and disabled people throughout the United States are encouraged to respond. Discussions span issues from access and health care to the institutionalization of disabled people and a range of other issues with much more nuance than they usually receive in mainstream media. Andrew Pulrang discussed the importance of these chats for centering different topics in the disability community that might not otherwise get much attention: "with our chats, we would take a little time each month to look at a topic that's important but maybe has fallen off the radar." (qtd. in "Activism"). As a result, #CripTheVote not only broadens the range of conversation around disability issues but also demonstrates how issues the general public might not consider as connected to disability are disability issues, like mass incarceration, gun violence, and education.

Through #CripTheVote, Wong, Pulrang, and Beratan were able to take a survey of disabled Americans and found—in their survey of over 500 disabled Americans—that the top five policy concerns related to disability were access to healthcare, civil rights/discrimination, accessibility, employment, and housing (Barbarin). From this information, and the additional commentary around it, policymakers were able to work *with* disabled people to craft more inclusive policy positions (Moss). #CripTheVote has enjoyed a degree of success in making disabled constituents visible, as American political candidates take notice and take up issues of disability policy in their own platforms: In 2020, for the first time, every major candidate in the Democratic primary had put together a disability policy plan, and in some cases, disabled candidates even worked closely with #CripTheVote to add a section on disability policy to their official platforms (Luterman). In 2020, #CripTheVote hosted candidate chats with Democratic Presidential Candidates Julian Castro, Elizabeth Warren, and Pete Buttigieg, which made it possible for disabled people to engage the candidates *and* their disability platforms directly, posing questions about their stances on important disability issues. Following these chats, each candidate collaborated with #CripTheVote organizers to revise their disability policies (Luterman) #CripTheVote also had a standing invitation to engage any candidate in a similar Twitter townhall (Luterman). Additionally, President Biden added a section on disability policy to his platform, working with many of the same policy advisors who helped craft policies for both Castro and Warren (see "Online"). While I don't pretend #CripTheVote is solely responsible for these changes, I do point to them as anecdotal evidence that the hashtag has had some impact on political considerations of disability. In what follows, I work to better understand the work of #CripTheVote, tracing how these disabled rhetors might challenge, inform, and (re)shape community listening practices.

## #CRIPTHEVOTE AS COMMUNITY LISTENING

As a disabled person interested in disabled advocacy and crafting crip space that might affirm disabled identity and build better futures for disabled people, I'm working to understand the work of #CripTheVote and to learn alongside fellow disabled community members. To do so, I seek to understand the community listening practices #CripTheVote draws upon to craft crip space. The ongoing work of #CripTheVote—through hosted chats as well as asynchronous posting and engagement—offers a means to foster disabled community, labor that has its unique rewards and challenges, and labor that should inform our understanding of community listening. Disabled lives and ways of knowing are often dismissed in American capitalist, colonialist, white-supremacist culture. But, as Ruth Osorio notes in her study of the #ActuallyAutistic hashtag as a site of resistance, "Disability-focused hashtags offer a discursive space to craft subversive stories, organize activist interventions, and affirm marginalized identities." I suggest that #CripTheVote has created crip space where community is formed and disabled identity affirmed, all while bolstering disabled people's collective political agency.

In theorizing community listening, Jenn Fishman and Lauren Rosenberg outline their evolving understanding of community listening as literacy practices that seek to understand everyday issues by engaging those affected by those issues (1). I assert that #CripTheVote employs community listening practices—carefully attending to issues by directly and deliberately engaging those most impacted—to build community, counter ableism and oppression, and exercise political agency. In what follows, I place the work happening in the crip space of #CripTheVote in conversation with community literacy studies to highlight three community listening practices through which crip space is crafted. As Lauren Rosenberg and Stephanie Kerschbaum have argued, more meaningful connections between disability studies and literacy studies are only possible by more careful attention to where disability and literacy "productively converge" (274). I look at these convergences through community listening practices of #CripTheVote, including difference-driven inquiry through empathic listening, pushing back against ableism through respectful listening, and finally drawing on political agency through hopeful listening. By putting existing community literacy in conversation with #CripTheVote, I hope to extend the scholarly conversations around community listening to be more mindful of disability.

## #CRIPTHEVOTE AS DIFFERENCE-DRIVEN INQUIRY THROUGH EMPATHIC LISTENING

In creating a hashtag and holding space for conversations around disability, #CripTheVote creates a crip space that affirms disabled identity and builds community among people with different disabilities and differing embodied disabled experiences. As Wong has said of the creation of #CripTheVote with Beratan and Pulrang, "We wanted to carve a space for thoughtful discussion about disability by us and for us" (qtd. in smith). Wong goes on to describe how, during 2015 when #CripTheVote began, most candidates didn't mention disability. There was also very little mention of issues faced by the disabled community and scant media coverage of policies that impacted disabled people. Wong outlines how #CripTheVote creates community, and I take up this project of disabled community building through community literacy scholarship to both understand how disabled rhetors might meet the challenges of disabled community building and advocacy and to highlight how the work of disabled rhetors might challenge and inform community literacy studies, which has too-frequently ignored matters of disability (Hubrig, "We" 145).

One important dimension of #CripTheVote with implications for community literacy studies is the careful attention to difference by disabled rhetors. To create rhetorical crip space, #CripTheVote tends to multiple registers of difference. For one, disability itself is an incredibly broad category, with one disabled person not necessarily identifying with or understanding the concerns of another disabled person with a different disability. And, as s.e. smith argues, "[T]here's also a high degree of intersectionality within the disabled community, because disabled people are rarely 'just' disabled." As smith goes on to explain, disabled people are more likely to be non-cishetero than their counterparts, and many disabled people are also BIPOC. Taking up these areas where disability intersects with other identities and, often, sites of multiple marginalization has been both a challenge for and goal of #CripTheVote (Mann 606).

As a community listening practice then, it's imperative to engage across these differences. To understand how community listening engages difference, Fishman and Rosenberg point to Linda Flower's work around intercultural dialogue. For Fishman and Rosenberg, intercultural dialogue "calls attention to how, when we listen, we must prioritize what others are saying and how they say it. We refer to the language people choose as well as the ways they embody that language and occupy the setting and moment in which they speak" (2). This attention to embodied difference is at the center of Flower's work: Flower describes how local publics are often called into being around a shared problem *and* underscores the importance of seeing difference in how the organization perceives the problem as an important site of rhetorical deliberation (309–310). Flower goes on to emphasize how those with truly dissenting opinions, those who understand this shared problem altogether differently, are frequently not consulted and—often because of systemic barriers—are left outside of the realm of deliberation. While Flower highlights how students are left outside the decision-making processes of universities, her argument about those missing perspectives seems especially salient considering the challenges for creating disabled community in a political system that has marginalized disabled people *while at the same time* underscoring the importance of seeking out multiply-marginalized voices *within* the disabled community.

I point to #CripTheVote's Twitter chat as an example of seeking out multiply-marginalized voices in action. Figure 2.1 depicts Wong posting the fourth question in this #CripTheVote chat session (labeled Q4), "How did your disability identity develop in relation to other identities you inhabit?" This question, posted with the #CripTheVote hashtag, allows others to answer, matching A4 (answer 4). It allows other users across Twitter to engage in conversations about difference while allowing #CripTheVote leaders to seek out multiply-marginalized perspectives on disability.

Here, #CripTheVote creates what Flower might recognize as a virtual deliberative Think Tank: Flower offers the rhetorical practice of a "deliberative Think Tank" as one iteration of which she calls "difference-driven inquiry." In a deliberative Think Tank, several different stakeholders are brought together to describe their differing understanding of a problem, working together to articulate the issue itself and possible solutions. Flower describes this process as resisting the "status quo version of the problem" that is often a "partial truth" (309) and argues,

*Figure 2.1. Image Description: A tweet from Alice Wong during one of the #CripTheVote chats.*

> The alternative perspectives we actually need belong to members of the community who are rarely consulted, lack standing, or speak a discourse divorced from power. We find ourselves facing an adaptive problem but playing without a full deck of cards—because competing the competing perspectives we require are absent and an inquiry into them must be provoked. (309)

With issues of disability, too often disabled people are not consulted, and inquiry into disabled perspectives needs to be provoked. #CripTheVote *is* such a provocation, and the crip space created by Wong, Beratan, and Pulrang offers a space specifically to capture this nuance. As Wong suggests, "Disabled voters are concerned about the same things as all voters such as employment, healthcare, education, and inequality, but these issues might impact them differently and those differences and nuances are important to highlight" (qtd. in Barbarin). In listening for the range of perspectives and presenting disability issues in nuance and complexity, #CripTheVote opens possibilities for difference-driven inquiry across disabilities.

But such possibilities are rife with challenges, including that the disabled community doesn't always see themselves as a community at all. As Pulrang has said about the difficulties of creating coalitions of disabled people: "There are many reasons why the disability community has previously 'punched under its weight.' Maybe the biggest is that most disabled people don't even consider themselves part of a larger disability community" (qtd. in Barbarin). Pulrang traces the political ramifications of disabled people being denied community where because the constituency is divided, politicians don't feel any pressure to address disability in their platforms or proposed policies. Christina Cedillo has stressed how the decentralized nature of the disabled community can make us invisible and has pointed to the importance of online spaces for creating disabled community because of this invisibilization, arguing that social media allows "disabled people to build embodied communities . . . where they challenge habituated beliefs and attitudes" ("#CripTheVote" 32). Building community is necessary, then, not just for the importance of community itself, but in being able to advocate for more equitable disability policies.

To meet the challenge of seeking out difference *while* crafting community, I once again turn to community listening practices to better understand the work of disabled rhetors. I understand #CripTheVote posts as practicing what Justin Lohr and Heather Lindenman call *empathic listening* as well as *disclosure* connected with empathic listening. Lohr and Lindenman identify the former as "a precondition for productive community listening" (82). Empathic listening as a community listening practice requires "allying with people whose life experiences are different from one's own" by mobilizing "community listening as the ability to recognize individual concerns as representative of larger collective concerns" (73). In the crip space created by #CripTheVote, empathic listening means fostering empathy across disabilities and lived experiences. For example, I am autistic and sighted. In conversations that have stemmed from #CripTheVote, I have discussed issues of political accessibility with disabled people who are neurotypical and blind. In these conversations, we have been able to inform each other's practices: me learning to better create image descriptions and alt text to better meet their access needs, and they learning to be more understanding of longer delays in responses to accommodate the time I might require as an autistic person to process their comments. While many of our access needs and concerns are quite different, we can talk *across these differences* and advocate for each other's access needs, while also attending to collective concerns.

Finally, for Lohr and Lindenman, an important site of emphatic listening is *disclosure*. While the word *disclosure* in disability studies often means to acknowledge the specific disability a disabled person has, often to gain accommodations (see Kerschbaum), it means something slightly different in community listening, though there is certainly some overlap. Lohr and Lindenman offer "emotional self disclosure" as a community listening practice, and they describe how sharing emotions or emotional information functions quite differently than sharing "facts" in creating audience motivation and fostering a "personal connection to the speaker" (76). Disabled organizer Tory Cross has remarked how this is a strength of online disabled community building because many disabled people have experience in creating online sites of community, recognizing "it's such a skillset to be able to quickly relate to someone and to connect to them emotionally" ("Q&A with Tory Cross").

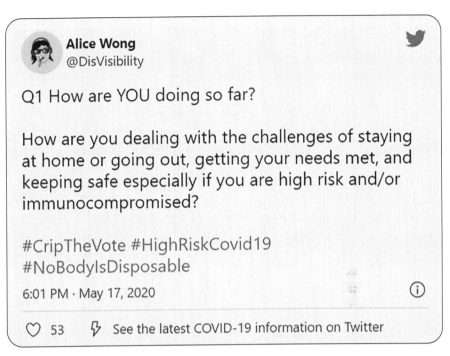

*Figure 2.2. Image Description: A tweet from Alice Wong as part of a #CripTheVote chat.*

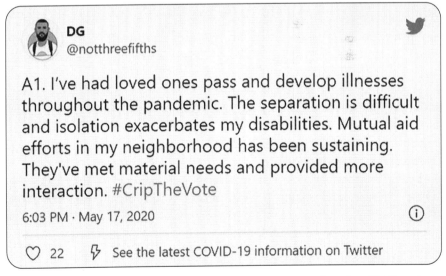

*Figure 2.3. Image Description: A tweet from DG as part of a #CripTheVote chat, answering Wong's question in Figure 2.2.*

We see how #CripTheVote consciously practices empathic listening and emotional disclosure in Figures 2.2 and 2.3, where Wong intentionally checks in with disabled people about their physical and emotional wellbeing during the COVID-19 pandemic, and DG responds with an emotional disclosure, explaining the emotional impact of isolation and the positive impact mutual aid has had. This exchange, characteristic of #CripTheVote chats, highlights how empathic listening creates space to share personal experiences and build community.

For #CripTheVote, this sort of difference-driven inquiry through empathic listening—as briefly demonstrated through Wong's check-in—helps foster disabled community across many sites of difference, including different disabilities and especially the perspectives of multiply marginalized disabled people. This, I argue, is the work of creating crip space, a place not just where disabled people can communicate, but where disability can be affirmed as a positive category. Crip spaces must be a community one would want to belong to—rather than reflect the deficit-driven narratives about disability that circulate outside of disabled communities. As Lohr and Lindenman argue, this kind of empathic listening across moments of disclosure both reifies agency as well as "foster[s] communal pride" (74). Building this crip space is the work of difference-driven inquiry through empathic listening.

## #CRIPTHEVOTE, RESPECTFUL LISTENING, AND PUSHING BACK AGAINST ABLEISM

Along with creating community across disabled positionalities, #CripTheVote faces rhetorical challenges from *outside* the disabled community that inform their community listening practices. Disabled people are frequently seen as expendable and dismissed by political systems—and so are how many disabled people politically engage, such as through hashtags. Though both disabled peoples' rhetorical agency *as well as* our methods of engagement are frequently dismissed, crip space pushes back against this double dismissal, affirming our rhetorical agency and methods for engagement.

I start with the ableist dismissal of disabled peoples' agency. Under capitalist, colonialist logics, disabled people are often disregarded and considered expendable. As disability justice collective Sins Invalid argues, "The same oppressive systems that inflicted violence upon Black and brown communities for 500+ years also inflicted 500+ years of violence on bodies and minds deemed outside the norm and therefore 'dangerous'" (18–19). Sins Invalid draws attention to the ways ableism operates while centering how ableism cannot be understood apart from other forms of oppression, which disproportionately harm multiply marginalized disabled people. These interlocking systems of oppression treat disabled people as expendable, and the rhetoric depicting us as expendable was only heightened during the COVID-19 pandemic, including commentary from elected officials who routinely described disabled people as expendable (Samuels). As Pulrang explains about the poor responses to disability during the pandemic, "It's part of disability rights rhetoric to say we're not valued, we're expendable. But it's not just rhetoric; it's real!" (qtd. in "Online"). From masking and social distancing policies that largely ignored disabled peoples' needs to the CDC director framing disabled deaths as "encouraging news" (Hubrig "Disabled Deaths"), the pandemic showcased many people's ableism—including some politicians and medical professionals—believed the loss of disabled lives were ultimately inconsequential.

The ableist devaluation of disabled lives is compounded by a frequent dismissal of online activism: In their own writing about "Crip Twitter," Sohum Pal pushes back against frequent critiques of hashtag activism as "slacktivism" or viewing online activist spaces as "a token act of support . . ." as "minimal-impact forms of virtue signaling." Focusing on disabled Twitter activism, Pal argues "such a register fails, first, by failing to consider the particular constraints that disability can place on forms of political action, and second by misunderstanding the metrics by which social movement can be judged." These restraints and barriers to political agency make #CripTheVote even more necessary. As Osorio has argued, "[F]or many disabled and autistic protestors, hashtag activism is the most accessible form of protest. . . . Traditional street activism—marches, rallies, sit-ins—are often inaccessible to disabled people." Importantly, this doesn't mean disabled people *don't* engage politically in these ways. In fact, many disabled people have done and continue to take part in disability activism in these ways. But for some disabled people, online discussions are a more accessible site of disabled activism. But the dismissal of this kind of activism is real, and harmful to disabled people who find political agency in this work.

Taken together, then, disabled people find ourselves in a double bind: both our political agency *and* our methods of engaging in the political are continuously brought into question. Addressing the dismissal of disabled bodyminds that casts disabled people as expendable, #CripTheVote also navigates barriers to access and communication, barriers which frame disabled people's participation as less-than. Taking up Krista Ratcliffe's work on rhetorical listening, J Logan Smilges has written about the intersections of disabled identity and the ableist assumptions of communication. Smilges draws attention to how expectations around listening are culturally created and how disabled people (Smilges centers on neurodiversity specifically) face political and social consequences if they are unable to *listen* in the ways that are culturally expected. Not only does this ableism impact disabled agency, but I pause for just a moment to point out how these ableist assumptions about rhetorical agency have implications for community listening—and composition and rhetoric more broadly (for more on ableism in the privileging of modalities, see Cedillo 2018, Jackson, Price, and Yergeau). In short, disabled people's methods of listening are dismissed along with disabled bodyminds—a dismissal that itself deserves more scholarly attention across disciplines.

In response to the double dismissal of disabled peoples' rhetorical agency *and* our methods for political engagement, I suggest #CripTheVote reasserts agency within the crip space they've established by practicing—and demanding of others—*respectful listening.* Here I draw on the work of Tiffany Rousculp's rhetoric of respect: "A rhetoric of respect for individual concerns, rather than relying on institutional definitions" (29). Rousculp describes how this rhetoric of respect runs counter to normal institutional understandings that privilege certain ways of knowing and dismiss others. In my own calls for community literacy studies to take up disability justice as we continue to reckon with how the field has continued to devalue certain epistemologies, I have pointed to the importance of respecting different ways of knowing: "Disability justice challenges the notions of what *counts* as expertise, what counts as knowledge" ("We Move Together" 146). Respectful listening understands that to undermine *how* something is communicated is itself an act of violence, of dismissing othered bodyminds. Instead, respectful listening affirms the rhetorical agency and methods of disabled people by seeking to create spaces where disabled people may speak across differences and modalities.

Through *respectful listening* practices, #CripTheVote specifically challenges ableist rhetoric and the eugenic notion of the expendability of disabled lives. In her study of the #ActuallyAutistic Twitter Community, Osorio has examined how autistic people resist anti-autistic violence by self-proclaimed "advocacy" organizations that have historically spoken over Autistic people and promoted violent "cure" arguments. Like this self-advocacy Osorio notes, the crip space created by #CripTheVote is both used to challenge ableist narratives about disabled people and policies that impact our lives *as well as* "circulate liberatory arguments" (Osorio) where disabled identity can be celebrated and crip community can be formed. As Osorio argues, "Hashtags allow for rhetors—especially rhetors who have been denied a public platform—to collectively create, share, and build upon stories that are not represented in dominant culture." Likewise, respectful listening pushes back against ableist violence and creates sites for conversations about disability that affirm disabled identity by allowing disabled people to circulate our stories, to be in conversation with one another, and to challenge ableist attitudes *on our own terms*, in formats created by and for disabled people.

Crafting Crip Space through Disabled Political Advocacy

Figure 2.4. Image Description: A tweet from Sarah Blahovec.

#CripTheVote pushes back against the dismissal of disabled people *and* the invalidation of our ways of protest. Consider the pushback to ableist coronavirus policies in California in 2020 through 2022: Often accompanying the #CripTheVote hashtag, Wong created the hashtag #HighRiskCA (followed by accompanying hashtags for other states). #HighRiskCA, began to address ableism and eugenic logics in policies, practices, and public statements that framed disabled people as expendable, that drew attention to the ways in which policies—like California's vaccination rollout (see Figure 2)—failed disabled people, and particularly disabled people at high risk from the coronavirus.

In using the crip space #CripTheVote has created a community in this way, disabled people are pushing back against the dismissal of disabled lives and embodied experiences *while* pushing back against the dismissal of disabled activist methods. The disability community creates crip space *not just* in building disabled community, but also by changing expectations of what counts as participation. Respectful listening tends to these alterations in *how* discussions happen. Smilges writes about how neurodivergence highlights disabled listening practices, and suggests "as a matter of access, listening might be delayed, split

59

into multiple sessions, or moved." Their work highlights the work of respectful listening, of opening more accessible spaces for community listening to take place, as demonstrated by Sarah Blahovec's tweet in Figure 2.4, which shows how the #CripTheVote hashtag as well as the related #HighRiskCA hashtag is used to push back against California Governor Gavin Newsom's COVID response plan that ignored the needs of disabled voters. By chronicling and linking stories with these hashtags, they may be—as Smilges suggests—split into multiple sessions and still archived as a whole.

The work of community listening—and the specific community listening practice of *respectful listening*—is not just the work of affirming disabled identity but the modalities through which disabled people engage and communicate. Respectful listening means realignment of listening practices; it means challenging the ableism and other forms of oppression that dismiss the forms of engagement used by disabled and otherwise marginalized rhetors. This realignment is central to how I understand community listening and why I believe it is important. Romeo García argues that the importance of community listening is that it reclaims space for speakers to address embodied experiences, pointing specifically to the crisis of whiteness that permeates academic discourse (13). García describes how academic listening forecloses rhetorical space through which those *not* credentialed by or recognized by academic structures can join conversations. This sort of academic listening—which García identifies as an iteration of Ratcliffe's rhetorical eavesdropping—creates an asymmetrical relationship, through which the only way for the person whose way of speaking and knowing has been devalued to engage is to speak and act on the terms of those with power (13). Academic literacies often foreclose possibilities for those without academic credentials to engage, and academic epistemologies frequently dismiss disabled ways of knowing and being, especially for disabled people who are multiply marginalized, while community literacy offers possibilities to decenter whiteness and the violent colonial epistemologies that foreground "academic" ways-of-knowing. For García, the difference between academic listening and community listening is tending to these asymmetrical relationships. Community listening means recognizing the agency of those academic listening would ignore, that those who are marginalized are "shapers of language, discourse, and modalities of agency" (13). I argue that in *respectful listening,* #CripTheVote engages in García iteration of community listening, specifically a version of community listening that creates crip space in which disabled people, our experiences, stories, and perspectives, as well as our *modalities* of engagement.

#CripTheVote changes our understanding of disabled political agency, not just pointing to ways we make the forms of protest nondisabled people engage in and making them accessible, but in *reframing* political engagement altogether:

in using #CripTheVote to value and recognize the political contributions of disabled people as well as the modalities in which disabled people organize and engage. As political organizer Tory Cross has said of disabled people's rhetorical savvy online:

> There's this misconception that online connections aren't real life, but I'm a real person, and you're a real person, and we're talking online. That's real life! Disabled people are so talented at eliminating that fake line between IRL [in real life] and online when it comes to community building. I think people who are abled bodied or have never been really isolated from their community sometimes find it stilted or difficult to build across digital space. ("Q&A with Tory Cross")

Disabled people often find new modalities to communicate and exercise political agency. Respectful listening recognizes this not as a deficit but a strength, a site of rhetorical invention. As Sins Invalid highlights, against the backdrop of ableism and other forms of oppression, many disabled people are isolated from other disabled people, and this is especially true of multiply marginalized disabled people who may find their communities celebrate *one part* of their identity while denigrating others (17). Respectful listening affirms both disabled identity and the modalities through which disabled people choose to engage.

## #CRIPTHEVOTE AS CRIP SPACE
## FOR *HOPEFUL LISTENING*

Finally, as a site of community listening praxis, #CripTheVote is a site where the labor of hope is carried out. To listen—both to craft this crip space for community listening and to engage with each other in this space—*is labor*. It takes organizational labor, effort, and time to read through threads from fellow crip community members and to respond over days that stretch into weeks, months, and years. It demands emotional labor to commiserate with others every time an ableist policy is brought to a legislative session or—on the most difficult days—these policies pass, to tell these stories, and to advocate for better futures for disabled people. But this is *hopeful* labor. Through building community among disabled people as well as resisting the limiting of rhetorical and political agency from those outside the disability community, #CripTheVote takes up what I'm calling *hopeful listening*. Hopeful not in the naive sense, but in the activist sense. Hopeful listening is listening that's done the required reading: hopeful listening is community listening that's brought a set of demands to the meeting.

In theorizing how #CripTheVote takes up hopeful listening, I draw on the work of Paula Matheiu, who describes hope as a community literacy practice, as acknowledging "the present as radically insufficient," and a necessary precondition for creating a more equitable future (19). For Mathieu, hope—as a verb— "is to look critically at one's present condition, assess what is missing, and then long for and work for a not-yet reality, a future anticipated" (19). Building on Mathieu's framework of *hope* in community writing, I suggest hopeful listening is the twin acts of listening for acknowledgments of what is "radically insufficient" in the present and listening to demands for a more equitable "future anticipated."

Beyond building community and rejecting ableism, #CripTheVote is actively engaged in the work of hopeful listening, and I would suggest #CripTheVote has been taking up this work from the moment of its creation. In describing the early work of #CripTheVote, Wong explains how the hashtag was only originally intended to go through the 2016 election cycle, but the co-founders decided to keep it going. Wong states: "[T]his community, there's still a huge need for it, and it's only gonna continue onward. It's much more than just about voting; it's about political participation. It's about having a voice" (qtd. in "Activism"). And the participation only grew: after the 2016 election, #CripTheVote held a number of chats on specific policies that impact the disabled community like the Farm Bill and Snap, Opioids and Chronic Pain, Immigration, and many topics. These chats—hosted on Twitter usually monthly—featured disabled people sharing how these policies impacted them, pointing both to how current laws and policies fail disabled people and imagining new ways forward. The community was listening to each other, across differences and intersectional disabled identities, engaging in what I call hopeful listening. Based on my reading of—and participation in—#CripTheVote, I describe hopeful listening as using listening practices to create new rhetorical spaces to foster community by attending to difference. Writing after Cheryl Glenn, who describes her hopefulness surrounding rhetorical feminism and the dismantling of patriarchal structures (196–197), I argue that hopeful listening is not naive in assuming there will be a better future for disabled people, but rather consciously chooses to listen across differences, abilities, and modalities to consciously create new rhetorical possibilities that might lead to such futures for disabled people and communities.

But #CripTheVote has *demanded* political candidates engage with their acts of hopeful listening. In an interview with the Disability Visibility Podcast, #CripTheVote co-creator Gregg Beratan describes the political impact #CripTheVote has had. Beratan suggests: "Before this, disability was a "tickbox" and not a community politicians recognized as a constituency, more something they used to signal their own goodness.... Something used to say "look I'm so good, I care about the disabled."

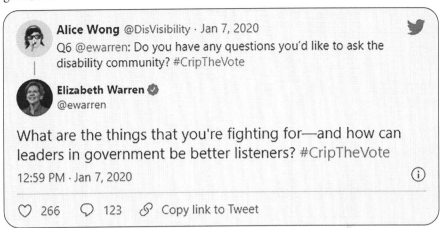

*Figure 2.5. A Tweet from Alice Wong to Senator Elizabeth Warren.*

Pulrang notes that #CripTheVote was meant to bring disabled people into conversations around disability policy, but then to push those conversations forward: "Our goal has been to foster discussion amongst ourselves, but then make those discussions noticeable to those running for office." (qtd. in "Online"). #CripTheVote has been successful in working alongside disabled organizers to have more nuanced, more meaningful conversations around disability with candidates and policymakers. In Figure 2.5, for instance, we see then-Democratic hopeful Senator Elizabeth Warren in conversation with a #CripTheVote chat, a conversation which led to Warren collaborating directly with disabled community members in drafting and revising disability policies in her campaign.

This move—a candidate in the presidential primaries seeking the input of the disabled community—itself marked a huge shift, as many candidates in past races only included simplistic, hollow orientations to disability if they mentioned the disabled community at all. As Pulrang noted about past candidates' political positions on disability, "[Y]ou can't really have disagreements over empty policy. You can't have disagreements over, 'I support the disabled.'" But #CripTheVote evoked political conversations about disability continue to evolve: In coordination with other disability organizers and activists, #CripTheVote has hosted conversations with political candidates and has offered critique of policy, compelling candidates to move from empty policy positions like "I support disabled people" to more robust policy plans in the 2020 presidential election as well as many down-ballot races. Pulrang draws attention to how these conversations around proposed policies and positions reflected the diverse positionalities of the disabled community: "one of the things I'll say about the better platforms . . . put out by candidates is there was a lotta love going around about the policies from various candidates, but also criticism from the community and even within the community" (qtd. in "Online"). This is the work of hope in community literacy that, as Mathieu describes it, is "active and critical" (19). As a community listening practice, hopeful listening attends to the inequalities by seeking out marginalized perspectives on real issues, decentering the epistemic violence of more "official" ways of knowing that frequently ignore disabled (and otherwise marginalized) ways of knowing. Hopeful listening is a community literacy practice of putting marginalized perspectives *first* in collaboratively imagining more just futures.

## #CRIPTHEVOTE, CRIP SPACES OF THE FUTURE, AND AN ABUNDANCE OF CAUTION

While I am grateful for the work of #CripTheVote, I understand that it isn't enough, and that disability community itself isn't a utopia that nullifies ableism and other forms of oppression. Leah Lakshmi Piepzna-Samarasinha underscores the limits of community in their writing on care webs, that "'Community' is not a magic unicorn" and that the only path forward for better futures for disabled people is "by not papering over the places where our rhetoric falls flat, where we ran out of steam, or where this shit is genuinely fucking hard" (35). In my optimism about #CripTheVote, I do not mean to paper over the difficulties, the shortcomings of disability community building.

I also know that the work of creating disabled community—while that space is invaluable and can be affirming of disabled identity—can also be deeply flawed and that disabled community can be as racist, sexist, trans and queer exclusive, etc., as any other space. I also recognize that as a white person, I have a great deal of privilege in these spaces. I try to listen to understand where disability community fails those less privileged, and I worry about the spaces in which current work like #CripTheVote recreates the same inequalities that the Disability Rights Movement hasn't fully grappled with, as Sins Invalid underscores, "The political strategy of the Disability Rights Movement relied on litigation . . . Rights-based strategies often address the symptoms of inequity but not the root" (15). Disability Rights frameworks have failed to fully grasp how their approach centers and privileges whiteness, a struggle shared with community literacy studies (García 13; Hubrig et al. 249; Jackson with Whitehorse DeLaune 40; Kannan et al. 29; Shah 11).

Despite these reservations, I'm optimistic about the work of #CripTheVote and the possibilities for community listening practices to further center marginalized perspectives, and I'm grateful to Alice Wong, Andrew Pulrang, and Gregg Beratan as the co-founders of that space as well as to the many disabled people who added their own stories, who flagged resources and articles, pushed back against ableism, demanded better futures for disabled people, and otherwise created a crip space for disabled community through the hashtag. When coverage about politics minimizes or outright ignores disability issues, to take part in disabled community through #CripTheVote is a site of solace, a place where I know I'm not alone and others understand these issues.

In their introduction to the special issue of *Community Literacy Journal* on community listening that began the conversations from which this collection was created, Fishman and Rosenberg describe the "complex, messy work of authentic engagement with community writing" (5), pointing to the complexities and rewards for scholars committed to community literacy work. Attending the community listening practices of #CripTheVote, as a member of that community, continues to make me a better teacher, scholar, and human. Engaging disability through the crip brilliance of disabled people—disability on our own terms rather than through the deficit-driven language of accommodations—productively challenges institutional norms of ableism but also cisheteropatriarchy, capitalism, and white supremacy. As I've argued before, being attentive to issues of disability—and especially disability justice—can help realize a more just version of community literacy studies (Hubrig, "We" 151). #CripTheVote demonstrates the ingenuity of a community that is frequently written off by nondisabled people.

## WORKS CITED

"A Q&A with Tory Cross." Disability Visibility Project, 2021.

Barbarin, Imani. "Come on Crips, Let's Get in Formation: #CripTheVote." *Crutches and Spice,* 2016.

Cedillo, Christina V. "#CripTheVote: Disability Activism, Social Media, and the Campaign for Communal Visibility." *Reflections: A Journal of Community-Engaged Writing and Rhetoric.* Special Summer Issue, 2021.

———. "Disabled and Undocumented: In/Visibility at the Borders of Presence, Disclosure, and Nation." *Rhetoric Society Quarterly*, vol. 50, no. 3, 2020, pp. 203–211.

———. "What Does It Mean to Move? Race, Disability, and Critical Embodiment Pedagogy." *Composition Forum*, vol. 39, 2018, (np). https://www.compositionforum.com/issue/39/to-move.php.

"Episode 1: Activism and the Disability Community." *Disability Visibility Project,* 2017.

"Episode 99: Online Activism." *Disability Visibility Project,* 2021.

Fink, Margaret, Janine Butler, Tonya Stremlau, Stephanie L. Kerschbaum, and Brenda Jo Brueggemann. "Honoring Access Needs at Academic Conferences through

Computer Assisted Real-Time Captioning (CART) and Sign Language Interpreting." In "Enacting a Culture of Access in Our Conference Spaces," edited by Adam Hubrig and Ruth Osorio. *College Composition and Communication,* vol. 72, no. 1, 2020, pp. 87–117.

Fishman, Jenn, and Lauren Rosenberg, editors. *Community Writing, Community Listening*, special issue of *Community Literacy Journal*, vol. 13, no. 1, 2018.

Fishman, Jenn, and Lauren Rosenberg. "Guest Editors' Introduction: Community Writing, Community Listening." Fishman and Rosenberg, pp. 1–6, https://doi.org/10.25148/clj.13.1.009085.

Flower, Linda. "Difference-Driven Inquiry: A Working Theory of Local Public Deliberation." *Rhetoric Society Quarterly*, vol. 46, no. 4, 2016, pp. 308–330.

García, Romeo. "Creating Presence from Absence and Sound from Silence." Fishman and Rosenberg, pp. 7–15, https://doi.org/10.25148/clj.13.1.009086.

Hirschmann, Nancy, and Beth Linker. "Disability, Citizenship, and Belonging: A Critical Introduction." In *Civil Disabilities,* edited by Nancy Hirschmann and Beth Linker, U of Pennsylvania P, 2015, pp. 1–21.

Hubrig, Ada. "Disabled Deaths Are Not Your 'Encouraging News': Resisting the Cruel Eugenics of Comorbidity Rhetoric." *Disability Visibility Project,* 26 Jan. 2022.

———. "Fear and Loathing—of Disability on the Campaign Trail." *Present Tense: A Journal of Rhetoric in Society,* vol. 9, no. 1, 2021.

———. "'We Move Together': Reckoning with Disability Justice in Community Literacy Studies." *Community Literacy Journal,* vol. 14, no. 2, 2020, pp. 144–153.

Hubrig, Ada, Heather Lindenman, Justin Lohr, and Rachael Wendler Shah. "The Work of the Conference on Community Writing: Reflections on the 2019 Philadelphia Conference." *Reflections: A Journal of Community-Engaged Writing and Rhetoric,* vol. 19, no. 2, 2020.

Jackson, Cody A. "How Does It Mean to Move? Accessibility and/as Disability Justice." *Medium*, 14 July 2019.

Jackson, Rachel C. with Dorothy Whitehorse DeLaune. "Decolonizing Community Writing with Community Listening: Story, Transrhetorical Resistance, and Indigenous Cultural Literacy Activism." Fishman and Rosenberg, pp. 37–54, https://doi.org/10.25148/clj.13.1.009089.

Kannan, Vani, Ben Kuebrich, and Yanira Rodríguez. "Unmasking Corporate-Military Infrastructure: Four Theses." *Community Literacy Journal*, vol. 11, no. 1, 2016, pp. 76–93.

Kerschbaum, Stephanie. "On Rhetorical Agency and Disclosing Disability in Academic Writing." *Rhetoric Review*, vol. 33, no. 1, 2014, pp. 55–71.

Lohr, Justin, and Heather Lindenman. "Challenging Audiences to Listen: The Performance of Self-Disclosure in Community Writing Projects." Fishman and Rosenberg, pp. 71–86, https://doi.org/10.25148/clj.13.1.009091.

Luterman, Sara. "Elizabeth Warren Has Made Disability Rights Central to Her Campaign." *The Nation,* 2020.

Mann, Benjamin. "Rhetoric of Online Disability Activism: #CripTheVote and Civic Participation." *Communication Culture & Critique*, vol. 11, 2018, pp. 604–621.

Mathieu, Paula. *Tactics of Hope: Street Life and the Public Turn in English Composition.* Boynton/Cook Publishers, 2005.

Moss, Haley. "Which 2020 Democratic Candidates are Taking Disability Rights Seriously?" *Teen Vogue,* 2020.

Osorio, Ruth. "I Am #ActuallyAutistic, Hear Me Tweet: The Autist-Topoi of Autistic Activists on Twitter." *Enculturation: A Journal of Rhetoric, Writing, and Culture,* 2020.

Pal, Sohum. "Crip Twitter and Utopic Feeling: How Disabled Twitter Users Reorganize Public Affects." *Lateral: Journal of the Cultural Studies Association,* vol. 8, no. 2, 2019.

Piepzna-Samarasinha, and Leah Lakshmi. *Care Work: Dreaming Disability Justice.* Arsenal Pulp Press. 2018.

Price, Margaret. *Mad at School: Rhetorics of Mental Disability and Academic Life.* U Michigan P, 2011.

Rosenberg, Lauren, and Stephanie Kerschbaum. "Entanglements of Literacy Studies and Disability Studies." *College English,* vol. 83, no. 4, 2021, pp. 267–288.

Rousculp, Tiffany. *Rhetoric of Respect: Recognizing Change at a Community Writing Center.* Conference on College Composition and Communication, National Council of Teachers of English, 2014.

Samuels, Alex. "Dan Patrick Says 'There are More Important Things than Living.'" *The Texas Tribune,* 21 Apr. 2020.

Shah, Rachael W. *Rewriting Partnerships: Community Perspectives on Community-Based Learning.* Utah State UP, 2020.

"Skin, Tooth, and Bone: The Basis of Movement is Our People." *Sins Invalid.* 2nd ed., digital ed., 2019.

Smilges, J Logan. "Bad Listeners." *Peitho,* vol. 23, no. 1, 2020.

smith, s. e. "'We Aren't Going Away Anytime Soon': A Q&A with the Organizers behind #CripTheVote." *Rewire News,* 2016.

———. "The Beauty of Spaces Created for and by Disabled People." *Catapult,* 22 Oct. 2018.

Wong, Alice. "Introduction to Disability Visibility: First Person Stories from the Twenty-First Century." In *Disability Visibility: First-Person Stories from the 21st Century,* edited by Alice Wong. Vintage Books, 2020, pp. xv-xxii.

———. "My Medicaid, My Life." In *About Us: Essays from the Disability Series of the New York Times,* edited by Peter Catapano and Rosemarie Garland-Thompson, Liverlight Publishing, 2019, pp. 27–30.

Yergeau, Remi. *Authoring Autism: On Rhetoric and Neurological Queerness.* Duke UP, 2018.

CHAPTER 3.

# KEEPING BAD COMPANY: "LISTENING" TO ARYAN NATIONS IN THE ARCHIVES

**Patty Wilde**
Washington State University, Tri-Cities

**Mitzi Ceballos**
University of Utah

**Wyn Andrews Richards**
Washington State University

*This chapter describes a collaborative archival research endeavor involving Aryan Nations propaganda, including newsletters and prison recruitment materials. Undertaken by two graduate students and their professor in Fall 2020, this project began when they learned that these documents were housed in the archives at their large, public university located in the Pacific Northwest. "[T]he most powerful organizing force for white supremacists in the United States" in the 1980s–90s (Balleck 40), the Aryan Nations established their headquarters in the "backyard" of their university, making these materials of "regional interest" to now-retired acquisitions librarians. While this propaganda targeted specific populations, its presence in the archive understandably alienates others, resulting in a tendency to ignore white power propagation. Using community listening as a non-neutral, embodied methodology to conduct their research and engage with community stakeholders, including the archivists at their institution, this chapter describes how they attempted to "take responsibility" for these materials.*

**Content Warning:** This chapter contains extreme words of racism and anti-Semitism drawn directly from Aryan Nations newsletters. Please read with care.

DOI: https://doi.org/10.37514/PER-B.2025.2531.2.03

"Community," writes Raymond Williams, "can be the warmly persuasive word to describe an existing set of relationships, or the warmly persuasive word to describe an alternative set of relationships. What is most important, perhaps, is that unlike all other terms of social organization (state, nation, society, etc.) it seems never to be used unfavourably. . . ." (40, emphasis in original). In this articulation, Williams alludes to a key tension of this "feel good" word: while there is considerable promise in community, however it might be defined or imagined, it is inevitably subject to the challenges and complications associated with conglomerations of people who have different views, values, and varying degrees of power. The promise and predicament of "community" was a point of conversation that repeatedly emerged as we, Patty, Mitzi, and Wyn, embarked upon a collaborative archival project on the Aryan Nations. Propaganda for this group of Christian Identity Theology believers is housed in the library of our large, public institution, Washington State University (WSU)—our most immediate academic community. As potential sites for community listening, what Jenn Fishman, Romeo García, and Lauren Rosenberg describe as the process of "emerging in and through the stories that acculturate us, including stories that transform, oppress, and liberate," archives give rise to narratives about our past that inform our present, shaping our environs and the structures of power that configure these places. While we did not want to claim the Aryan Nations as members of our community, their legacy reverberates throughout the region, which is reified for us most immediately by their presence in the archives and library at our university.

Our work with the Aryan Nations materials began in the context of ENGL 597: Rhetorics of the Archive, the graduate-level course that Patty, then assistant professor of English, taught in the fall of 2020, at a time in which institutions were beginning to reckon with their implicit and explicit connections to white supremacy. Mitzi and Wyn, both English graduate students, enrolled in the small course.[1] As a result of the COVID-19 pandemic, we faced significant constraints. Our class took place via Zoom, and because the Manuscripts, Archives, and Special Collections (MASC) was closed to the public, we were not able to examine physical artifacts in person. We leaned heavily on two very accommodating archivists to help us overcome these hurdles. After consulting the archive's finding aid, we requested that the archivists provide copies of sample materials from three different collections that potentially aligned with our commitments to doing antiracist work in the archive. These included the "Washington State Office of Commissioner of Public Lands Land Grant Ledgers" from 1901–1912,

---

1    In addition to Mitzi and Wyn, there was one other student enrolled in English 597: Rhetorics of the Archive, but they opted out of composing the chapter.

the "WSU Police Officer Papers" from 1967–1972, and the "Racism Workshop Papers" from 1970–1971. The archivists generously provided scanned copies of these materials, but it was during one of the class consultations that they mentioned that MASC also counted among its collections Aryan Nations propaganda, specifically newsletters that spanned from the 1970s to the early aughts. Because these materials are cataloged both as rare books and periodicals at our institution, they did not appear in our review of the finding aids for MASC. In this way, these documents constitute an archive more in the "vernacular" meaning of the word, what Peter B. Hirtle explains is "anything that is old or established, be it collections of old movies . . ., a journal that publishes what the editors hope will be papers of enduring value . . . or even rock-and-roll oldies on cable television" (10). But as critical archive scholars Jeanette A. Bastian and Ben Alexander remind us, "records in all their manifestations are pivotal to constructing a community, consolidating its identity and shaping its memories" (xxi). Though classified as lower-case "a" archives, the Aryan Nations propaganda is illustrative of the commemorative power of the material, functioning as the basic matter that begets the narratives that help define our community.

After much deliberation, we, as a class, decided to pursue an archival project involving the Aryan Nations newsletters. Driven by a similar impulse that spurred Kenneth Burke to examine Adolph Hitler's *Mein Kampf*, we wanted to get a better sense of the "snakeoil" (165) that these texts offered readers. As we grappled with the damaging rhetoric of this white supremacist propaganda, we thought deeply about how archives can function as places for community listening that "re-situat[e] the individual within constellations of stories, genealogies, ghosts, and hauntings," as García explains ("Creating Presence from Absence and Sound from Silence" 7). A wellspring of remembrance, archives are, in the words of Charles Morris, "rhetorical sites and resources, part of a diverse domain of the usable past that, despite the sincere if not conceited espousals of disinterested custodianship by its representatives, nevertheless functions ideologically and politically, and often insidiously" (146). The power associated with such sites, as Joan M. Schwartz and Terry Cook maintain, informs "the shape and direction of historical scholarship, collective memory, and national identity, over how we know ourselves as individuals, groups, and societies" (2). A product of Euro-American epistemologies that privilege material and discursive records, archives are highly curated collections that (often white) archivists[2] deem worthy of preservation. The Aryan Nations collection held in our university's library is a manifestation of that power, "necessarily mean[ing] that other records will not

---

2    According to a 2012 survey conducted by the Society of American Archivists, the archival profession overwhelmingly trends white, representing 89% of those who participated in the study ("Member Needs and Satisfaction Survey, 2012" 14).

be preserved" (Jimerson 11). And while that gives us pause, especially in the fraught context of higher education where students of color have not always been welcomed or well-received, we also see the collection's presence as problematically necessary, as it documents the region's white supremacist history that might otherwise be subsumed by the more ubiquitous contemporary narratives that paint this corner of country as "liberal."

Because community listening calls us to examine "the privileges we inherit and enact and the privileges we want—and need—to reckon with" (Fishman, García, and Rosenberg), we felt compelled to listen to this archive, however contemptible it may be, and tell its story, which is our story, too. But the rhetorical power of the archive is located not only in what is preserved, but in how those materials are organized, described, and dispersed, as KJ Rawson elucidates. As we learned more about the accession of Aryan Nations materials and how they are managed in our library, we grew increasingly concerned with their exhibition: these documents circulate with surprisingly little intervention at our university's library. The story that we tell, then, is also about our attempt to use community listening to encourage the archivists to further contextualize this collection and, more broadly, adopt antiracist archival practices. Making such requests raises important questions about disciplinary boundaries and reminds us, as Michelle Caswell has rightly observed, that there is a general propensity to overlook the expertise of archival scholars properly. Though we kept these critical concerns in the forefront of our minds, we were nevertheless moved to intervene to take responsibility, however imperfectly executed, for the varying acts of latent and overt white supremacy embedded in our community.

While archives are inevitably shaped by those who create them, they are what Barbara Biesecker calls "scene[s] of a doubled invention" ("Historicity" 124, emphasis ours), where researchers' embodied experiences are also brought to bear on the collections they study and the narratives they craft. As we collaboratively tell the story of the Aryan Nations archive and our experiences with it, we recognize that this account is inescapably slant, informed by the intersections of our own individual identities. A white, cisgender woman of relative means and privilege with Catholic and working-class roots, Patty came to this research as a pre-tenured professor, challenging her work with this project, as she tried to balance her commitments to social justice and intersectional feminism with the demands of being both a teacher and colleague. But born and raised in Portland, Oregon, Patty keenly recognized the discrepancy between the progressive perceptions of the Pacific Northwest and its racist past. These formative experiences contributed to her understanding of the project. As both a practicing Catholic and an Idahoan, Mitzi felt a sense of urgency in taking up these materials, though her ability to do this was complicated by being the only person of color working on this project. She felt that her racial identity and status as a then-master's student impacted the power dynamics, and she held back during the writing of this chapter. Her hope is that her silence will also create a sound that other communities can hear, one that reverberates past the writing. From her position as a highly privileged white, Anglo-Saxon, Protestant, cisgendered woman, Ph.D. student, Wyn, felt a deep responsibility to work on this project due to her driving ideology of radical racial justice. Because Wyn is not directly targeted by the bigoted hate of Aryan Nations, she recognized her important role of reader of these archival items. Though she was dispirited to consider these people part of her community, they are. She must listen to current white supremacists with the hope of disrupting the ruinous consequences of racialized hate.

Though we occupy different "politics of location," to borrow the phrasing of Adrienne Rich, we all agreed to undertake the work of analyzing and collaboratively writing about these deeply racist texts that have propagated hate and helped inspire tangible acts of violence. Such an endeavor, we believed, would render legible the rhetorical strategies employed by white supremacist groups and, more broadly, call attention to the role that archives play in buttressing past, present, and future mechanisms of power. But engaging with these vile documents also necessitated that we intently listen to each other as poured over these trauma-inducing texts. Though we did not always agree and there were layers of power to navigate, an "ethics of hope and care" informed our collaborative research and composing practices, as we sought to "listen and speak, not just with our heads by with our hearts, backbones, and stomachs" (Royster and Kirsch 146).

## ARCHIVES AS SITES FOR COMMUNITY LISTENING

Attending to the ways that physical place and space define community and inform community listening practices, we began our research on the Aryan Nations propaganda by first asking, "Why are these materials *here*?" The location of archives function as what Greg Dickinson, Brian L. Ott, and Eric Aoki call "experiential landscapes" where "the larger landscape (and of attendant sites) spill over into specific sites" (29). Shaping hermeneutical approaches, archival scenes influence cognitive and affective interactions with materials, as scholars such as Malea Powell, Gesa E. Kirsch, and Liz Rohan, among others, have observed. But relatedly, place also can determine the records that archivists seek to collect, illustrative of a desire to connect local communities with views of regional pasts. As such, these repositories function as potential sites for community listening where particular narratives of the past co-constitutively shape and are shaped by the places in which they emerge and reside.

WSU is located in Pullman, Washington, on the eastern, more agrarian, side of the state. A land grant institution, it was founded in 1890 and built upon the ancestral lands of the Niimíipuu and the traditional homeland of the Pelúuc Band of Indigenous People. Although it is a predominantly white institution, as Victor Villanueva observes, "WSU's history has always included, from its inception, American Indians, African Americans, Chicanos, Latinos, Pacific Islanders, Asian Americans, no less than the many hard-working White Americans of the state" (N.P.). For some, the university's location in the Pacific Northwest may conjure notions of "blue state" politics, but the region is very much shaped by both implicit and overt white supremacy, which continues to haunt Washington, Idaho, and Oregon in a variety of ways. Most pertinent to our discussion of archival places, however, is the university's proximity to Aryan Nations headquarters which, until 2001, was located in Hayden Lake, Idaho, approximately 100 miles away. This area was specifically chosen by the founder of Aryan Nations, Richard Butler, because of its distance from "the mongrel masses" (Day).

Today, the population of Idaho consists of approximately 93% people who identify as "white," according to the US Census Bureau data from 2019. This racial makeup is a direct result of intentional efforts to create a white stronghold, which largely began with the "white flight" that took place after the American Civil War. As historian Jill Gill explains, after the war, Southerners who sought to preserve their way of life moved to the Pacific Northwest; legislation was introduced to help promote this brand of white supremacy ("Why Idaho's Racist History Matters"). Oregon, for example, passed Lash Laws that called for non-enslaved Black people in the state to be whipped for merely existing within its borders (Nokes). In Idaho, Jim Crow-type laws were established to help control Black populations, but additional exclusion laws were enforced to deter other people of color from settling there ("Why Idaho's Racist History Matters"). It was this homogeneity of whiteness that drew Butler to Hayden Lake where he later established Aryan Nations headquarters in the late 1970s.

The geographical proximity of Hayden Lake to WSU contributed to a long-retired librarian's decision to acquire Aryan Nations propaganda, reminding us that "all archival programs and institutions are the contingent products of their time and place," as Adrian Cunningham explains (55). While some finding aids are more transparent about the "archivists' invisible hands" (Morris and Rose 52), including statements of accession and provenance, because of how the Aryan Nations materials are classified at WSU, no such details about the collection are available. This omission called us to employ community listening principles and dig more deeply into the origins of this archive so that we might better understand the construction of this archive. When we asked the current archivists about the acquisition of these materials, they contacted several now-retired employees to help us find answers to our questions. According to the archivists' contacts, the materials were of interest to the now-deceased acquisitions librarian who wanted to preserve a range of voices that characterized the region. While some might debate the value of housing such racist materials, we agree with the assessment articulated by archivist Richard J. Cox:

> if we are doing our job well, we often will hold archival materials challenging the identity or role or even value of other groups. We want the records of both the National Association for the Advancement of Colored People and the Ku Klux Klan. . . . They are all bellwether issues for our society, and if our objective is to leave for future generations a reasonable documentation of what our society represents, we need to be deliberate and public about efforts to encompass a wide range of perspectives, activities, organizations and institutions. (257)

Of import, artifacts such as the Aryan Nations materials enable researchers to track unambiguously oppressive organizations, a necessary step to reckoning with past and present wrongs. Without records of the Aryan Nations' propaganda, this unfortunate legacy that haunts the Pacific Northwest would be less conspicuous. But while these documents preserve the region's troubling past, in listening for the ways in which power informs the logic of this acquisition makes perceptible a common, though increasingly disputed, ideological commitment to fair and balanced treatment of all sources regardless of the message espoused. In characterizing these materials as just a local perspective without addressing their explicit racist messaging neither accounts for the sway these documents continue to hold nor takes responsibility for the place they now occupy in a research university's library. So while we deem such collections necessary, how these materials are organized, described, and displayed should appropriately respond to the white supremacist content in accordance with reparative archival practices that "reckon with the past by repairing the harm that was done," as critical archive scholar Lae'l Hughes-Watkins maintains (4).

In applying community listening practices to the archive to learn more about the story behind the story, we uncovered more about the problematic acquisition of the Aryan Nations propaganda. When we started this project, we assumed that the Aryan Nations sent their literature unsolicited, but as we sought to better understand the collection's relationship to the university, we learned that the library paid for the materials. This was confirmed when one of the former librarians recalled that when the Aryan Nations newsletters ceased before the subscription was complete, the organization wrote to the library, asking if they would donate the remainder of subscription fee to their cause in lieu of a refund.

The librarian found it satisfying to decline this request, noting that it was a matter of principle, not money. Though only a nominal amount, the funds used to purchase the subscription inescapably supported the Aryan Nations publication. And while troubling, without this material record, our ability to document the evolution of this white supremacist group, its violent rhetoric, and its lingering presence in the region would be impeded. To be sure, there is a long legacy of institutions that have acquired materials in ethically dubious ways, but community listening, and its attention to the gaps and silences in the stories we tell, calls us to consider such dimensions of the archive but also bring them to light. Here, we are again reminded of how reparative archival practices "acknowledg[e] these failures and engag[e] in conscious actions toward a wholeness that may seem to be an exercise in futility but in actuality is an ethical imperative for all within traditional archival spaces" (Hughes-Watkins 4).

For this archival project, community listening also called us to consider the ways in which artifacts are housed within a particular institution or organization and the implications of that positioning, as display and arrangement, too, are rhetorical and imbued with meaning. In the libraries at WSU, the Aryan Nations materials are kept in two places: in special collections, which means that some copies are kept in storage and require potential users to view them in person within MASC's reading room. But at our institution, these documents are also available in the public stacks. Located among books that discuss hate groups, *Calling Our Nation* circulates publicly in a series of nondescript mauve or brown hardcovers. Patrons can pull these collections off the shelf and leaf through them, whether intentionally or by chance; they are also available for checkout. Their placement in these public stacks, with no label, explanation or contextualization, is predicated on a supposed spatial objectivity, but as the explicitly racist contents of these materials make clear, how they are displayed in the library and what that signifies merits greater consideration.

While we find the easy accessibility of this propaganda troubling, as it ostensibly neutralizes the content contained therein, such positioning has afforded patrons the opportunity to "talk back" to these documents. Listening, as García encourages, "for humanity in stories and memories in between cultures, times, and spaces" ("Creating Presence from Absence" 7), we noticed in our study of these materials how some patrons reinscribed meaning of these texts. Someone, for example, penned "Fuck You Whitey" on a page, while another wrote "Assholes" next to the word "Aryan." Though the institution approaches these texts from a seemingly impartial perspective, these individuals subverted authority and voiced their own disapproval of these materials. Through such acts of disruption, they make visible the different cultures of the university but also the nonlinear and participatory nature of community listening as employed within this archival collection.

*Figure 3.1. Cover Page of WSU-Bound Edition* Calling Our Nation, *No. 67.*

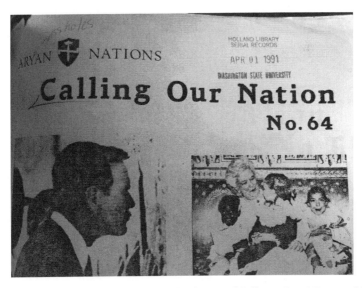

*Figure 3.2. Cover Page of WSU-Bound Edition of* Calling Our Nation, *No. 64.*

The photographs in Figures 3.1 and 3.2 capture the "disruption" found within the bound copies of *Calling Our Nation*.

## COMMUNITY LISTENING AS ARCHIVAL METHODOLOGY

As we began examining the Aryan Nations' general newsletter *Calling Our Nation*, it became clear that *how* we listen is very much by context. In addition to living through the COVID-19 pandemic, we witnessed local and nation-wide demonstrations that called for police accountability and the need for police reform; unprecedented wildfires burned around us so closely and intensely that the sky was dark and smoke crept in through our doors and windows, and a contentious presidential election was underway. These experiences greatly impeded our ability and desire to listen to the Aryan Nations propaganda: we struggled to "stan[d] under" these discourses (Ratcliffe 28), to "suspen[d] judgment" (Fishman and Rosenberg 2), and to engage in "empathetic listening" (Lohr and Lindenman), prompting us to recalibrate our approach. Inspired by García's use of community listening in the settler archives, we aimed "to create presence from absence and sound from silence in the name of justice" ("A Settler Archive" 7). For us, this meant reading the Aryan Nations documents against the context of the given moment, seeking explicitly to put these artifacts into conversation with the events that were unfolding around us. A publication "of, by and for the White 'Aryan Nations' kinfolk of people on this earth," as stated on the title page, *Calling Our Nation* is clearly only concerned with the voices of Christian Identity Theology and white supremacy. "No pretense is or will be made as to any so-called 'objectivity' concerning any other peoples, their beliefs, doctrines, customs or so-called gods," the publication continues to explain. The clear intent of the Aryan Nations newsletter is historically dishonest and realistically warped propaganda. These were challenges we faced as we wrestled with our responsibilities to practice community listening in the context of an overtly racist archival collection. Though the Aryan Nations documents are abhorrent and detestable, we must listen to these sources to confront the racist legacy that continues to haunt the Pacific Northwest and avoid the kind of white supremacy propagation that occurs when such ugly voices are routinely ignored. For this reason, we made the difficult decision to include excerpts from these materials in the section herein. While we struggled with the politics of such citations, we ultimately concluded that it was important to unequivocally demonstrate why these texts are so violent.

Commencing our work with this project, we first read issue #28 of *Calling Our Nation*. One of the earliest editions available in our library, it was published in 1979. From the first issue our class reviewed until the last, a common theme found within these newsletters was the supposed false narratives conveyed by the media. To illustrate, Colin Jordan writes in a reprint of "Great Lie of the 6,000,000," "From the moment the National Socialists came to power in Germany in 1933, Jewry—through its colossal power over the press, radio and cinema of the remainder of the globe—began the greatest campaign of distortion and fabrication which the world has ever seen" (19). Given our time of reading within the final year of the Trump presidency, we could not help but see similarities between the views championed by both Aryan Nations and the Trump presidency concerning the media. While *Calling Our Nation* doesn't have a quick catchphrase, like "Fake News" or "Alternative Facts," as we witnessed from the Trump administration, the skewing of history and historical quotations alongside dishonest claims of the persecution of the white man, racialized scapegoating, and Jewish media domination, the same tactics have been utilized in many corrupt and fascist governments.

Though some governments' uses of these tactics are more subtle than others, through the publication of *Calling Our Nation*, Aryan Nations makes its worship of Hitler and the Third Reich very well known. Hitler's government scapegoated Jews, Romani people, and other "racial inferiors," the Trump administration scapegoated Mexicans, Central Americans, and Muslims. The Third Reich, Aryan Nations, and the Trump administration all worked to discredit intellectuals, communists, and those with left-leaning politics. While the Third Reich and Aryan Nations exclusively employed rhetorics of fear concerning communists, the Third Reich deployed a fraudulent appropriation of the word "socialist." Trump's GOP and its supporters called everyone with humanist opinions "communist and/or socialist," almost exclusively in error. Aryan Nations clearly adopted the Third Reich's rhetorical maneuvers of misleading political and historical context. Each of us in class found it easy to connect these dots.

Relatedly, we noticed the many ways in which history was appropriated, distorted, and otherwise falsified in the effort to generate support for the Aryan Nations. In an article from *Calling Our Nation* #89, "Caucasian Genocide: What will it take to save the White race from Extinction," author Gerhart Hauptmann (most likely a pseudonym stolen from a Nobel prize-winning German naturalist dramatist and novelist) writes, "All of this is neither theory nor opinion, but rather, documented fact supported by an abundance of documentation for anyone willing to investigate the evidence." However, the only evidence provided in this article is opinion and anti-Semitic conspiracy theory. When we were reading this issue, the similar tone peddled by coronavirus deniers and popular QAnon conspiracy theories, such as Pizzagate and the false narrative of US Democratic party members as pedophiles and baby eaters, the similarities could be laughable were it not for the violence and death these conspiracy theories spawn.

As we studied this propaganda, the human casualties were never far from our hearts and minds. In an effort to listen to the voices most affected by the hate speech contained within those documents, we reflected on the rise in harassment and violence that people of color and Jews endured. As Wyn observed, the Aryan Nations are "equal opportunity racists; they hate anyone who isn't white, heterosexual, cisgender, Christian, and male." As we read through the hate-filled pages of *Calling Our Nation* that rhetorically "othered" and subjugated non-white, non-Christian people, we collectively turned to the many examples of hate crimes and violence that we had recently witnessed, connecting violent rhetoric with physical acts of violence, for as Fishman and Rosenberg remind us, "Community listening arises from the recognition that none of us is ever outside of our communities. We are never teaching or researching or organizing or writing unmoored from the communities to which we belong, from what surrounds us, or from the people with whom we engage" (3). Hate crimes have been on the rise since 2014, according to the FBI statistics, which can be directly correlated with an increase in dehumanizing rhetoric. The acts of violence that we witnessed the summer prior to our class, particularly the murder of George Floyd and Ahmaud Arbery, are forever burned into our brains, but we know, too, that so many instances, macro and micro, were not recorded or given the platform warranted. As we reflected on these matters, we thought, too, about the systemic flaws that enabled COVID-19 to disproportionately ravage Black, Indigenous, and Hispanic and Latinx populations, all while Donald Trump and other political leaders added insult to injury with their racist characterizations of the virus that contributed to a notable increase of anti-Asian sentiment.

While no racial, ethnic, or religious group was left untouched, Jews were particularly targeted in the issues that we reviewed. In issue 73, for example, the re-print from *Gothic Ripple* in *Calling Our Nation,* "The Enemy Within," notes that the "InterNational Jewry, a Corrupt & Malignant Tree Bearing No Godly Fruit. It Blots out THE LIGHT and strangles God's Living" (6). We grappled with this kind of ubiquitous dehumanization as we acknowledged the considerable uptick in anti-Semitic harassment and hate crimes that have occurred since 2019. This matter was brought to a head for us when, in Dec. 2020, the Idaho Anne Frank Human Rights Memorial, located in Boise, was vandalized with stickers displaying swastikas and the phrase, "we are everywhere" ("Idaho Anne Frank Memorial"). This upset all of us, but Mitzi was particularly affected. Born and raised in Boise, she used to walk past the memorial every day. She had proudly told the class that it's the only place in the U.S. where you can see the entirety of the Universal Declaration of Human Rights on display, and it's one of only 11 sites in the U.S. to have received a sapling from the Anne Frank chestnut tree in Amsterdam. To Mitzi, the monument was a reminder that even though she was dealing with racism every day, there was hope for intersectional parity. In response to this hate-filled vandalism, Mayor of Boise, Lauren McLean said acts of hatred are not the Boise way. "Bad actors who use racist and violent rhetoric are not welcome in this community" ("Idaho Anne Frank Memorial"). While many of us wish to deny that these "bad actors" are part of the community, as their stickers indicated, they are everywhere. For us, community listening is "a way to *be-with* others," (García, "Presence from Absence" 7), a sharing of responsibility that requires us to accept the "bad actors."

This reality was, unfortunately, reaffirmed a few months later when, in February 2021, in Spokane, Washington, fewer than one hundred miles from WSU, Temple Beth Shalom was vandalized with painted swastikas. However, this most recent incident in the Spokane synagogue was not the first. In 2014, "a swastika was painted on a concrete wall during a service on Yom Kippur, the holiest day of the year for the Jewish community" (Riordan). Rabbi Tamar Malino said, "Our community is in shock and in grief, and trying to be strong. It's very difficult to know that there are people that hate you that much for being Jewish and have intention of expressing that. It's very important for our community to continue living meaningful, strong, and Jewish lives and not be afraid to continue being who we are" (qtd. in Riordan). Christian allies from Spokane decried this vandalism. The dean of St. John's Episcopal Cathedral, Heather VanDeventer, stated, "We pray for our neighbors at Temple Beth Shalom. We pray for an end to anti-Semitism and other expressions of hate which hurt and demean our siblings. We pray for continued strength, focus, and determination as we seek to walk in the Way of Love and to build the Beloved Community" (qtd. in Riordan). This statement of support is a far cry from Aryan Nations' Christian Identity Theology. Perhaps because of our reading of Aryan Nations messages of hate combined with the persistence of anti-Semitism found in current regional white supremacist groups, such as the One Percenters, Oathkeepers, and the Proud Boys—many of whom participated in the attempted insurrection at the US Capitol building on January 6, 2021—we were deeply saddened and sickened, but we were not surprised.

In the case of Aryan Nations' legacy, the greatest failure in community listening is the inclination for the broader members of the community to ignore white supremacist groups. It is the act of ignoring these communities that perpetuates the cycle of hatred and violence, as is evidenced by their continued existence. According to the Southern Poverty Law Center, there are 22 hate groups, primarily white supremacist, in Washington alone; 838 in the United States ("Hate Map"). James Baldwin famously said, "Not everything that is faced can be changed, but nothing can be changed until it is faced." To disrupt this fatal cycle, community members must contribute to the ongoing work of listening, learning, and resisting; they must not ignore this harmful offshoot of the community. As many well-intentioned white non-racists are wont to say, hate isn't born, it is taught. But to be truly antiracist, we must address this teaching of hate, and learn how to decompose these organizations and their actions of hate.

## COMMUNITY LISTENING AS INTERVENTION

As we grew more acquainted with the Aryan Nations propaganda, we became increasingly concerned with the lack of context that accompanied these inflammatory materials. Residing both in MASC and in general circulation stacks, these documents are cataloged under *Calling Our Nation*. The entry for this periodical is rather sparse: there is no summary, no additional notes, no discussion of acquisition; it contains only basic information, including the author's name, date of publication, and subject headings, neutralizing the gravity of these documents and the serious harm for which they blatantly advocate.

Further, because of their classification as both rare books and general periodicals, facsimile copies of these documents circulate in the general stacks, a practice that deviated from other institutions that managed these same materials much more carefully. In our library, though, issues of *Calling Our Nation* are bound together into a series of hardcover books that are readily available to the public; there is no explanation of these sources, no acknowledgment of their misleading and violent statements, and no content warning. These consequential omissions, born out of status quo archival practices, prompted us to bring our concerns to the archivists who introduced us to these artifacts. In this way, we sought to share the responsibility that the archivists inherited with the *Calling Our Nation* newsletters as an act of community listening.

In many ways, this chapter would not have been possible without the archivists. They found the materials for us, and they did additional, extraordinary work, such as emailing former archivists and librarians to help us learn more about the acquisition of the documents. Our archivist colleagues met with Patty several times in preparation for the visits with the full class and exchanged emails with her throughout the semester and beyond; they even agreed to read this essay, offering valuable feedback. Importantly, we recognize, as Magia G. Krause observes, "only people who work in the archives really know the collections" (404). Although we appreciate their generosity of time and energy, we also had some challenging questions, which the archivists graciously answered during two separate class meetings; both conversations became strained. While this tension was palpable for all parties, we follow Fishman and Rosenberg's idea that the purpose of community listening "is to find ways to make relationships more productive and substantial with the goal of meaningful change" (5).

In our first conversation, we learned that a former librarian had paid a subscription fee for the newsletters. The conversation turned tense when we asked the archivists if this contribution could be taken as supporting a then-prominent white supremacist group, but pointing to their email correspondence with former librarians, they saw this more as an attempt to preserve a wide range of viewpoints, even those deemed unpalatable. Though library sciences have long encouraged professionals to remain objective, such decisions illustrate how, in the unequivocal words of historian Howard Zinn, this "supposed neutrality . . . is a fake" (21). To be clear, the archivists with whom we worked were not part of this decision-making process; they had inherited the problem that we were bringing to them. But while we agreed that the area's history of white supremacy shouldn't be denied, we wondered how these sources were interpreted by patrons.

The next step was to ask if the materials had an introduction or content warning. They answered no, explaining that if teachers assigning Aryan Nations propaganda wanted a trigger warning, it was up to their own discretion to provide one. The archivists abided by a similar practice in MASC, giving student workers the option of not scanning the materials if they felt uncomfortable, so while there was recognition that these materials warranted greater care in some contexts, there was no move to attend to these concerns in broader, public application. We invited the archivists to return to our class because we had additional questions for them, and despite the discomfort we all felt during our first conversation, they agreed to another meeting. At this point, our understanding of community listening was informed by Karen Rowan and Alexandra J. Cavallaro's idea of listening being the "work before the work" (27). Drawing from Krista Ratcliffe's scholarship on rhetorical listening, they explain that there is a "need to listen beyond individual intentions to 'historically situated discourses . . .'" (Rowan and Cavallaro 26). Prompted by this insight, we reflected on why our previous conversation with the archivists had felt tense and what this tension meant for us and the broader WSU community. Why, for example, were we upset that this propaganda sits unattended on the self? Why were we bothered about the lack of a content warning in the newsletters? And why did we feel angry that there was no transparency regarding the accession of these documents? Such questions and the emotions that haunted them informed our next steps.

As the instructor of the course, but also as a colleague who hoped to build a relationship with the archivists, Patty wanted to ensure that they did not feel ambushed when they spoke with the class during the second visit, so she emailed them in advance with some of the questions that had come up in class. In asking them to discuss MASC protocols for sensitive materials, she acknowledged that the class had "do[ne] a little research [and] noticed that other libraries limit access to [*Calling Our Nation*]—that is, [these documents] are for "library-use" only.

Are there policies that inform why [the library] allows them to circulate more freely? Are there any documents in the archive that are more difficult to access because of their sensitive nature?" As Patty further explained, "We are interested in learning more about how [MASC] and archives more broadly handle these kinds of materials." In response to these questions, the archivists reminded us that the Aryan Nation materials are in two places at WSU: the original publications are housed in MASC, overseen by the archivists, but the bound facsimile copies are shelved in the library, falling under the purview of university librarians. As noted by the American Library Association, even "hate speech is protected by the First Amendment." We tried to clarify that we weren't asking for the materials to be removed, but rather, we strongly believed that these physical documents warranted greater contextualization. But we also asked why there weren't more institutional controls in place for accessing these materials, again pointing to the precedent established by other universities holding Aryan Nations periodicals. Patrons wanting to view these documents either needed to request access to them because of their archival status or check them out in two-hour increments. The archivists reiterated that their mandate was to preserve history and serve the community, though our lessons in community listening had us asking ourselves what members of the community are prioritized with such directives. We went around in circles like this, failing to find a way forward that satisfied us all.

But discussing the availability of these documents wasn't the only uncomfortable moment in our conversations. The tension deepened again when we asked if there was talk about implementing any library protocols on how to address racist materials, similar to the plans of action put forth by the National Archives[4] and the University of California Los Angeles (Smith), among others. Though, as Elizabeth Yale maintains, "No archive is innocent" (332), antiracist archival practices specifically call institutions to acknowledge their role in acquiring and disseminating materials that contribute to systemic oppression; develop finding aid descriptions sensitive to the implicit and overt racism that lives in the archives, including transparent context statements about accession and provenance; appropriately manage known white supremacist materials with content warnings and reasonable control of access; and create a concrete plan of action for when oppressive materials inevitably emerge (National Archives). We continue to recognize the web of complications associated with such a request, especially when budgets and personnel are scarce. The conversation remained locked until one archivist nodded to the "white fragility" of the matter: "we could start working on this stuff and get feedback."[3] Finally, the

---

3    According to Robin DiAngelo, white fragility is "[a] state in which even a minimum amount of racial stress becomes intolerable, triggering a range of defensive moves" (57).

tension snapped like a rubber band as the archivists laughed and admitted to feeling uncomfortable.

We'd like to retrospectively unravel this moment in the conversation because the archivists effectively opened portals into community listening, though we failed at the moment to recognize them. Justin Lohr and Heather Lindenman contend that self-disclosure can invite empathetic listening, to "hear the collective refrains and struggles that often present themselves in individual voices" (72). Confessing to something as vulnerable as white fragility and discomfort invited our two mini-communities to "be with" each other to understand our different positions. Lohr and Lindenman propose empathy as a steppingstone to community listening. It was easier to withhold judgment and have an openness to understand the archivists' perspective because they were willing to be open with us. As García writes, "Responsibility, then and now, meant listening to know and to learn" ("Creating Presence from Absence" 10). Part of our responsibility was listening with that openness, and that also gave us hope that our working relationship could be meaningful and productive—that together, we could "know and learn" to better serve our shared communities.

Mitzi would like to draw attention to the close of what was, at the time of writing, the last conversation with the archivists. They responded to a question about accessibility of the materials. "Do we want to interrogate people every time they want access to any material, though?" they asked. The response, Mitzi thinks, might be, "Who will be responsible for the hurt that comes when somebody accesses material containing hate speech, material that is presented as neutral?" The library shelf in a university has an undeniable ethos. This matters to Mitzi because, on the shelves of her undergraduate institution, she once found a doctoral thesis arguing that students of Mexican descent are underachieving because they are lazy. The unspoken authority in the thesis' placement communicated that the university supports or at least tolerates racism. What is the inadvertent message sent in a bound volume of Aryan Nations propaganda sitting unsupervised on the shelf with no statement of context?

These struggles taught Mitzi, Patty, and Wyn their first lesson in the limits of community listening. They were uncomfortable and dissatisfied with how the conversation flowed, particularly with what they interpreted as a reluctance on the archivists' behalf to move toward changes in contextualizing, handling, and housing of the material. Rowan and Cavallaro contend that community listening work "entails more than envisioning a better world, but rather, using that vision as 'an ethical guide for the practical work that must be done in the here and now' [in the words of Paul Feigenbaum]" (27). Wyn had entered the conversation believing that the archivists were going to readily see our perspective, and she found the pushback galling. Patty tried to listen to the archivists but was hoping for more immediate results; worthy of note, she felt conflicting obligations, as she tried to be a good teacher and colleague, while also following her conscience. As the only person of color involved with this project, Mitzi had her walls up. Erica Stone posits that we all bring different identities and roles to community listening—the self brings history to community that we are attempting to listen to (20). Our idea of being open was challenged as we thought about how we had closed off—were we truly open to listen if we shut down when the archivists weren't on the same page?

Months after our second conversation, we continued to engage in community listening when the archivists sent us an invitation to a webinar they thought would interest us. We attended a panel titled, "When Collections are Considered Controversial," where we were introduced to the article "A Reconsideration of Library Treatment of Ethically Questionable Medical Texts: The Case of The Pernkopf Atlas of Anatomy." Scheinfeld et al. investigate the handling of the *Pernkopf Atlas*, a medical atlas created with "a disregard for human life and informed medical consent" by an active member of the Nazi party (165). The *Atlas* has Nazi symbols on many pages of illustrations, the authors write, "Though these facts are extremely distasteful, censorship of distasteful material is not part of the mission of libraries. What makes the *Atlas* a work of which libraries should be aware is that individuals depicted in the anatomical drawings were likely victims of the Nazi regime" (Scheinfeld et al. 165). The text also echoed many concerns we heard from the WSU archivists, such as the avoidance of censorship and the risk of vandalism "or mutilation [of controversial texts]" (166). However, the article concludes that "Situational meaning created by location is balanced by curatorial and cataloging decisions that provide additional context to the work" (170). We understand community listening to be a non-linear, recursive process that involves both past and present selves. Part of the discomfort in our conversations with the archivists was caused by knowing that other libraries have more control over controversial materials, and this discomfort resurfaced again as we read the article on the *Atlas*. Wendy Hinshaw points out that "Community listening also means recognizing our limitations, the barriers of listening created by our subject positions" (67). We recognize that the listening we invited and engaged in with the archivists is complicated by the fact that our community is impacted by white supremacy. In tangling with our shared responsibility and discomfort, we hope to better understand ourselves as community members. How do we bring our individual positionalities into the listening in a way that respects all?

We honor our relationship with our archivists and echo the participants from the Krause survey, who note that archivists are "probably the best suited people to highlight what [primary sources] mean to our cultural heritage to enhance people's appreciation for that cultural resource" (404). In our case, providing context and transparency about the acquisition of Aryan Nations materials is a matter of acknowledging WSU's entanglement with the white supremacists in our backyard, a way of providing information student researchers should consider in their work. Finally, as Rowan and Cavallaro suggest, "Our approach to community listening must be ongoing, reflective, and subject to revision" (34). We understand that community listening is not over once this chapter is finished. We hope to continue the dialogue with the archivists and with each other to work collaboratively toward meaningful change in our community.

## REFLECTIONS ON KEEPING BAD COMPANY

As Fishman and Rosenberg explain it, community listening is a process "that involves deep, direct, engagement with individuals and groups working to address urgent issues in everyday life, issues anchored by long histories and complicated by competing interpretations as well as clashing modes of expression" (1). In positioning archives as sites of community listening, we were committed to attending to the unfortunate but very real legacy of white supremacy in our local and regional communities. While the explicit racism that the Aryan Nations propaganda espouses is understandably alienating, the ensuing sense of disidentification that subsequently emerges tends to ignore white power propagation.

Listening to these collections, for us, also further exposed the socially negotiated nature of such collections and the narratives that emerge from these places of memory and history—including the story that we've offered here, which is informed by our own collective and individual values and embodied experiences. Originating in the archive, our account is illustrative of what Rodney Carter calls "[a]chival power," which, "is, in part, the power to allow voices to be heard. It consists of highlighting certain narratives and of including certain types of records created by certain groups" (216). While Carter's observation largely rings true in theory, it is not always executed in meaningful ways in practice, as our experience with the Aryan Nations collection suggests. Moved by a sense of responsibility to our community, a defining tenet of community listening, we attempted to enact change through our requests to contextualize these explicit racist documents and develop protocols for addressing future similar occurrences. While we were largely unsuccessful in these endeavors, we are reminded of bell hooks' observation: "To build community," she writes, "requires vigilant awareness of the work we must *continually* do to undermine all the socialization that leads us to behave in ways that perpetuate domination" (36, emphasis ours). In this spirit, we are hopeful that the conversations have only just begun.

## WORKS CITED

American Library Association. "Hate Speech and Hate Crime." https://www.ala.org/advocacy/intfreedom/hate. Accessed 15 Sep. 2021.

Balleck, Barry J. *Hate Groups and Extremist Organizations in America: An Encyclopedia.* ABC-CLIO, 2019.

Bastian, Jeanette A., and Ben Alexander. *Community Archives: The Shaping of Memory.* Facet Publishing, 2009.

Biesecker, Barbara. "Of Historicity, Rhetoric: The Archive as Scene of Invention." *Rhetoric & Public Affairs,* vol. 9, no. 1, 2006, pp. 124–131.

Burke, Kenneth. *The Philosophy of Literary Form: Studies in Symbolic Action.* 3rd ed. U of California P, 1973.

Carter, Rodney GS. "Of Things Said and Unsaid: Power, Archival Silences, and Power in Silence." *Archivaria,* vol. 61, 2006, pp. 215–233.

Caswell, Michelle. "'The Archive' is Not an Archives: Acknowledge the Intellectual Contributions of Archival Studies." *Reconstruction,* vol. 16, no. 1, 2016, https://escholarship.org/content/qt7bn4v1fk/qt7bn4v1fk.pdf?t=ox1knk.

"Christian Identity." *Anti-Defamation League*, https://www.adl.org/resources/backgrounders/christian-identity. Accessed 13 Apr. 2021.

Cox, Richard J. "The Archivist and Community." *Community Archives: The Shaping of Memory*, edited by Jeannette A. Bastian, Neil-Schuman Publishers, 2009, pp. 251–64.

Cunningham, Adrian. "Archives as a Place." *Currents of Archival Thinking* (2nd edition), edited by Heather MacNeil and Terry Eastwood, 2017.

Day, Meagan. "Welcome to Hayden Lake, Where White Supremacists Tried to Build Their Homeland." *Timeline*, 4 Nov. 2016, https://timeline.com/white-supremacist-rural-paradise-fb62b74b29e0.

DiAngelo, Robin. "White Fragility." *International Journal of Critical Pedagogy*, vol. 3, no. 3, 2011, pp. 54–70.

Dickinson, Greg, Brian L. Ott, and Eric Aoki. "Spaces of Remembering and Forgetting: The Reverent Eye/I at the Plains Indian Museum." *Communication and Critical/Cultural Studies*, vol. 3, no. 1, pp. 27–47.

"The Enemy Within." *Gothic Ripples.* (1989): 3–6. Rpt. in *Calling Our Nation.* N.A. 73, 20 (1994).

Fishman, Jenn, and Lauren Rosenberg, editors. *Community Writing, Community Listening*, special issue of *Community Literacy Journal*, vol. 13, no. 1, 2018.

García, Romeo. "Creating Presence from Absence and Sound from Silence." Fishman and Rosenberg, pp. 7–15, https://doi.org/10.25148/clj.13.1.009086.

———. "A Settler Archive: A Site for a Decolonial Praxis Project." *Constellations*, no. 2, 2019.

"Hate Map." Southern Poverty Law Center, https://www.splcenter.org/hate-map.

Hinshaw, Wendy. "Writing to Listen: Why I Write Across Prison Walls." Fishman and Rosenberg, pp. 55–70, https://doi.org/10.25148/clj.13.1.009090.

Hirtle, Peter B. "Archival Authenticity in a Digital Age." *Authenticity in a Digital Environment.* 2000, pp. 8–23.

hooks, bell. *Teaching Community: A Pedagogy of Hope*. Psychology Press, 2003.

Hughes-Watkins, Lae'l. "Moving Toward a Reparative Archive: A Roadmap for a Holistic Approach to Disrupting Homogenous Histories in Academic Repositories and Creating Inclusive Spaces for Marginalized Voices." *Journal of Contemporary Archival Studies*, vol. 5, art. 6, 2018, pp. 1–17.

Jimerson, Randall C. *Archives Power: Memory, Accountability, and Social Justice*. The Society of American Archivists, 2009.

Jones, Dustin. "Idaho Anne Frank Memorial Defaced With Nazi Propaganda." *NPR*, NPR, 10 Dec. 2020, https://www.npr.org/2020/12/10/945150729/idaho-anne -frank-memorial-defaced-with-nazi-propaganda.

Jordan, Colin. "Great Lie of the 6,000,000." *National Socialist*. no. 7, (1964). Rpt. in *Calling Our Nation* (1979) 19–20.

Kirsch, Gesa E. "Being on location: Serendipity, place, and archival research." *Beyond the Archives: Research as a Lived Process*, edited by Gesa E. Kirsch and Liz Rohan, Southern Illinois UP, 2008, pp. 20–27.

Krause, Magia G. "'It Makes History Alive for Them': The Role of Archivists and Special Collections Librarians in Instructing Undergraduates." *The Journal of Academic Librarianship*, vol. 36, no. 5, 2010, pp. 401–411.

Lohr, Justin, and Heather Lindenman. "Challenging Audiences to Listen: The Performance of Self-Disclosure in Community Writing Projects." Fishman and Rosenberg, pp. 71–86, https://doi.org/10.25148/clj.13.1.009091.

Morris, Charles E. "Archival Queer." *Rhetoric & Public Affairs,* vol. 9, no. 1, 2006, pp. 145–151.

National Archives. *The Archivists Task Force on Racism: Report to the Archivist*, Apr. 2021, https://www.archives.gov/files/news/archivists-task-force-on-racism-report .pdf.

Nokes, Greg. "Black Exclusion Laws in Oregon." *Oregon Encyclopedia*. Oregon Historical Society. 6 Jul. 2020. https://www.oregonencyclopedia.org/articles/exclusion _laws/#.YI3jkGhlBHQ.

Powell, Malea. "Dreaming Charles Eastman: Cultural Memory, Autobiography, and Geography in Indigenous Rhetorical Histories." *Beyond the Archives: Research as a Lived Process*, edited by Gesa E. Kirsch and Liz Rohan, Southern Illinois UP, 2008, pp. 115–127.

Rawson, KJ. "The Rhetorical Power of Archival Description: Classifying Images of Gender Transgression." *Rhetoric Society Quarterly*, vol. 48, 2018, pp. 327–51.

Ratcliffe, Krista. *Rhetorical Listening: Identification, Gender, Whiteness*. Southern Illinois UP, 2005.

Rich, Adrienne. "Notes on a Politics of Location." *Blood, Bread, and Poetry*. Norton, 1989, pp. 210–31.

Riordan, Kaitlin. "'In Shock and in Grief': Spokane Synagogue Vandalized with Swastikas." *Krem.com*, 9 Feb. 2021, https://tinyurl.com/2c8hptpt.

Rohan, Liz. "Stitching and Writing a Life." *Beyond the Archives: Research as a Lived Process*, edited by Gesa E. Kirsch and Liz Rohan, Southern Illinois UP, 2008, pp. 147–153.

Rowan, Karen, and Alexandra J. Cavallaro. "Toward a Model for Preparatory Community Listening." Fishman and Rosenberg, pp. 23–36, https://doi.org/10.25148/clj.13.1.009088.

Royster, Jacqueline Jones, and Gesa E. Kirsch. *Feminist Rhetorical Practices: New Horizons for Rhetoric, Composition, and Literacy Studies*. Southern Illinois UP, 2012.

Scheinfeld, Laurel, Jamie Saragossi, and Kathleen Kasten. "A Reconsideration of Library Treatment of Ethically Questionable Medical Texts: The case of the Pernkopf Atlas of Anatomy." *Library Faculty Publications*, vol. 64, no. 32, 2020, pp. 165–176.

Schwartz, Joan M., and Terry Cook " Archives, Records, and Power: From Theory to Performance." *Archival Science*, vol. 2, 2002, pp. 1–19.

Society of American Archivists. "Member Needs and Satisfaction Survey, 2012." http://files.archivists.org/membership/surveys/saaMemberSurvey-2012r2.pdf. Accessed 24 Mar. 2021.

Smith, Michelle C. "Thoughts on Conserving Racist Materials in Libraries." *UCLA Library.* 29 Sept. 2020, https://www.library.ucla.edu/about/news/thoughts-on-conserving-racist-materials-in-libraries/.

Stone, Erica M. "The Story of Sound Off: A Community Writing/Community Listening Experiment." Fishman and Rosenberg, pp. 16–22, https://doi.org/10.1353/clj.2018.0018.

United States Census Bureau. "Quick Facts: Idaho." https://www.census.gov/quickfacts/ID, Accessed 27 Mar. 2021.

Villanueva, Victor. "Celebration of Diversity: Strive to Honor the Past, Celebrate [the] New, and Look to the Future." Unpublished paper.

"Why Idaho's Racist History Matters: Part 2." *Boise State Public Radio*, 13 Aug. 2020. https://tinyurl.com/2ybhuzfw.

Williams, Raymond. *Keywords*. Duke UP, 2007.

Yale, Elizabeth. "The History of Archives: The State of the Discipline." *Book History*, vol. 18, pp. 332–359.

Zinn, Howard. "Secrecy, Archives, and the Public Interest." *The Midwestern Archivist*, vol. 2, no. 2, 1977, pp. 14–26.

# PART 2. STORIES OF SUSTAINING COMMUNITY

This section advances our understanding of community listening through stories of sustaining community in deliberate and intentional ways. Notably, if coincidentally, each of the following chapters situates readers across the Southwest landscape. Chapter 4 "The Public Art of Listening: Relational Accountability and The Painted Desert Project" by Kyle Boggs contends with the role of art within the Navajo nation of Arizona and highlights how relationality has nuanced community engagement. Chapter 5 "The DJ as Relational Listener and Creator of an Ethos of Community Listening" by Karen R. Tellez-Trujillo carefully reckons with the role radio DJs play in El Paso, Texas, and illuminates the intentional centering of relationality by the DJ to inform, give form to, and even transform ways of thinking and being amongst marginalized communities across space and time. Chapter 6 "Listening In: Letter Writing and Rhetorical Resilience Behind Bars" by Alexandra J. Cavallaro, Wendy Hinshaw, and Tobi Jacobi reflects on prison letter writing programs in Colorado and explores how relationality can help navigate the challenges of thinking with and from incarcerated writers. Of no coincidence, the theme this section addresses is relationality and the role relationality can play in sustaining a community otherwise, which authors explore from various positionalities and potentials.

CHAPTER 4.

# THE PUBLIC ART OF LISTENING: RELATIONAL ACCOUNTABILITY AND THE PAINTED DESERT PROJECT

**Kyle Boggs**

Boise State University

*Public art thrives when it reflects the community in which it is situated and engages its audience in meaningful dialogue. Public art serves as advocacy and community writing, translating community needs and struggles into visual mediums. The process of community listening, integral to public art, fosters relational accountability, building solidarity, and provoking action. Chip Thomas, also known as Jetsonorama, exemplifies relational accountability through his public art on the Navajo Nation. His work, characterized by large-scale photographs, captures everyday life and cultural elements of the community, fostering a dialogue between artist and audience. Thomas's process, described as an "evolving dialogue," emphasizes community listening and relationality, echoing Indigenous research paradigms articulated by Shawn Wilson. Thomas navigates cultural sensitivities by celebrating aspects of Diné culture recognized as beautiful by the community. Thomas's murals highlighted in this chapter address various themes, including sacred site protection, the legacy of resource extraction, and health solidarity during the COVID-19 pandemic, amplifying community voices, connections, and concerns. His work invites viewers to engage in reflective dialogue, fostering deeper connections within and among communities. Community listening, as demonstrated by Thomas's art, encourages audiences to listen further and differently, triggering reflective processes within individuals and communities. This ongoing dialogue, rooted in relational accountability, challenges systemic structures and amplifies marginalized voices. Through public art and community writing, communities assert their identities, needs, and struggles, shaping public discourse and fostering collective action against the ongoing effects of colonialism.*

DOI: https://doi.org/10.37514/PER-B.2025.2531.2.04

Public art thrives when a community can see themselves reflected in the work and the art itself assembles a listening audience. Independent newspapers, chapbooks, newsletters, broadsides, zines, and more remain crucial for their interventions into public discourse, their articulations of identity and sense of place, and their capacity to provoke public debate and challenge institutional dominance over the public sphere through radical and democratic action. Public art has also been established as a meaningful form of advocacy, a valid mode of community writing. It catalyzes a particular kind of community listening that is expressed uniquely through the mediums of art that reflect community, its values, goals, lived experiences, histories, and identities; it has the power to translate the community's needs and struggles as well as its joys. These characteristics, expressions, and orientations are made visible in public art that is engaged in community listening and, in turn, produces a viewer that becomes a listening audience. Whether the viewer engages or ignores the work's provocations, they nonetheless persist, perhaps long after they return home.

Public artists establish structures of accountability, where both positive and critical feedback is not only welcomed but necessary to cultivate public trust. Community listening as a practice/process is fundamental to how I understand the formation of accountability and relationality, and it is central to cultivating what Shawn Wilson calls "relational accountability," a means of building solidarity and provoking action that focuses on the process of *how* (99). When I think of relational accountability in public art, I'm recognizing how listening is communicated visually and what that reveals about the artist's process of representation and their relationships with the community. When public art appears in shared community spaces, when peoples or their cultures, practices, and histories are depicted/reflected in the work, it is the community that ultimately decides whether the work will continue to stand. This measure of community listening, foregrounded by accountability and relationality, is not something that can be achieved overnight. However, community listening practices and processes can also be meaningful in a particular moment. For example, recall "the people's mic," or the "community microphone," as it was also referred to, which became the signature form of amplification during the Occupy Wall Street protests in 2011. The practice refers to a large group of people gathered around a speaker with no microphone. Each line shouted by the speaker is promptly repeated by the group, thus amplifying the message of the speaker to those in the back. As each listener moves back and forth between roles as listener and speaker, their relationship to each other extends from their shared participation and solidarity with the message.

Whether confrontational or invitational, varying degrees of critical self-reflection is an important effect of public art. Focusing on community listening scholarship on community writing and public art has helped me find ways to recognize, contextualize, and process the ways we are implicated by our research and by those we interview, how we are situated in the topic, and it allows us to articulate difference in terms of consequence: what is at stake for those we engage with might be vastly different from what is at stake for us or to our readers. Public art, especially that which is unconventional and unexpected, may similarly provoke this kind of reflection. While scholarly work on visual rhetoric has long maintained that the production and rhetorical effect of images can certainly do the same persuasive work that written texts do (Foss et al.; Hill and Helmers), I also understand what visual texts like public art can do to produce forms of community listening that activate and engage the public in ways that are dynamic and meaningful. I understand this claim as synesthetic in nature, as community listening works across senses synergistically, producing new forms of engagement as it participates in complex sense-making processes that are folded into the work.

## THE VIEW FROM THE ROAD

Around 2009, I noticed Chip Thomas's murals when driving up 89, the road that goes north from Flagstaff, Arizona, through the Navajo Nation. One, then a few months later, another installation would pop up somewhere else, breathing new life into a structure I had hardly noticed before. In the years that followed, they were everywhere: large-scale photographs, most of them black and white with splashes of accent color. I saw images of a woman herding sheep, a close-up of a man's face laughing, a toddler with eyes inquisitive and mischievous, children laughing hysterically, grazing sheep, a child's eyes gazing upward toward a big piece of raw coal, a woman on a swing smiling with her head upside down, a close up of hands, a man standing proudly next to stalks of corn (and lots more sheep!). Sometimes the work featured text, sometimes written on subject's faces and other times below, off to the side, or overlayed. At the time, I recognized how this text often worked in tandem with the image to convey meaning that would not otherwise be possible through either the image or the text alone (see Figure 4.1). Because of the contrast between the landscape, quiet and still, and the vibrancy of the images, I found myself compelled to pull over, to turn off my engine, and to listen. The images clearly had something to say, stories to tell and communicate about that place and the community it represented, they quite literally animate the landscape, making it talk, making it move.

The work of Chip Thomas brings the concept of relational accountability into focus as a useful framework for community listening. In his own words, Chip Thomas, aka Jetsonorama, is an "artist, activist, and physician," a "visual storyteller" (Bell).[1] He's an "intentional provocateur, putting work out that people might not expect to see in a particular space" (KQED Arts). I met Thomas and wrote about his art when I was a journalist in northern Arizona, where his work is primarily situated where he lives and works on the Navajo Nation. I found that Thomas' visual work not only constitutes community writing, but in a lot of ways it transcends what I was able to do as a journalist. This chapter analyzes the visual and material rhetoric of his murals to emphasize community listening, as both a process-oriented and relational practice, and something that shows up visually in the work, and is thus necessary to the process of relational accountability.

## RELATIONAL ACCOUNTABILITY AND LISTENING

In *Research is Ceremony: Indigenous Research Methods*, Wilson articulates an Indigenous research framework assembled by traditional Indigenous practices that center relationality and relational accountability. One who is accountable to their relations recognizes the ways they are implicated in the consequences of the work. For Wilson, relational accountability refers to the process by which one becomes accountable to and respectful of all relationships, including relationships between individual people, human and nonhuman communities, ideas, and land. It's a process that should feel organic, less like a prescription and more like building a relationship. Accountability in this framework refers to the process by which one forges meaningful relationships and establishes trust through working together, collaborating, and learning from one another. The effect of becoming accountable to one's relations creates the conditions from which work that is wanted, needed, and celebrated by that community is imagined; it means one is open to criticism because they want to do right by that community, to find ways to connect on deeper levels, to forge stronger connections that provoke, inspire, and challenge. These practices and processes scaffold structures of accountability over time and are intimately connected to community listening.

I am invested in community listening that mobilizes public engagement against settler and white supremacist systems. What does it mean to be a settler on stolen Indigenous land? I am interested in new rhetorical approaches that find ways to articulate the landscapes in which we engage as the palimpsests of culture and history that they are. This requires modes of thinking that disrupt and complicate what we see as anything but simple physical spaces, but rather

---

1    "Jetsonorama" refers to his street artist name, associated with his work with "The Painted Desert Project" and other past and ongoing collaborations and installations.

an amalgamation of stories, competing histories, and contested spaces. The view from the road on the Navajo Nation, a view that is vast and made to feel empty, reflects colonial logics that sustain silences that are strategic and systemic. Thomas's work proves that a rusty old silo or abandoned building can be reclaimed and transformed into something that works against these silences. Listening, when it attends to culture and relationality, when nurtured by the kind of intention exemplified by the words of Shawn Wilson when he wrote— "I come to you with a good heart"—listening can indeed be translated into a language that is visual, responsive, and has the power to provoke action (7).

The work of Chip Thomas, and more specifically, the process through which he creates his work, which he described to me as an "evolving dialogue," applies the same responsible relational engagement that has been articulated through Indigenous research paradigms as articulated by Wilson. Relationships, for Wilson, are themselves an "ongoing process," within which "all intelligible action is born, sustained, and/or extinguished" (xv). But Wilson also doesn't view us and our practices as "being *in* relationship" but writes that "we *are* the relationships that we hold and are a part of" (80). Community artists and writers literally embody the relationships reflected in their work as they recognize how they are implicated and intimately connected in ways that are unique to them. "I identify as a visual storyteller," says Thomas (New Mexico PBS).

Emphasizing Thomas' public art on the Navajo Nation as a form of visual storytelling, I agree with Rachel C. Jackson, who based on conversations with Dorothy Whitehorse DeLaune, understands stories "as a kind of community listening" and "call us to consider the ways in which community writing occurs beyond the colonialist implications and limitations of printed text" (42). As an Indigenous scholar, Jackson is concerned with the ways that Western academic discourses impose a "rational order on otherwise organic ideas and spontaneous meanings," and I'm drawn to her understanding of community listening as a praxis that "invites us to listen without limitations" (40). For Jackson, storytelling "depends on community listeners for collaborative meaning making," asking listeners to "imagine possibilities," attend to "potential meanings" and "actions," and to examine the "relationships between the past and present situation, between peoples and places, between 'then and now' and 'us and them'" (40). While considering visual stories in the same light, I am drawn to Jackson's analysis of Kiowa storytelling in that it "invites us to listen differently, *with* a community rather than *to* a community or *for* a community" (42). Jackson's analysis of Kiowa storytelling not only challenges our understanding of community writing itself but mobilizes it toward Indigenous solidarity and resistance to settler colonialism. By focusing on the visual storytelling of public art, this chapter is invested not only in expanding our understanding of what "counts" as community writing but mobilizes community writing to work against settler colonialism by using visual storytelling in ways that move "historical legacies into the present" (38). And when those legacies are thrust into the present, they demand to be listened to and reckoned with in the present.

After introducing Thomas and demonstrating these relationships in his work generally, this chapter analyzes three of the themes his work addresses: the protection of sacred sites, the legacy of resource colonialism, and health solidarity during the COVID-19 pandemic. Each of these works underscores the profound relationship between community listening, visual art, and meaningful public engagement. In representing Thomas in his own words, I rely primarily on film and print interviews and profiles; I also weave in moments from my own interviews with him when I was a journalist and more recently. The result is a personal reflection of his work over many years, which exemplifies my observations about community listening as a process built from long-term commitments. Thomas's murals further emphasize new ways that a community that is listened to can speak through the work, where the art—like all meaningful community writing—speaks *with* and not *for*. With this phrasing, I am recalling Linda Alcoff's discussion of the problems of speaking *for* and speaking *about* in her 1991 essay, "The Problem of Speaking for Others." As I analyze Thomas' visual stories, I am reminded of Alcoff's observation that "Who is speaking, who is spoken of, and who listens is a result, as well as an act, of political struggle" (15). While she calls for more research into practical ways to speak *with*, or at least "lessen the dangers" of speaking *for* or speaking *about*, this chapter constitutes one of the ways community listening, particularly through public art, can contribute to this larger discussion (24). By listening to Thomas and observing his work, I learned to be a different kind of listener who is more attuned to the multiple stories and converging relations a work can communicate. Thomas' visual storytelling reflects these commitments in ways that depict the intensive listening moments that he experienced so that others may experience them, too.

As a journalist, I learned to think of myself as a community listener as well. My responsibility as a storyteller necessarily relies on community listening, and the work produced through a deep community listening process is also better positioned to challenge systemic colonial structures. A storyteller who engages in community listening that is relational, that is focused on building long-term connections, that creates spaces where the community can speak to each other, community listening can clarify needs that can then be pursued as more stories that the community wants, will benefit them, and through which they can see themselves accurately represented.

## JETSONORAMA AND THE PAINTED DESERT PROJECT

Thomas is a Black physician, photographer, public artist, and activist originally from North Carolina. While he has recently retired and moved to Flagstaff to concentrate on his art full time, he had lived and worked on the Navajo Nation in northern Arizona, practicing medicine since 1987. After finishing medical school in the mid-1980s, Thomas came out to Arizona to serve as a physician on the Navajo Nation through the National Health Service Corps, a program that connects physicians to places around the country with limited access to healthcare. Although he finished his obligation in 1991, he had fallen in love with the people, the culture, and the landscape of northern Arizona, and he decided to stay. Today, he continues to work on the reservation as both a physician and an artist. In the latter role, he is part of the Painted Desert Project, where he works with other artists to create works across the region. As many of the examples below will show, he often draws inspiration from his relationships with patients and co-workers, most of whom are Diné, who have shared stories with him about their lives, their struggles, and their joys.

Having grown up admiring the photojournalism of people like Eugene Smith and Gordon Parks, whose work regularly appeared in *Life* magazine and *Look* Magazine in the 1960s and 1970s, Thomas became a photographer. "I just loved turning the pages and looking at the images and seeing how people lived in other parts of the world," he said. "People who were being documented and photographed weren't necessarily famous people, but just everyday people; so I came away with a sense that everyone has a story to tell" (New Mexico PBS). He often asked people on the reservation if he could photograph them, and his work appeared in some regional exhibitions, but as a street artist himself, he always wanted to "go bigger," to create art "where the people in the work got to see themselves represented," to "create work that reminds people of the beauty they've shared with me over the last thirty years" (KQED Arts). Between the craft of his photography, his interest in street art, and the relationships he has cultivated with the Indigenous communities with which he lives and works, he asked, "Is there a way that I can bring that medium to a place that has never had it, and can I do it in a way that is respectful and appreciated by the people whom I am representing" (Bell)?

Thomas told me that he thinks of his process as an "evolving dialogue." What follows are three visual stories, examples of Thomas' work spanning nearly a decade from 2011 to 2020. I refer to them as visual stories, not only to animate Thomas' own identification as a "visual storyteller," but also to draw attention to the fact that each of these examples is the culmination of a process that begins with community listening—building meaningful relationships, community belonging, accountability, and trust, before responding visually and artistically in a way that is public and provocative. Community listening is embedded in the work itself, through visual cues that reflect relationality: private moments captured through smiles, home settings, family intimacy, and daily practices— all of which typically reside outside of public view. This is community listening that is evidence of a healthy relationship, one built on trust cultivated over many years. That these private moments are displayed publicly and embraced by the community, as evidenced through the overwhelmingly positive feedback Thomas has received, is further evidence of community trust and relationality.

This doesn't mean he has never faced pushback over the years, but ultimately being open to the nuance and situatedness of cultural identity is necessarily part of the listening process. "I started this project in 2009 without any guidance on how to pursue 'street art' on the Navajo Nation." So when he posted a photo of a peyote bud cupped in the hand of a friend he wanted to support who was studying to become a roadman in the Native American Church, what he didn't realize is that the roadside stand belonged to a born-again Christian. "That piece lasted 24 hours." Of course, "no community, tribe, race or culture is monolithic," he told me, and described how after that experience, he pasted images he considered "safe," such as representations of "Code Talkers, sheep, and elders," he said. "Over the course of several years and working with safe imagery people began to appreciate the work," empowering him to do more, accepting invitations to put work up in specific locations. Some tribal members fully embrace traditional Hopi and Diné spiritual practices, but there are also many Christians as well, and like any group of people, have different experiences, priorities, and values. He described to me some pieces he put up in response to the proposed tourist destination at the confluence of the Colorado River and the Little Colorado, a one-mile tram and supporting amenities sought by a wealthy developer from Scottsdale, AZ. While the project was largely unpopular as the site is sacred to the Diné, Hopi, and other regional tribes and was ultimately defeated (at least for now—the developer said he would be back), in a region plagued by unemployment rates that hover around 60%, some local tribal members were excited about the employment opportunities. In his art along the road in that region of Arizona, he "opted to represent the position of the traditionalists," and the work quickly got tagged, or painted over. "A lesson I learned," he said, "is that as long as I'm celebrating what the Diné recognize as beautiful about their culture, I'm good."

As a matter of affect, work produced through community listening, in turn, encourages an audience to listen further and listen differently, both to themselves and the those depicted.[2] Thomas' articulation of his work as an "evolving

---

2    By choosing *affect* here, I am signaling the theoretical framework known as affect theory that attempts to explain the relationships between nonlinguistic forces that shape people and culture.

dialogue" is also a useful way of thinking about community listening as a back-and-forth between listening and reflecting. When he is installing a piece, Thomas said that it is common for people to stop, and they talk about their reactions to it, how it made them feel, why they decided to stop. This indicates a strong and meaningful level of engagement that first requires listening to trigger a reflective process. And that process continues after that person has driven away, within and among their home communities.

## Visual Story One. "What we do to the mountain we do to ourselves"

*Figure 4.1. Panoramic photo of the entire installation in an alleyway in Flagstaff in 2011. Photo credit: John Running, 2011. Used with permission of the author, Chip Thomas*

As a journalist in northern Arizona, I extensively covered a regional controversy over development on the San Francisco Peaks—a mountain held sacred in different ways by at least 13 Indigenous tribes[3] of the southwest—by the Arizona Snowbowl ski resort. Over the course of a decade, I learned how the Peaks, as they are referred to locally, are woven into creation stories, and they serve as a marker of one of the four directions, and they are the home of important deities. I learned that ceremonies are performed there, medicinal herbs and plants are gathered there, that there are shrines in undisclosed locations all over the mountain range. In 2002, resort shareholders sought to build a 13-mile pipeline from the city's wastewater treatment plant out of town, up the mountain, and into a reservoir where it would be pumped to make snow. Beyond the absurdity of committing water resources to a ski resort in the dry and drought-prone southwest or introducing contaminated water to a fragile alpine eco-system, the proposal was unacceptable to those who hold the Peaks sacred, who collect medicinal herbs and plants on the mountain, who gather for ceremonies there, who pray to the Kachina who

---

3   This includes the Navajo (Dinè), Hopi, Havasupai, Yavapai (Apache and Prescott), Hualapai, Tewa, White Mountain Apache, San Carlos Apache, Acoma, San Juan Southern Paiute, Zuni, and Fort McDowell Mojave.

inhabit this place and make snow.[4] In 2011, during a year of Indigenous-led non-violent direct actions, road blockades, and demonstrations against the City of Flagstaff and the US Forest Service's approval of reclaimed wastewater to make snow on the San Francisco Peaks, I wrote articles while Thomas worked with area activists, photographers and artists to create an installation that combined black and white photography with text drawn on subject's faces. While I was previously aware of Thomas' work, this was the first time I met him and encountered his work in the city in which I lived, centered on an issue I covered extensively.

The installation appeared in a public walkway in downtown Flagstaff at the height of this controversy, featuring several Indigenous and non-Indigenous people together, with writing scrawled across their faces that they each composed. John Running, a long-celebrated regional photographer, wrote, "Consider the San Francisco Peaks are Sacred to Natives and to Non-Natives," a message positioned in solidarity with Indigenous peoples, literally alongside. One man, Sam, wrote, "faces are sacred, faces are beautiful. We walk on the face of the Earth. The Mountain is a beautiful sacred place that needs to be protected. In beauty I walk." Another woman, Stephanie, connected the protection of the Peaks with global issues of concern, bridging the concern over contaminated snow with climate change and the poisoning of our global environment. She writes: "I am the change. Industrialization, pollution, and drought. Water, air, earth. Fake snow. CO2." This installation is a great example of the writing *with* community writing that is foregrounded by concerns and connections that the community wants and needs—messages they literally wrote themselves—that transcend the limitations of traditional "ink on paper." This is achieved by literally and figuratively having these messages attached to bodies, to identities, reflected in body language, expression, and emotion. Writing *with* and thinking through what that process looks like in different ways according to the needs of a community, is, therefore, integral to the practice of community listening.

---

4    For examples of this coverage and writing, see Boggs, "The Material-Discursive Spaces of Outdoor Recreation: Rhetorical Exclusion and Settler Colonialism at the Arizona Snowbowl Ski Resort." *Journal for the Study of Religion, Nature and Culture* 11, no. 2 (June 8, 2017): 175–96. https://doi.org/10.1558/jsrnc.18841; Boggs, "Anti-Snowbowl Direct Actions Intensify Alongside Construction." *The Noise: Arts & News*. September 2011. 10–11; "Arizona Testbowl: Denying Human Rights and Experimenting with the Ecological Integrity of the San Francisco Peaks," *The Sustainability Review*. February 28, 2010. https://www.thesustainabilityreview.org/articles /arizona-testbowl-denying-human-rights; "Storm Clouds Darken Over the San Francisco Peaks as the City Debates Water for Snowbowl," *The Noise: Arts & News*, September 2010: 10–11, 37; "Storm Clouds Darken Over the San Francisco Peaks as the City Debates Water for Snowbowl, Part 2," *The Noise: Arts & News*, October 2010: 10–11. For more context, also see Benally, Klee and R.T. Cody, dir. *The Snowbowl Effect.* 2005; Flagstaff, AZ: Indigenous Action Media.

The Public Art of Listening

*Figure 4.2. Klee and Princess forehead to forehead wearing bandanas. Photo credit Chip Thomas, 2011.*

One part of the larger installation featured Princess Benally and her partner, Klee Benally, a prominent Diné activist and musician whose family has been instrumental in resisting development on the Peaks since the 1970s. In this photo, they are forehead to forehead. His eyes are closed while her hands cup the back of his head. A message is scrawled directly across their faces in thick black letters: "WHAT WE DO TO THE MOUNTAIN WE DO TO OURSELVES." The message is written across both of their faces as if it were one canvas. This choice visually connects Klee and Princess as they express this statement together. It is a powerful message that illustrates the idea of sacredness, skipping over any need to define it, and instead hones on affect and consequences, declaratively. It conveys a deep cultural and spiritual connection that cannot be denied or dismissed. Both Klee and Princess are wearing bandanas across their faces, which were often worn during the Indigenous-led direct actions and demonstrations against the resort, which were ongoing at the time of the installation—the bandanas signal this moment of quiet reflection during the resistance. Skiers, snowboarders, and others who support the resort's developments would often stand annoyed and confused at such demonstrations against ski infrastructure, asking, "why are you trying to ruin people's fun" ("The Material Discursive Spaces of Outdoor Recreation" 176)? Listeners of this image are asked to weigh their commitments to outdoor recreation against the cultural

103

and spiritual survival of regional Indigenous peoples who hold the mountain sacred in profound ways. Complimenting the actions happening in the streets, characterized by signs reading, "defend the sacred" and "no desecration for recreation," Thomas' work in this context deepens a kind of cognitive dissonance that is productive and provocative. The disconnect between recreation and desecration forces outdoor enthusiasts to reckon with the ways they are caught up in colonialism in the present, that one can help to sustain colonialism without a conscious commitment to it.

## Visual Story Two: Hope + Trauma in a Poisoned Land

*Figure 4.3. A black and white photo of Cyndy Begaye's hands holding a black and white family photo of her father working in a uranium mine on the Navajo Nation. Photo credit, Chip Thomas 2017.*

In the fall of 2017, the Coconino Center for the Arts in Flagstaff, Arizona, invited installations that addressed the history of uranium mining on the Navajo Nation. During the period following World War II through the Cold War era, most of the uranium mined to create nuclear bombs came from the lands in and around the Navajo Nation, and the majority of the miners were Dinè people. Thomas came to know about this history through his patients, their families, and his coworkers. One of these co-workers and friends is Cyndy Begaye, whose father, Kee Roy John, died in 2001 from cancer that formed as a direct result of working in the uranium mines for decades. "He had good intentions to provide for his family," Begaye told the filmmakers (KQED Arts). "He worked for close to 20 years in the mines not knowing the effects years on down the road that this would have on him and on us," she said. (KQED Arts). Because of his relationships with his community through his work as a physician, Thomas learned more about the history of uranium mining on the reservation. "As early as the 1950s," he said in a short video documentary, "scientists and public health workers knew of the dangers of radiation exposure," Thomas (quoted in KQED Arts). "Yet little was being done on the reservation to tell workers about these dangers and to protect them" (quoted KQED Arts). Those former minors who are still living come to his clinic every six months to get examined to get recertified for their required benefits from a settlement detailed in the 1990 Radiation Exposure Compensation Act. Thomas knew that he wanted to figure out a way to bring those stories to the show in Flagstaff (RECA).

Begaye had found an old picture of her father operating some machinery in a mine, and she worked with Thomas on the photo together, which captured the essence of love and loss that she felt, the tragedy of extractive resource colonialism[5] that still looms large in her community. Thomas took a black and white photo of Begaye holding this photograph, and around the edge of the photo, they added, in her writing, "Dad—working the Slick Rock Mine to provide for his family during the cold war. Early 1960s." Thomas added four neon green symbols of radiation floating around the scene to indicate the invisible exposure. Thomas worked closely with Begaye, whom he had known for over 16 years, to memorialize her father. Thomas teared up on camera, remembering the conversations they had about her dad, "It just really touched me, the history, the personal impact it had on this family, of someone I know closely" (KQED Arts).

The impact of uranium mining on Navajo people and the landscape continues to be immense. Despite President Joe Biden's establishment of Ancestral Footprints of the Grand Canyon National Monument, which protects the area surrounding the Grand Canyon from future uranium mining—which includes large swaths of the Navajo Nation—it doesn't include clean-ups of previously established mines. At large, there are 524 abandoned uranium mines on the Navajo Nation today that continue to poison aquifers and affect remote communities in profound ways (EPA). Like radiation, itself invisible—a kind of

---

5    While this chapter doesn't focus specifically on "extractive colonialism," otherwise known as "resource colonialism," as a framing concept and thus I will not be returning to it, this terminology refers to the past and present colonial framework in which corporate and governmental control over sovereign indigenous lands persists for the purpose of extracting resources, often at the expense of community human and environmental health. See Gómez-Barris 2017 for more of an expanded analysis.

present absence—community grief and resilience are not visible from the road. Yet Thomas' work of community listening portrays all this and more for passersby to see and grapple with, a powerful intervention for those who support nuclear energy but have not had to reckon with its legacy. For Thomas, I've observed that his work begins with listening intensively with people he encounters in the community, then he represents those listening experiences in his art. The image in this story captures one of these moments of intensive listening, a moment in which Thomas was shown a personal family photograph. Thomas is able to recreate this intimate moment in a way that transposes his perspective as a physician and friend to a public audience, inviting them to contend with what he understood and felt in that moment.

## Visual Story Three. ". . . creating an environment of wellness in the community."

*Figure 4.4. A black and white photo on a roadside stand on the Navajo Nation in Black Mesa. Photo credit, Chip Thomas 2020.*

The first wave of the COVID-19 pandemic hit the Navajo Nation particularly hard. There was a moment in the summer of 2020, when adjusted for population, the Navajo Nation had the highest rate of infection and death in the United States. The reasons why the reservation was hit particularly hard are varied and complex. When I was a journalist, I learned that much of the Navajo Nation lacks basic amenities, with close to a third of the population live without electricity or running water. Furthermore, nearly half of the population lives below the poverty line, and healthy fruits and vegetables are not easy to come by locally in the region which is marked as a "food desert."[6] All of this means that "shelter-in-place" is simply not a realistic option. Social distancing is also harder given the increased likelihood that multiple generations might be housed together. Further, Indigenous peoples are more likely to be disproportionately affected by health conditions such as diabetes, chronic respiratory diseases, and other diseases of the heart and the liver. Once COVID-19 entered the community, it spread quickly, and the results were devastating.

Outside of the context of the COVID-19 pandemic, Thomas' role as a community physician means that the types of photos he typically works with often prioritize mental and physical wellness and he has recognized the impact his art has in lifting people up. "In my medical practice," says Thomas, "when I see people, I am attempting to create an environment of wellness within the individual, and in the community with the pictures, I'm putting up reflecting to the community the beauty they've shared with me, I'm attempting to create an environment of wellness in the community" (Bell). By reflecting back to them their strength in the face of so much adversity, Thomas attempts to depict visually the listening process he has spent decades cultivating. "Living here, seeing how many people realize they haven't been treated fairly, but they still live in a way that honors creation and the earth—that example keeps me grounded, and I feel really fortunate to have found this means of expression through art" (KQED Arts). These are the commitments Thomas has brought to his art in the framework of the pandemic, attentive to the context of culture and health, demonstrating the ways listening as a physician and as an artist are complimentary.

While promoting the health guidelines recommended by the Centers for Disease Control, he does so in a way that is attentive to culture and his personal knowledge of the community in which he engages—this is a community physician communicating through the language of art. Throughout the pandemic, particularly during the summer of 2020, Thomas worked with local families to push back against the dominant narrative, reinforced in the media, that life on the reservation was bleak and hopeless. A child wearing a face mask made from a bag of Blue Bird flour, the preferred brand for many Diné fry bread recipes, therefore functions rhetorically as a symbol of belonging. The cultural symbol unifies while the child and the baby bunnies communicate hope for a healthy future. Another Diné man named Ryan, is masked-up next to the Center for Disease Control's recommendations for mask wearing, hand washing, social distancing, etc.

---

6    The poverty line is marked by the Federal Poverty Threshold, which is $12,760 for individuals and $26,200 for a family of four (2020 Poverty Guidelines).

*Figure 4.5. A black and white photo of a man named Ryan masked up beside health protocols. Photo credit, Chip Thomas 2020.*

The two together tell a story of resilience and shared experience during unprecedented times. Diné people are invited to see themselves in the ways they have shown to Thomas, a process based on decades of intensive listening, reflecting back dignity, strength, and resilience. To triangulate the images above and below within the context of community listening, Thomas is both an artist and a physician who understands the unique challenges posed by the pandemic to Diné communities, one who has listened intensively to a community invested in keeping each other safe, and who carefully depicts those moments of listening in a way that is culturally responsive. It is a visual expression of concern and safety characterized by rhetorical choices curated toward a specific audience. For passersby, the work represents a moment of listening, animating the idea that the pandemic is culturally distinct in this space, that the communities there face a unique set of challenges, and those who enter should leave their own assumptions about the severity of the pandemic at home.

## ". . . ART CHALLENGES THE WAY WE PERCEIVE THE ORDINARY" [7]

*Figure 4.6. Rose Hurley with her great grandson. This is a black and white photograph of the work on a roadside stand on the Navajo Nation. Photo credit, Chip Thomas 2018.*

In his 2017 analysis of graffiti writing, Charles Lesh calls for broader understandings of community publishing that "include a wider range of texts, rhetorical strategies, and communities" that have been "historically unrecognizable" to the disciplinary mainstream (64). While unconventional, even illegal, forms of community publishing like graffiti writing may have been historically dismissed by scholars, they have nonetheless functioned as "an inventive rhetorical-material process by which networks are produced, sustained, or challenged by the specific genres of writing that move through them" (70). In other words, despite the lack of attention by scholars and its status as mostly illegal, graffiti writers and street artists have been doing the rhetorical work of community publishing anyway, work that has constituted place-based belongings in ways that are meaningful, unexpected, and at times, confrontational in the sense that "encountering public art is not entirely elective. . . . we go to private art, but public art is

---

7   Quote in context: "I like to think that art challenges the way we perceive the ordinary" (New Mexico PBS).

109

come upon" (Hein 55). Thomas' work is certainly "come upon" in this way, and it coheres to Lesh's articulation of street art as a form of rhetoric that depends as much on discourse as it does the physical, material world. But there is a relationship between Thomas' rhetorical-material work that engages audiences in community listening.

Thomas's photographs often adorn small structures positioned within a sea of red desert and blue sky, a landscape that is otherwise quiet and vast. Thomas revises these quiet places, creating small interruptions that invite audiences to listen in new ways—curated by Thomas and the culture and community in which he engages. In a landscape that is riddled with colonial myths and misconceptions, the photographs disrupt and demand to be listened to. They radiate a dignity of being, an honesty, a vulnerability that invites an empathetic response, and they resonate with a powerful sense of shared humanity and relationality.

This is achieved by depicting people and their relationships as they are, yet appearing in unexpected places, where the image and the landscape cohere and necessarily constitute one another. The image above, which depicts Rose Hurley with her great-grandson, seems like a simple family picture, but against the backdrop of open high desert, the photo works against the colonial logic that would prefer passersby not see or recognize the experience, the presence, and the dignity of Dinè people. Further, the candid image itself, which represents not a photo shoot event where everyone might be dressed up and smiling for the occasion, but rather, a regular, everyday occurrence communicates to me that the photographer is a trusted friend with whom the son and his great grandmother are sitting comfortably and at home.

The art itself also produces a kind of reciprocity in that the work is for those white settler visitors like me who pass by, but it is also embraced as a gift to the communities depicted as well. This speaks to the affective possibilities of rhetoric, which is to say that the art is produced through years of ongoing listening interactions between the artist and the community, but the art also potentially affects those who see it, like me, from outside of the community. For passersby, the cultural connection to the landscape is brought into focus, potentially harmful myths are challenged, and a greater sense of accountability is activated. For those who live there and are accustomed to viewing Thomas' work displayed in the landscape, "his murals reflect back our everyday life; I know that he gets it, he understands it" (KQED Arts). Not everyone who passes by will see it operating in this way, however. While the rhetoric of the mural against the backdrop of the desert does intervene, interrupt, and provoke, the work itself constitutes a mere invitation for engagement, not the promise of it.

## "... SHARE THEIR STORY IN A WAY THAT HONORS THEM"[8]

Thomas elaborated on how other aspects of his life, his career as a community physician and his activism, are connected to his identity as a storyteller. "In medicine, you know, we start with a history, and we hear people's stories; as a photographer and an activist, I'm attempting to tell stories as well" (*Outside Magazine*). As a physician Thomas describes his careful attention to his patients, and over time has begun to unravel the ways that medical history is woven into the cultural history of the patients and communities he serves, a colonial history that continues to structure the present.[9]

As a function of settler colonialism in this context, historically, the view from the road—where Thomas' art often appears—has rhetorically silenced Indigenous peoples. While the occasional billboard might advertise an attraction, those images often rely on and sustain settler colonial logics through Indigenous caricatures, such as the case with a casino or a trading post, for example. One of the challenges Thomas confronts in his work is how to represent voice, or how to visually reclaim voices from the settler colonial structures that prevent them from being heard on their own terms. To do so, he must work in and with the absences and silences produced by settler colonialism. The public art produced by Thomas exemplifies community listening as described by Romeo García, that it "pushes us to both take up the traces left behind of the past and people and work toward creating presence from absence and sound from silence" (7). Thomas' work answers the absences and silences with images of Indigenous peoples in the present on their own terms. Those images demand viewers reject false caricatures of Indigenous peoples trapped in a mythic past. Krista Ratcliffe discusses the ways in which James Phelan and Andrea Lunsford theorize listening as relating to "voices speaking or not speaking within written texts" (18).

This relation between listening and speaking/not speaking is useful for this analysis as it positions listening within a similar framework of inclusion/exclusion that Thomas' public art addresses. Thomas proves that public art has the potential to disrupt this silence, that listening is a means of reclaiming the voices of Indigenous peoples living under the spatial, material, and cultural conditions of settler colonialism in the every day. Thomas' visual storytelling

---

8    Quote in context: "It's really a matter of developing a relationship, a trusting relationship with people such that you cannot only hear their story, but you can present their story, and share their story in a way that honors them" (New Mexico PBS).

9    Here I am recalling Wolfe's (2006) observation that settler colonialism is a structure, not an event, as well as a multitude of Indigenous scholars who discuss the simple and complex ways that the structures of colonialism operate in simple and complex ways in the present.

Boggs

challenges the terms of those conditions by placing Indigenous peoples in those spaces on their own terms, unexpectedly, and in ways that demand to be seen. In the same way that a rhetorically "loud" billboard wants to be heard, the struggles, joys, and everyday experiences of Indigenous peoples portrayed in Thomas's work also demand to be heard. Through this work as a storyteller, Thomas has recognized how his own role as an artist and physician on the reservation is an identity that is bound up in the lives of the community in which he lives, loves, and works.

As I gesture toward this chapter's conclusion, I return to some of my initial observations about the synesthetic qualities of public art, and how this analysis of Thomas' work maps out new pathways toward understanding the broader possibilities of a community listening praxis. Public art is a "hybrid" of material and discursive elements that cut across "a variety of polarities," allowing it to transcend boundaries of perception, specific sensory receptors, or mediums (Hein 50). While it is certainly true, as Hinshaw observes, that "the sounds of a place and space orient us, teach us and help us connect," the emphasis on sound obscures the multitude of ways cultural and community knowledge can be transmitted and received, how places and spaces themselves can orient, teach, and connect us in a myriad of ways that don't rely on the ability of our ears (Hinshaw 64). Our understanding of what counts and what doesn't count as community listening need not be limited to one way of perceiving the world. "Public art compels both artists and public to refine communicative skills" (Hein 55). To describe the communicative process as a simple back-and-forth between speaker and listener obscures other ways we can be present as we listen to and show up for each other, how we acknowledge our understanding/misunderstanding, how we process and communicate cultural knowledge. When it is rooted in building trust, reflecting a relational process that establishes structures of accountability, community listening becomes a mode of perceiving, reflecting, and responding that is personal and situational.

A community that is heard is a community that is first listened to; I have demonstrated some of the ways evidence of listening shows up in Thomas' work. To be a responsible and effective storyteller, to tell stories that demand to be heard, yet are not one's own, the process of listening necessarily precedes that story. Thomas lingers on this notion of process and community listening. "It's really a matter of developing a relationship, a trusting relationship with people such that you can not only hear their story, but you can present their story, and share their story in a way that honors them" (New Mexico PBS). His observation echoes Wilson's assertion that "the relationship with something (a person, object, or idea) is more important than the thing itself" (73). The art of Thomas,

The Public Art of Listening

while aesthetically stunning, is itself a reflection of a relationship, and a move toward cultivating other relationships, and, therefore, more stories. Without the relationship, the art loses its meaning and productive power, therefore, relationality takes precedence over the "thing itself" (7). "It's all about the process of creating with good intention and with love," Thomas told PBS, which I understand as another way of articulating Wilson's idea of relational accountability (New Mexico PBS). Deep, intensive listening is necessarily part of this process and as community writers, work like Thomas' models the forms of trust and compassion we want to cultivate.

Community listening not only foregrounds the process of meaningful artistic creation, but it is also productive in that it engages audiences in new ways. This chapter helps to establish that community listening can take on visual forms, as a process seen, and therefore not limited to a verbal (e.g., heard, read) phenomenon. Being heard—a statement that implies a level of fulfillment and effectiveness—is not just a result of listening, but how one listens. Community listening as a visual engagement invites others to interpret those images in the context of their own lives, inviting many forms of listening that are situational, personal, and generative. I agree with García's observation that "how we listen no doubt tells us something about our ways of seeing, being, and doing. We are constituted differently, and yet, strung together by a universe of stories, stories-so-far, and the possibilities of new stories" (7). When we listen, as passersby viewing an art installation in an unexpected place, we bring ourselves to that process—our culture, history, identity—and positionality here matters. The public art of community listening provokes critical reflections about how we are constituted differently by colonial structures. The result is public engagement that invites stronger, more empathetic alliances across differences.

It is important to note that not all public art is inherently successful in the ways I describe it in this chapter; it is my hope that through my analysis of Thomas' work, I have sketched out some of the ways that community listeners might gauge the effectiveness of public art in their own communities. When looking at public art elsewhere, Thomas' work has taught me to simultaneously listen as well. I listen for the voices that want to be heard, the competing histories that appear as stories. I listen for that which reveals something about the relationships between the artist, those depicted, and the landscapes in which the work is situated. I listen for the questions the work asks of me, and I try to answer them. And the moment I start doing that, by engaging in the public art of listening and the back-and-forth exchange it elicits, I recognize the work's productive power, its potential to alter perceptions, shake up realities, provoke responses, deepen commitments, and change minds.

113

## ACKNOWLEDGMENTS

I would like to thank Chip Thomas for giving me permission to use his images and for his openness in discussing his work with me throughout the process of writing this chapter. I also want to note that during the course of writing this chapter, Klee Benally—a friend and fierce protector of the Indigenous sacred sites, including the San Francisco Peaks—sadly passed away at the end of 2023. I hold Klee's partner, Princess, and his family in my heart as I continue to be inspired by him.

## WORKS CITED

"2020 Poverty Guidelines." ASPE, https://tinyurl.com/bdcvy98a. Accessed 4 Oct. 2021.

Alcoff, Linda. "The Problem of Speaking for Others." *Cultural Critique*, no. 20, 1991–1992, pp. 5–32.

Bell, Brooklyn. "Outside Magazine: Chip Thomas, Telling Navajo Stories with Street Art." *YouTube,* 2020, https://www.youtube.com/watch?v=vD_3p4UIcE8.

DeLuca, Kevin Michael. *Image Politics: The New Rhetoric of Environmental Activism.* Routledge, 2012.

Dobrin, Sidney I., and Sean Morey. *Ecosee: Image, Rhetoric, Nature.* SUNY P, 2009.

EPA (Environmental Protection Agency). "Navajo Nation: Cleaning Up Abandoned Uranium Mines." 12 Apr. 2019. https://www.epa.gov/navajo-nation-uranium-cleanup.

Fishman, Jenn, and Lauren Rosenberg, editors. *Community Writing, Community Listening*, special issue of *Community Literacy Journal*, vol. 13, no. 1, 2018.

Fishman, Jenn, and Lauren Rosenberg. "Guest Editors' Introduction: Community Writing, Community Listening." Fishman and Rosenberg, pp. 1–6, https://doi.org/10.25148/clj.13.1.009085.

Foss, Sonja. "A Rhetorical Schema for the Evaluation of Visual Imagery." *Communication Studies*, vol. 45, no. 3–4, 1994, pp. 213–224.

García, Romeo. "Creating Presence from Absence and Sound from Silence." Fishman and Rosenberg, pp. 7–15, https://doi.org/10.25148/clj.13.1.009086.

Gómez-Barris, Macarena. *The Extractive Zone: Social Ecologies and Decolonial Perspectives.* Duke UP, 2017.

Grohowski, Mariana. "Community Literacy for the 21st Century: A Review of Adela C. Licona's Works." *Community Literacy Journal*, vol. 5, no. 2, 2011, pp. 183–190.

Hein, Hilde. *Public Art: Thinking Museums Differently.* Rowman Altamira, 2006.

Hill, Charles A., and Marguerite Helmers. *Defining Visual Rhetorics.* Routledge, 2012.

Hinshaw, Wendy. "Writing to Listen: Why I Write Across Prison Walls." Fishman and Rosenberg, pp. 55–70, https://doi.org/10.25148/clj.13.1.009090.

Jackson, Rachel C. with Dorothy Whitehorse DeLaune. "Decolonizing Community Writing with Community Listening: Story, Transrhetorical Resistance, and

Indigenous Cultural Literacy Activism." Fishman and Rosenberg, pp. 37–54, https://doi.org/10.25148/clj.13.1.009089.

KQED Arts. PBS NewsHour | Street Artist Portrays Navajo Life with Large Scale Murals | Season 2018. video.kqed.org, https://tinyurl.com/yk74svrm. Accessed 29 May 2021.

Lesh, Charles. "Writing Boston: Graffiti Bombing as Community Publishing." *Community Literacy Journal*, vol. 12, no. 1, 2017, pp. 62–86.

New Mexico PBS. "NMPBS ¡COLORES!: Golden Migration at Valle de Oro with Chip Thomas" *YouTube*. https://www.youtube.com/watch?v=6899P_APxqM. Accessed 29 May 2021.

Peters, Jason. "Public Art as Social Infrastructure: Methods and Materials for Social Action at Environmentally Contaminated Sites." *Reflections: A Journal of Public Rhetoric, Civic Writing & Service Learning*, vol. 19, no. 2, 2019/2020, pp. 106–29.

Ratcliffe, Krista. *Rhetorical Listening: Identification, Gender, Whiteness*. Southern Illinois UP, 2005.

Wilson, Shawn. *Research Is Ceremony: Indigenous Research Methods*. Fernwood Publishing, 2008.

Wolfe, Patrick. "Settler Colonialism and the Elimination of the Native." *Journal of Genocide Research*, vol. 8, no. 4, Dec. 2006, pp. 387–409.

CHAPTER 5.

# THE DJ AS RELATIONAL LISTENER AND CREATOR OF AN ETHOS OF COMMUNITY LISTENING

**Karen R. Tellez-Trujillo**

California State Polytechnic University, Pomona

*This chapter explores the concept of relational listening by examining the interactions between a Sunday radio show DJ, Mike Guerrero, and his listeners along the Borderland, including the author. By exploring the community engagement of members of the Borderland with the DJ, and listeners of "The Fox Jukebox," the chapter highlights how relational listening fosters a sense of belonging across temporal and spatial boundaries. Through engagement with callers' emotions and experiences, listeners reaffirm their connections to their communities and identities. The author's personal experiences with her father, music, and "The Fox Jukebox" serve as a lens through which to explore the practice of relational listening and its transformative potential. While encouraged by DJ Mike, relational listening emerges as an impactful process that enables listeners to revisit memories and create new memories through music. By maintaining this culture of relational listening, DJ Mike sustains the community of the radio show, inviting new generations to participate in its communal experience as relational listeners. This process points back to the author's early experiences with listening to music with her father, mother and grandparents, as she learned to be a relational listener.*

Hi, Mike Guerrero reminding you to join me for The Fox Jukebox this Sunday. We'll be in the studio eight full hours with your El Paso style classics. The hits from early years of rock and roll, the doo wop, the old school. Your requests, your dedications, birthdays, anniversaries, saludos, all that. And then we'll play the best from the sixties, seventies, late eighties. A little bit of this, a little bit of that. We'll throw it all in together and it becomes what it has been for the last twenty-one years. The Fox Jukebox on a Sunday afternoon.

– Mike G.

DOI: https://doi.org/10.37514/PER-B.2025.2531.2.05

It's Sunday evening in Southern California and I'm moving between the kitchen where dinner is on the stove and the dining room where I plan Monday classes. Of the many pages open on the web browser of my laptop, one is a recording of a James Brown song in which he pleads "Please, please, please." I pause in the kitchen and sway to the slow beat of the song, my mind traveling back to the summer I turned thirteen, when the DJ, Steve Crosno, played James Brown every weekday during his lunchtime oldies hour radio show. The song was already familiar to me at thirteen, as I'd been listening to oldies with my dad for as long as I could remember.

I didn't have a lot in common with my dad, but the love of music was something we shared. Early on, he taught me to listen to music actively, to keep a beat, to pay attention to lyrics, to listen to the instruments in a song, and to attach songs to moments. While my mom often played music in the background of our lives, my dad listened to music intentionally and encouraged his kids to do the same. Each of my five siblings, Luis, Carlos, Gil, Kathryn, Eric, and I pause in the same way to take in music. We listen to each other as we share the reasons for loving a song and appreciate the stories that are sometimes attached.

The Fox is a station out of El Paso, Texas, that spans the Borderland comprised of two countries: the United States (U.S.) and Mexico; three cities predominantly: El Paso, Ciudad Juarez, and Las Cruces: and three states: Texas, Chihuahua, and New Mexico. Online, the station can be heard around the world. I listen to The Fox Jukebox, an oldies radio show on The Fox in an act of community listening, an "active, layered, and intentional practice," as it's described by Jenn Fishman and Lauren Rosenberg in their Introduction, "Community Writing, Community Listening" (1). For me, community listening means coming together to honor people, places, and memories through music. I think I have been listening in this way my whole life. I have listened with the purpose of connecting with fellow listeners through their stories and recollections surrounding the music that is the soundtrack of their lives while simultaneously creating my own soundtrack.

Tuning in to the music and giving attention to the listeners of The Fox Jukebox means that I attend to "not only the sensory, embodied experience of sound" that Steph Ceraso describes in "(Re) Educating the Senses: Multimodal Listening, Bodily Learning, and the Composition of Sonic Experiences," but also "the material and environmental aspects that comprise and shape one's embodied experience" through the emotions conjured by music and the memories that are tied to it for me (105). Taking in the sounds and songs of The Fox Jukebox involves what Ceraso describes as multimodal listening. It is, in her words, "a bodily practice that approaches sound as a holistic experience, making use of more than my ear" (105). As I listen, I access people that are out of reach, listening through my body, moving my body, and being emotionally moved as acts of remembrance of my past, my family, and my culture (Royster and Kirsch).

In this chapter, I posit that active listeners of The Fox Jukebox use music and opportunities to call in or communicate using social media as a way of relating with others. I argue that the listeners engage in "relational listening," a new term I apply that suggests listeners acknowledge callers' feelings and experiences as they enact community listening. Listening also takes place as a way of reasserting one's identity with one's community, in this case, a reminder to the self of belonging to a people and place.

When we engage in relational listening, it is like community listening in that it is personal, affective, and engaged. Relational listening requires that a giver and receiver show up as who they are in that moment, without set roles, as the caller can both give and receive from other callers, and listeners don't ever have to be callers or givers. While there does not need to be a dialogue, nor does one trade something for another thing, those who choose to give of themselves do so without expectation, and those who show up to receive are integral to the interaction. Relational listening is a form of community listening that involves both transactions and transformations, although neither is required. The listeners of the show are not required to give anything in return, no matter how much they take away from the experience of listening. The callers, however, give something to the listeners of the show by calling in, while they don't require anything in return. Relational listening also has the potential to be transformational, in that the listeners can use their experience to transform their memories and experiences attached to the music.

As an early relational listener, I think of the way I was taught to recognize when it was time to sit quietly while music was playing, giving other listeners a chance to feel, and talk about the music. There were opportunities to dance, sing, and have conversations, but relational listening required that I pick up on the cues for when it was time to behave accordingly. As a way of letting others know they are listening on The Fox Jukebox, listeners send saludos, or their regards, to others and impart deep sentiments expressed through the songs of their request and dedications. Most of the calls are motivated by celebration, remembrance, expressions of love, or attempts to repair a relationship using a song as an apology, all of which are performances of emotion, as well as enactments of relational listening. Reception is a key part of the practice of relational listening, as it is as important to listen to the DJ, the music, and to the callers of The Fox Jukebox whether one responds on air or not. Without the listening or the sharing, there would not be relational listening, as both sharing and listening are required for this to take place. The sharing and receiving are actions that enable The Fox Jukebox community to honor the past attached to the music while forming new memories and new collective relations. It also becomes possible to reframe the past by taking music from the past and attaching it to present moments. This is something I find myself doing, as oldies were often attached to memories shared by my father, and slowly became songs attached predominantly to my new experiences with the music.

It's interesting to me that I feel closest to my dad when I listen to this radio show because it was not a show he listened to. Most of his listening came from his own music collection and mixes he made from individual tapes and CDs. We most often listened to radio shows on road trips and stayed silent between singing to be entertained by the DJ and listening to what the callers had to say. Casey Kasem, Wolfman Jack, and Dave Michaels of Dave's Diner radio show stand out most in my memory. There was something magical about being in the car on I10 West, pulling up to Los Angeles at 10:00 pm in the backseat with my little brother, Eric, while listening to a woman call into the show from Iowa while her children were asleep to talk about deeply missing her husband, knowing that the DJ would play a song that would help her feel less lonely, if only for the next three to five minutes. It was meaningful to me that I felt I was connecting to a stranger and was also part of the comfort being offered, although I was a stranger, hundreds of miles away.

Listening to The Fox Jukebox isn't just a way that I spend time imagining that I am connecting with other strangers, or with my 84-year-old dad through the music we both love. It is also the way that I travel digitally from southern California to Las Cruces, New Mexico—to the places and people to whom I belong, relate, and identify. By listening to The Fox Jukebox with other listeners from El Paso and Las Cruces, I spend time with many people who "get" me, other Chicanos, others who have attachments to music of the past, and to the Borderland. It is also how I tune back into the memories of myself and my children surrounding music. I conjure Van Morrison playing "In the Mystic," as my son, Jon, stands on the coffee table to dance with me, or the chill of my brother Luis's garage, where we stop to dance to "La Puerta Negra" on a winter morning, for no reason other than because it is what we do when that song plays, and we identify with the music as being part of our heritage.

Kevin Adonis Browne writes in the Introduction to *Tropic Tendencies,* "A Jour Ouvert," that identification is "a fundamental carnivalesque process because it functions as an articulation of collective agency and cultural intention . . . as the expression of a realistic desire for successful participation in contemporary society and the benefits promised by it" (7). It's important to me that I identify with my home and those who live in the Borderland, mostly because I think it's a way of remembering who I am, and that although there is distance between me

The DJ as Relational Listener

and my family, I need to pause to remember that there are people who love me, and to remind myself through music that they are not forgotten.

Using The Fox Jukebox to connect with home is common for its listeners. An online listener who is seeking a way of feeling close to home posted to a message board for The Fox Jukebox, on April 1, 2021, "I get to listen to my hometown, although I live in New Jersey and feel like I'm home. Thanks." Another listener shares on July 3, 2021, "We love . . . the oldies every Sunday. We have been in Tucson, Arizona and now in Ft. Worth, Texas. We love all of our gente from Chucotown. Can't get enough of this music. Much love from the . . . family in Ft. Worth!!! El Paso strong, por siempre. We love you all. God bless all of us. Take care and stay safe!!!" ("The Fox"). This act of looking and listening toward home and sharing the connection by calling or writing in reflects the strong context for personal exchanges that Mike, the DJ of The Fox Jukebox, has built through relational listening. Relational listening is taking place in that this caller not only remembers where they came from and wants to connect with home and one's people, but they want to impart love, blessings, care, and a reminder that if one is listening, they are part of a family by virtue of shared place, and a shared love of music. The Fox Jukebox also creates the possibility for the long-distance caller to feel that they are still part of their community and can still create memories surrounding the music that is attached to a particular place and time.

Kevin Adonis Browne also writes of a particular social formation, which, for him, is comprised of Caribbean people." The Fox Jukebox and the Borderland, as social formations, are made up of Hispanics, predominantly. There is not one way to belong in or to the Borderland, to identify with, or to participate in this space. Similarly, The Fox Jukebox is its own carnival, as the listeners do not all listen for the same reasons. The Fox Jukebox's DJ, Mike's audience uses The Fox Jukebox as a place for listeners to don their masque, not as a way of hiding "but to display and be displayed" (23). On this radio show, the caller is not seen, but can "be seen" through the words they leave on social media, the website or through calling in. This invisibility of sorts can be important to situations in which citizenship or lack of confidence are issues, as well as for the sake of anonymity, where a caller has a need but does not want to be tied to the request. Browne further notes that those involved in carnival want to "engage in forms of individual and collective activity that will allow them to navigate the currents of other discourses—power for instance, or politics—if not change course altogether to their benefit . . . being seen requires action . . ." (28), a form of epideixis or "vernacular epideictic rhetoric" (24). The radio show allows for the listeners to act in such a way that they do not need to be seen, but can still be a part of a group, belong to something, and push against physical and language borders, as well as the confines of nostalgia by creating new memories.

121

I listen on this Sunday to take part in the carnival I've created in my home, to be moved by the lamentations across sound waves, to join with people and places, and to spend time with my father who lives seven hundred miles away, using the memory and the music of the Borderland. By listening this way, I connect with my community and across generations in a way that creates a bridge that has become more necessary as he and I have both gotten older. Listening in this way creates the possibility for me to be a part of my father's life without being physically present in the Borderland where he lives.

## THE BORDERLAND AND ITS LISTENERS

It is important to note that the border of which I write is the geographical area that Gloria Anzaldúa describes as "una herida abierta," the wound "where the Third World grates against the first and bleeds. And before a scab forms it hemorrhages again, the lifeblood of two worlds merging to form a third country—a border culture" (3). The geographical area is marked by trauma, such as disease and raids by Apaches and Spaniards that have left a mark on the descendants of the Piro-Manso-Tiwa tribe in Las Cruces and the Tigua tribe in El Paso that reside in the Borderland to this day. This space is complicated with a history of nationality, race, ethnicity, and class, for instance, and important to this history is the value of calling attention to the places in which there is solidarity and unity. Anzaldúa also writes of the Borderland, "On one side of us, we are constantly exposed to the Spanish of the Mexicans, on the other side we hear the Anglos' incessant clamoring so that we forget our language" (1029). This region faces numerous civil and social problems, such as those of the right to citizenship, the lowest wages in the United States, and long-held arguments over who has rights to the water in the Rio Grande River.

Issues centered on the politics, the past, and power struggles between the U.S. government and Mexico are put aside by callers of the show. The show is about family, good times, get-togethers, delicious food, and love for the Borderland and its music. It is also about opportunities to reconnect, such as when the callers do so, for the sake of letting their family in the Borderland know they are thinking of them. The callers share which high school they went to, the side of town they live on, the places they frequent, and the names of their loved ones, both romantic and those of their parents, siblings, and children.

This Borderland is its own unique family, comprised of more than 80% of residents who identify as Hispanic or Latino, and is made up of a rich culture that celebrates Mexican and Indigenous heritage. It is home to universities, numerous historic sites, Ft. Bliss Army base, and art influenced by Mexican and American cultures. El Paso also has its own style of oldies made up of songs by artists such as Fats Domino, Otis Reding, Smokey Robinson, and Marvin Gaye. These details are important because The Fox Jukebox is a radio show where Borderland residents can express their relationships to these identifiers, regardless of on which side of the border they reside or if they communicate in English, Spanish, or both languages at the same time. As relational listeners who engage in community listening, the listeners of The Fox Jukebox are active parts of the radio show, co-creators integral to maintaining it as a space to which others return week after week.

## RELATIONAL LISTENERS AS SHOW CO-CREATORS

Relational listeners are involved in the activity of co-creating the show by making requests, sending dedications, and sharing their stories that take place inside and outside the Borderland that are ultimately tied to the music. These relational listeners build local community by taking in the interactions, ads, media, and nods to businesses as a form of participation throughout the course of a Sunday by layering music, call-in interactions, advertisements, and participation across numerous media, for instance. By participating in this way, the relational listeners gain a place to which they belong, knowing that the music, language, and Borderland cultural references are familiar and consistent.

There are frequent occasions for the DJ to express gratitude to listeners who feed him and invite him to events around El Paso. Eating and sharing meals is an activity integral to community making in the Borderland. The relational listeners of The Fox Jukebox have found ways to integrate eating and feeding others into their practice. Mike frequently gives a shout-out to Marco's Pizza, saying, "In the house, hooking us up. Thank you, Marco's Pizza, for stopping by with your delicious salads, subs, and pizzas" (August, 2019) and contributes consistent nods to the Tropicana Café through photos posted to social media. Where the business aspect of the show is concerned, in addition to the social, Mike acknowledges the show's sponsors. This is the business of the radio show, but also a solidification of the community as he celebrates local dishes, employees, and sides of town with which the listeners identify and relate.

Both on social media and on the air, Fox Jukebox listeners leave messages entirely in English, Spanish or in Spanglish. While listening in June 2021, a man leaves a message on the station website in both Spanish and English, recognizing his father as a listener and as a chance to say hello to his family in Texas, as well as to let anyone reading the message that his father is the best in the world.

> My dad is a huge fan and the most loyal listener . . . Saludos a
> mi familia Tejada!! I still listen too, all the time, desde Austin,

> Texas! Happy Father's Day al papá mas fregon del mundo
> who listens from Juarez Chihuahua!! Please play the "When I
> See You Again" song!! Dedicated to my dad . . . can't wait to
> see you papi! Best Radio Station!!! ("The Fox")

This is just one example of a listener displaying moves between English and Spanish, using slang and formal language. He does not leave the actual name of the song, but a description of it, knowing that the DJ will know the song to which he refers. The message sender uses "papi," and "dad" to describe his father in English and Spanish, and from this message, we learn of this fan's loyalty but also of his affections for his Borderland community and his father. Every part of the radio show, from the listeners to the social media platforms, is important to maintaining this space as a consistent home for listeners to return to. The radio show makes time and space travel possible, even if it is only through the airwaves, with the DJ guiding the journey.

There are numerous moving parts to a radio show, from the sponsors who keep the show going to the DJ who makes sure that listeners return each week. The Fox Jukebox is a place where community listening is encouraged, with an emphasis on kinds of remotely mediated relationality. In the sections that follow, I talk through some examples of Mike, the DJ of The Fox Jukebox, as an active participant in the listening process and will explore the significance of the roles he fills as a fellow relational listener, community builder, digital rhetorician, guide, and curator of memory for the Borderland.

## MIKE, DEL CHUCO

As a lifelong resident of El Paso, Mike knows Borderland inhabitants, as well as of the music of The Fox Jukebox, and upholds the values of the Borderland, which some might refer to as, someone who is adept at "keepin' it real" (Brown and Lewis). He is a graduate of an El Paso high school, and a former student of an El Paso college. Mike belongs to the Borderland in the way that Art Laboe belonged to California and their "Killer Oldies," honoring the language and cultures of the Borderland, which are important markers of regional identity, as well as of Mike's role as a relational listener. When callers share their feelings or experiences as residents of the Borderland, Mike understands where they are coming from, and most of what they share does not need explaining because of this.

He stays true to the genres of music expected by his listeners and to the Spanish and English languages used in the Borderland. As a local Chicano, Mike injects border jargon into his announcements to include shortening of names for schools, e.g., "Jeff," for "Jefferson High School," or to refer to neighborhoods such as San Juan to denote the neighborhood surrounding the San Juan Bautista Catholic Church. Mike also expresses sentiments of thanks in Spanish, saying "Muchas gracias," and calls El Paso "El Chuco," a name of endearment pointing back to the history of zoot suit-wearing pachucos in the area (Martinez). These injections of border jargon locate the listeners as part of a family or group to which they belong through sharing the love of music and language that is all their own. The ethos Mike is constructing is dependent on relational listening that confirms that one belongs to their community, and sharing language is an active way of belonging to this group in a way to which not everyone has access.

Mike's word choices are in line with that of the colloquial or "old school" Chicano (although he is often chided for the way he pronounces his last name with an anglicized accent). His knack for switching between English and Spanish aligns him with border residents, showing that he is an insider and reaffirms their language and way of being. For example, when inviting listeners to a free, large event held in El Paso in early June of 2022, Mike announced, "Just one of the incredible local bands we will be featuring LIVE on stage this Saturday, June 4th at Raves Club, Dulce Mal. Bring your dancing shoes and partner, and get ready to get your cumbias on with these beautiful talented ladies and their amazing band. Si se vale bailar." Words and Spanish phrases used commonly in association with music such as, "bailar," or with requests, such as "gracias" or "por favor," are often used in conversations between Mike and callers. By peppering messages with Spanish words and phrases, Mike maintains an ethos of home place. Similarly, questions such as, "¿Como estas?" or "¿Que paso, Mike?" come across the air too often to track and are accepted as popular greetings regardless of how many times Mike has let callers know that he is, "Bien, bien." The ethos of home place maintained by Mike gives people a familiar place to belong and to return to, as the self that they are at any given time is welcome. Because the homeplace is static, listeners are free to change, are free to form new memories around the music and join the listening community as strictly listeners. This is possible because the music never changes, nor does the language or rules for relational listening.

By playing the music that the listeners have attachments to, as a Chicano community, as well as staying true to the artists valued by the community, Mike is and remains a central figure of his listening community. He does not stray from the comfort that his consistency offers his listenership by keeping it real but also keeping it old school. Playing music that draws on Chicano style, oldies songs, or "the classics," he keeps relevant popular references to this genre to include the terms "low rider music," "golden oldies," and simply "oldies." He proclaims, however, that the music he plays is El Paso-Style Oldies, saying, "I'll be spinning some Friday night oldies, old school!" based on the location of the station and the style of music that El Pasoans of a certain generation prefer. The term "El Paso-Style Oldies," was coined by the late DJ Steve Crosno and "covers everything from Sunny and the Sunliners' 'Carino Nuevo' to 'Angel Baby' by Rosie and the Originals: slow ballads that you can dance to, usually cheek to cheek" (Renteria). Mike honors artists such as Little Joe y la Familia, Malo, and other Chicano artists, and his playlist is also a collage of sorts in that it includes music from various eras as styles such as those classified as Motown, Spanish-language, funk, and soul.

## MIKE, EL DJ

Mike, as DJ, maintains the ethos of the listening community by encouraging relational listening, as well as by being a relational listener. He encourages those listening to the station to "Give a shout out" and to "Give a listen to" both the music and the callers. He reminds them that this is a place and people to which they belong and can always return. Reflecting on ethos, Kenneth Adonis Browne writes, "Embedded in every rhetorical exchange is an ethos on which the conversants rely to make their interactions not only comprehensible but meaningful, convincing, familiar, and authentic" (162). As DJ, Mike upholds the ethos of community listening, in the style of Browne's description, involving the Borderland listeners in performances that include calling to make requests, dedications, announcements, and to share a bit of their story surrounding music.

Mike further engages the listenership as part of a praxis by encouraging the listeners to cocreate and sustain a community listening ethos by balancing his voice with that of the music and of the callers. Mike activates in his listeners some of the key relational aspects of community listening through active relational listening, which is fundamental to how community listening works in this and perhaps other listening communities. While on the air, Mike invites listeners to call in, saying, "Let's hear from the Borderland. Give us a call at The Fox Jukebox." Mike uses ads and a radio commonplace to build his relationship with local sponsors. He also uses social media, which is another means by which he engages listeners. These common practices operate as something distinctive in that relational listening requires that those participating make communication possible through multiple media, reaching as many listeners as possible and meeting them where they are as they engage with the show.

## MIKE, THE RELATIONAL LISTENER

Mike reveals relational listening in action, as he "does" relational listening. He makes relational listening audible to listeners via the ways he performs relational

The DJ as Relational Listener

listening and gets them to perform in response. Mike regularly invites listeners to share news about events, including that of a gathering in remembrance of a listener and well-known community member; he honors the memory of the old-ies, as well of events occurring in the lives of the listenership. An example of this is the posting of a listener's funeral services on The Fox Jukebox Facebook page on September 23, 2022, labeled "Pete's Last Ride." A flyer, with a picture of a man on a motorcycle, lists the details regarding a visitation, mass, and reception in the deceased's honor. Mike is tagged on the posting with a message from the poster, "Here is the info for his services," indicating that Mike has requested this information for himself but also for other listeners who knew Pete. This type of sharing makes it possible for listeners to share condolences, further strengthen-ing the bonds of the listening community. Mike is not just a businessperson who shares information but is part of the community, a friend of Pete's, and a friend of those who are gathering to honor him.

By inviting messages such as the one included above, Mike is also an invoker of narrative and is a conductor of emotions felt for the Borderland as home, expressed through the nostalgic music of yesterday. In less than a minute, at Mike's prompting, the listener can gather a story about family as a parent calls in for her children on June 5, 2022, and asks, "Can my kids say something?" At Mike's encouragement and approval, the kids yell, "Happy Birthday to our grandpa and grandma. They're both of them 80!" As listeners, we become part of a birthday celebration between three generations. All the while, this inclusion of a new generation of listeners guides young callers through the performance expected of radio show listeners and welcomes participation of younger gener-ations. Through invitation and hospitality as the DJ of The Fox Jukebox, Mike models a variety of ways that listeners engage in relational listening.

I find it thought-provoking that the material, the music, that brings together this community is not new, but new occurrences are motivated by the music and by the younger generations, such as when a child calls the radio show and speaks to the DJ for the first time. This sounds like, "Hi, Mike. Can you play the birthday song by the Beatles for my grandma Mary?" asked by a young caller. "Did I do that right?" he whispers to someone, likely an adult in the room with him, "Yes, you did that right," Mike answers with laughter in his voice (April, 2016). In this example, the grandchild wants to be sure that his performance as a listener was correct. There are consistently new responses to old songs, and new memories are formed, layered with the memories that the songs have been a part of over decades. There is something special about initiating kids into the listening community, in that this practice adds to relational listening by provid-ing kids a way to relate to and strengthen relationships with their elders in ways that can't be manufactured outside of spending time together, listening with

127

intention, and creating opportunities for memory making. Mike welcomes the kids into the relational listening family. Hierarchies fall away when listening, as the kids and adults are all listeners, and not separated by age or position in the family. My grandpa Manny, my father's father, would fill an empty and cleaned Budweiser can with white landscaping rocks and tape the opening with black electrical tape. This homemade instrument allowed me to dance and shake along to the beat of the music, and while this was happening, I wasn't just the granddaughter or daughter. For a moment, I was a member of the band, hanging out, and taking in the music and conversations flying by and around me.

Mike actively builds the ethos of community listening by engaging in certain kinds of relational listening and utilizes his authority to choose his callers, emails, letters, and social media requests for reading on air. He keeps the communities of the Borderland united through shared memories and a shared love for the genre of music specific to the El Paso region. Maintenance of the commitment and emotional closeness of nearby cities is encouraged when Mike gives thanks to callers outside of El Paso by naming them as such as when he says, "Thank you to our Las Cruces caller," or, "We just heard from James from Clint." Also, Mike acknowledges his online listenership and invites them to call in from outside the Borderland region. When speaking and when writing on social media, Mike enacts relational listening by using certain words and phrases to engage his listeners in jargon that is familiar to the listeners, relating to them through the slang of the Borderland, as well as with familiarity with the community and the people within the community.

As a way of keeping musical heritage intact, Mike creates a space on a particular Easter Sunday, when a dedication from a male voice shared, "I'd like to make a dedication to my mom—I love you." The song following the dedication, a polka ranchera "Las Nubes," ("The Clouds") by Little Joe Y La Familia, which has been spoken of as an anthem to Chicanos and migrant workers everywhere in the Southwest. The listeners can relate to this request, especially on this day when the workers are resting and celebrating family and the resurrection recognized by this majority Catholic population. Mike responds affirmatively, following the dedication with the song that is important on this day, and also a well-loved and anticipated song every Sunday that mentions struggle, Texas, and God. The lyrics tell of a man who dreams of his childhood days, would rather die than suffer any longer, and would rather cry than sing but he gets relief when the clouds stop to rain on him to brighten his soul. In the lyrics, it is also told of the man that, "His heart's still back home in Texas, beneath its beloved sky," a feeling with which those who miss Texas can relate. This song from the radio show's archive will be appreciated widely by the Border listening community, as well as by numerous generations from whom love for the song has been inherited. This is also one of the songs to which my sister, Kathryn and I learned to dance polka rancheras with our dad, uncles, and brothers, adding a layer of personal nostalgia for me. It's these memories that, in large part, keep me returning to the show.

By playing songs from a range of genres, styles, and social movements that have taken place from the 1950s to the 1980s, Mike is host to a listenership that spans at least three generations. He encourages active participation and, between songs, converses with the audience, most often by leading the caller with questions such as where they are, what they are doing, or the reasons for their request or dedication. Mike recognizes the voices of frequent callers, remembers names, and makes consistent mention of locations throughout the Borderland, such as neighboring cities, high schools, restaurants, and other El Paso businesses, Mike reminds the listeners of those to whom they belong. These relationships are not only Mike's but also the listeners', as through relational listening, they too come to recognize people and locations. It's not uncommon for Mike to call out to someone casually, such as, "Hey, Adrian! I haven't seen you in a while." It is also expected that a caller will send out music to their hometown, such as, in this case, San Elizario, a city in El Paso County. The caller says briefly, "'Mockingbird,' from Inez and Charlie Foxx, going out to our friends in San Eli" (June 2020). Listener requests and comments illustrate the community listening interaction as the music serves intimate functions, such as reinforcing the listening community by enacting nostalgia and commemoration of important dates, as well as celebrating important events as an extended family.

Unlike the national DJs to whom I grew up listening, Mike is accessible as a local DJ, and because of his style of interacting with callers, he is a relational listener and encourages relational listening by sharing his life with the El Paso community. When he came up on a milestone birthday, he shared his celebration with the twentieth anniversary of The Fox Jukebox in 2021 with hundreds of listeners. The celebration was held a year late due to COVID-19, but was a grand event, advertised on the radio, as well as all social media outlets. At the event, Mike recognized the community in an announcement, "Thank you very much to all the gente that came out from out of town, from the Segundo, from Central, from Northeast El Paso, los de Fabens que vinieron, los de Ciudad Juarez tambien los que vinieron. People came from Cruces, thank you very much, We're one big happy family on a Sunday afternoon. I want to thank you from the bottom of my heart for a great twenty years. Let's see if we can do twenty more. A ver" (EPTCruising).

In the same way that the listening community includes Mike by sharing details of their personal lives when calling into the radio show, they also know details about Mike's life and health, his friendships, and about a major illness experienced almost ten years ago, the information shared predominantly through social media. Most DJs spend time in their communities making guest appearances, but Mike also has an online presence through Instagram, Twitter, and three Facebook pages, adding another dimension to his contact with listeners outside of radio. In these ways, Mike is involved with the listening community through his voice, through his physical presence, and through sharing photos, videos, and messages. While it is important to take notice of Mike's involvement on the local level, he also has a national listenership that speaks to the ethos of community listening that he has created. As he models relational listening, this encouragement is far-reaching for listeners outside the borderland, who feel welcome to participate in relational listening and feel closer to home as a result.

## CONCLUSION

Mike and the listeners of The Fox Jukebox's listeners take active, intentional roles in upholding the values within the community. His interactions with the listenership constitute relational listening, as he shares language, knowledge, and history with the listeners while encouraging their participation and gives them a listening home to return to each Sunday. Through participation, the listeners build upon memories carried from the past, associated with music by layering new memories, created each Sunday. This relational listening happens as the result of listeners coming together through an intentional decision to tune in to The Fox Jukebox, to listen to the music, to Mike, and to the participants of the show who belong to the Borderland and to The Fox Jukebox, some of whom who have belonged their entire lives.

On November 15, 2021, a mother shared a video of her daughter's wedding day on Facebook, writing:

> When I was pregnant with Juliandra, Grandma Yvette had already picked out her song, Suavecito by Malo. Since she was born Yvette has called in a dedication into 92.3 The Fox and our wonderful friend Mike G. would play it for them both for every birthday, Sunday, all the time. So, it was only right to have Mike G be the one to dedicate and introduce their song as a surprise. Thank you for making the moment so special Mike.

This is an example of the consistency of The Fox Jukebox as part of El Paso family life, as well as Mike's relationships with the listeners as DJ, family, and community members involved in the upholding and sharing of memories, as well as in memory making. This message is an example of the ethos of community listening that Mike upholds, the sharing of a story in exchange for a song, the commitment to history that is enjoyed at present, and the valuing of generations that serve as a thread from the music's beginnings to today. Through his willingness to share details of his life, by showing an interest in the stories of the callers, and by staying close to the values of the Borderland culture, the relationships Mike has built with his listenership have helped him to build an ethos of community listening. The listeners want to share with Mike and with each other.

Every so often, between songs, the show is interrupted by the bursting voice of a radio announcer who declares, "It's an El Paso tradition, oldies on Sundays" and there is comfort in knowing that as a listener, there will always be a place to be and belong on Sunday. Through relational listening, the community of The Fox Jukebox reaffirms that they have a place and people to belong to, and to which they can return. I return because community listening means coming together to honor people, places, memories, and moments through music.

Consistent in my practice of listening to oldies on Sunday, and dependent on The Fox Jukebox to transport me back to my hometown and to memories of my family, I recall one of my first memories where I learned to operate a Hi-Fi radio set in a large, walnut console at my Grandpa Manny and Grandma Lupe's house in El Paso. With me as DJ, the family would listen on weekend summer nights. Although we didn't call into the show, my parents, grandparents, little brother, and I would interact with the callers on our end of the radio. When certain oldies would play, my dad would say, "Oh man, I like that one. It reminds me of this one time . . . ," and my mom would say, "Ooh, remember that one? I haven't heard that one in forever." The stories connected through songs were some of the only ways I got to know my dad. For him, music was connected to blocks of time in his life, although some artists and songs remained constant throughout. Sharing his memories and stories helped me to relate to him, to see him as a man who was once a teen, a Marine hanging out on leave in San Diego, a young man falling in love to the music of Fats Domino, rather than just my dad who worked the grind of the Post Office or was the disciplinarian.

Engaging in community and relational listening takes more than a dad who teaches his children to love music. It is helped along by a DJ who loves the music he represents, respects the stories and memories of the listeners, who cares about and understands the community, and who is willing to push the next generation into learning how to belong to the listening community to create a space like The Fox Jukebox. I would nod as a child, in agreement with my parents' comments on the music we listened to on Sundays. Although I didn't know it then, many years in the future, I would use music as a way of traveling home and would respond in their absence with, "I like that one too, dad," and to my mom, "I remember and won't ever forget."

131

# WORKS CITED

Anzaldúa, Gloria, editor. *Making Faces, Making Soul/Haciendo Caras: Creative and Critical Perspectives of Feminists of Color.* Aunt Lute Books, 1990.

Banks, Adam Joel. *Digital Griots: African American Rhetoric in a Multimedia Age.* Southern Illinois UP, 2010.

Brown Jr., James J. "Composition in the Dromosphere." *Computers and Composition,* vol. 29, no. 1, 2012, pp. 79–91.

Brown, James, and Johnny Terry. "Please, Please, Please." *Please, Please, Please,* Federal Records, 1959.

Browne, Kevin Adonis. *Tropic Tendencies: Rhetoric, Popular Culture, and the Anglophone Caribbean.* U of Pittsburgh P, 2013.

Ceraso, Steph. "(Re) Educating the Senses: Multimodal listening, Bodily Learning, and the Composition of Sonic Experiences." *College English*, vol. 77, no. 2, 2014, pp. 102–123.

Facebook. 92.3 The Fox. Covid. 23 Jan. 2021. https://www.facebook.com/thefox923. June 2022.

———. 92.3 The Fox. Marco's Pizza. 13 Aug. 2019. https://tinyurl.com/4ccyymfn. June 2022.

———. 92.3 The Fox. Planet Fitness. 23 May 2022. https://tinyurl.com/ymrd4rpt. June 2022.

Facebook, Mike Guerrero. Daughter's Wedding. 15 Nov. 2021. https://tinyurl.com /3zsutkrk.

———. Mike Guerrero. Birthday and Mom Request. May 2022. https://tinyurl.com /2p2vuj48.

———. Mike Guerrero. Danny Trejo. 22 Apr. 2022. https://tinyurl.com/2p2vuj48.

———. Mike Guerrero. Little Mike and Steve Salas. 11 Feb. 2022. https://tinyurl .com/5n6s3dfv.

———. Mike Guerrero. Patti Diaz. 3 June 2022. https://tinyurl.com/ycx4p3fz.

———. Mike Guerrero. Skyline Lounge. 26 May 2022, 8:49 a.m. https://tinyurl.com /msw7w5f4.

Fishman, Jenn, and Lauren Rosenberg, editors. *Community Writing, Community Listening*, special issue of *Community Literacy Journal*, vol. 13, no. 1, 2018.

Fishman, Jenn, and Lauren Rosenberg. "Guest Editors' Introduction: Community Writing, Community Listening." Fishman and Rosenberg, pp. 1–6, https://doi.org/10.25148/clj.13.1.009085.

The Fox Jukebox with Mike Guerrero. 92.3. El Paso, Texas. 2012–2022.

García, Ofelia. *Bilingual Education in the 21st Century: A Global Perspective.* John Wiley & Sons, 2011.

———. "The Curvas of Translanguaging." *Translation and Translanguaging in Multilingual Contexts*, vol. 5, no. 1, 2019, pp. 86–93.

García, Ofelia, and Jo Anne Kleifgen. "Translanguaging and Literacies." *Reading Research Quarterly*, vol. 55, no. 4, 2020, pp. 553–571.

García, Romeo. "Creating Presence from Absence and Sound from Silence." Fishman and Rosenberg, pp. 7–15, https://doi.org/10.25148/clj.13.1.009086.

Hernandez, Jose Maria de Leon. "Las Nubes." *Discos Joey*, 1972. https://tinyurl.com /2y8unmex.

Hierro, Victor Del. "DJs, playlists, and Community: Imagining Communication Design Through Hip Hop." *Communication Design Quarterly Review*, vol. 7, no. 2, 2019, pp. 28–39.

Long, Trish. "Rudy Salas, Tierra Band Leader and Cofounder, Dies at 71." *El Paso Times* 30 Dec. 2020. https://tinyurl.com/2hvrjj82.

Nicotra, Jodie. "'Folksonomy' and the Restructuring of Writing Space." *College Composition and Communication*, vol. 61, no. 1, 2009, pp. W259-W276.

Nielsen.com. "Fan Favorite: Radio Listeners Spend 58% of Their Tune-I Time with Their Favorite Station." Dec. 2017. https://tinyurl.com/4szyedkt.

Pough, Gwendolyn D. *Check It While I Wreck It: Black Womanhood, Hip-Hop Culture, and the Public Sphere*. Northeastern UP, 2015.

Martinez, Aaron E. "El Paso Muralist Tino Ortega Unveils New 'Chuco' Mural at Chuco Relic Store." *El Paso Times*, 5 Apr. 2021.

"Mike Guerrero's Birthday & 20 Year Jukebox Celebration/" *YouTube*, Uploaded by Mike Drone, 28 Sept. 2021. https://www.youtube.com/watch?v=h8FSl-mGOcM.

Renteria, Ramon. "Mike Guerrero Spins the Hits, El Paso- Style." *El Paso Times*, 20 Dec. 2008, Entertainment sec.

Richardson, Elaine, and Sean Lewis. "'Flippin' the Script'/'Blowin' up the Spot': Puttin' Hip-Hop Online in (African) America and South Africa." *Global Literacies and the World-Wide Web*, edited by Gail E. Hawisher and Cynthia L. Selfe, Routledge, 2000, pp. 251–276.

CHAPTER 6.

# LISTENING IN: LETTER WRITING AND RHETORICAL RESILIENCE BEHIND BARS

**Alexandra J. Cavallaro**
California State University, San Bernardino

**Wendy Hinshaw**
Florida Atlantic University

**Tobi Jacobi**
Colorado State University

*This chapter centers on a study of prison letter-writing programs and advances a version of listening referred to as community-centered listening. The authors demonstrate the challenges in navigating relationships with incarcerated writers, the limitations of interpreting meaning in and from carceral spaces, and the importance of establishing listening relationships.*

Thank you for the books and I thank you even more for your personalized response. Out of the other five or six places that I write, this is the first time I've had someone take the time to make me feel like a real person and not some charity case.

– LGBT Books to Prisoners letter archive

Letters—more than any other form of literacy-related prison activity—are a prime indication that prisoners are inordinately successful in their endeavors, and not only display and use their literacy talents but use them in a way specifically designed to retain a sense of social identity in an institutional world (197).

– Anita Wilson, "'Absolutely Truly Brill to See from You': Visuality and Prisoners' Letters"

Though much of the world has moved on from physical letters in favor of faster, digital modes of communication, such letters remain a crucial lifeline between

DOI: https://doi.org/10.37514/PER-B.2025.2531.2.06

incarcerated people and the outside world. As the letter writer in the epigraph above attests, connections to outside communities—real and imagined—are life-sustaining for people experiencing incarceration. In fact, so prized are letters that when leaving prison, even as many people discard personal items they have accumulated, letters almost always go with them to the free world (Wilson 192). Mail provides an essential connection to the outside world despite the many limitations imposed upon how people in prison can receive and send correspondence (see "Writing to Someone in Prison"); as Janet Maybin argues in her study of death row penfriends, letters allow for the negotiation and reassessment of identity that stands in stark contrast to the "intentional dehumanization of the prison" (162). In this way, physical artifacts, including letters, postcards, pictures, etc., preserve the humanity of senders and recipients by preserving familial and community lifelines.

Limitations on how people in prison can communicate are part of the ever-present carceral control of literacy practices that determine who can read and write, what they can read and write, and with whom. Paid services like JPay have extended email access to some incarcerated people, thereby enabling them to access some forms of digital communication, and yet these same technologies also threaten to replace physical mail altogether, as the Federal Bureau of Prisons and increasing numbers of state prison systems move to digitize all prison mail. Such moves, made ostensibly in the name of security and convenience, threaten one of the few means of communication that people who are incarcerated have available to them, and overlook the particular kinds of physical and emotional closeness that the exchange of physical letters embodies. Letters allow writer and reader to imagine presence across place and space boundaries, a fundamental feature of epistolary discourse that Esther Milne refers to as a "dance between absence and presence" in which "writing a letter signals the absence of the recipient and, simultaneously, aims to bridge the gap between writer and recipient." While bridging gaps of time and place drives the purpose of any letter exchange, letters written from within carceral spaces make particularly apparent the boundaries that letter-writers must overcome, as well as the strategies writers employ to listen for and enact community. Such letters reveal the "active, layered, intentional" practices that we recognize as the core of community listening (Fishman and Rosenberg 1). In the discussion that follows, we build on methods of community listening to center the kinds of practices produced by and required for listening within carceral spaces. We carve out a specific space for community-centered listening to letter-writers behind bars to recognize the ways in which writers form community—however fragmented or partial—and enact practices of rhetorical and material resilience through listening.

This chapter offers readers windows into the complex system of discipline, punishment, and human interactions that the U.S. prison system makes visible through letters written to, within, and from confined spaces; such letters embody a resilient and critical community listening that demonstrates resistance to state- and culturally-imposed identities and demand a community-centered solidarity. The letters come from several sources: the first is the archives of LGBT Books to Prisoners housed at the University of Wisconsin-Madison. For over ten years, this organization has been sending books to queer- and trans-identified incarcerated people across the United States. While incarcerated people can simply request books they are interested in, many letters go far beyond that, providing important insight into the lives of queer and trans people in prison and instantiating membership in global communities. Other letters also informed our understanding of rhetorical resilience in writers inside, including pairings of open letters written by trans people in prison and letters that respond to the specific cultural moment of incarceration at the beginning of a global pandemic. Writers and educators in programs we are directly involved with, as well as writers responding to the PEN Prison Writing and Justice Program annual writing contest, turned to letter writing to seek and maintain connections with communities of support. As Lori Lebow describes, "letter writing involves the writing self as a joint venture undertaken by the writer and reader. Writer and reader construct identity from textual cues based on the received responses from the selected audience" (75). In the context of letters from carceral spaces, we understand such "textual cues" as listening-centered practices that invite writer and reader to imagine presence across place and space boundaries and co-create relationships and understanding based on an interpretative negotiation of presence/absence. In line with other community writing scholars taking up the call to attend to listening as central to our work, we attend to the cultural logics as well as the available actions that shape our access and responses as listeners. While there is now an established field of scholarship devoted to reading incarcerated writers, including significant collections of letters (e.g., Castillo, Furio, Gramsci, Kennedy, Thompson), less attention has been given to the listening relationships formed through letters from prison. This site of writing is crucial to examine because the institutional constraints of prison result in communication that is often fragmented, interrupted, and subject to the whims of an institution whose core goals result in disconnection and isolation.

As prison literacy educators and researchers, we are accustomed to the restricted circumstances of carceral writing: we have each taught in conventional college classrooms and behind bars, have written alongside people serving time, and have participated in research focused on prison literacies. The community-centered listening we practice here is an effort to contribute to methods of rhetorical community listening that resist extractive relationships with historically marginalized people. We have learned that the rhetorical resilience emerging from community-centered listening enables connection but cannot on its own enact it. For example, in "Writing to Listen," Wendy uses listening as a strategy to "tune to the material conditions of speaking and writing" in a writing exchange between prison and university classrooms (57). In this case, "writing to listen" provided a strategy for invention and connection for two groups of students to exchange writing and communicate across the physical, institutional, and geographic boundaries of a prison-university writing exchange, as well as a framework for thinking about the "absences that we are left to listen into" in such exchanges (58). But, as Romeo García points out, listening for such absences does not preclude the colonial memories that animate many rhetorical listening practices, particularly the "haunting legacies of seeing and hearing the 'other' in and on the academic scholar's terms" (García "Haunt(ed/ing) Genealogies" 240). For García, listening practices that presume the ability to stand outside of one's own position, such as Krista Ratcliffe's tactic of "eavesdropping," represent a "simulacrum of whiteness, a 'tactical,' but not ethical practice, akin to colonial gazing" (García "Creating" 13). Where Ratcliffe's tactic for listening from outside one's own identity position fails to attend to the limits in our ability to transcend or move across identity positions, García's approach to community listening tunes into the absences and "hauntings" in prison writing to "find solace both with the inability to extract and foreclose upon all knowledges and the inaccessibility for some of community listening" ("Creating" 7). Alexandra and co-author Karen Rowan address some of these absences in "Toward a Model for Preparatory Community Listening," in which they utilize community listening as a way of preparing to listen to historically and geographically-situated discourses to "make political and ethical assessments of these discourses' impact and our own responses to them in the work we undertake" (26). In this way, Rowan and Cavallaro adapt community listening as not only a means for engaging with the community but also a means for identifying "the (un)conscious presences, absences, unknowns" that shape listening relationships (Ratcliff 206, qtd. in Rowan and Cavallaro 26). Listening to letters pushes us to sharpen our attention to these unknowns, foregrounding the gaps in communication that so often characterize writings emerging from behind bars. Letters from inside prison can document experiences of incarceration and reframe them, but letters are also partial communications that contain within them the traces (hauntings) of sender, reader, and circumstances.

Our approach to community-centered listening helps us navigate our relationship with the incarcerated writers we read and the writing we help to amplify, as well as the limits of what we can know through this writing. What follows is a critical reading of letters from an LGBT Books to Prisoners letter archive, contemporary open letter exchanges between activists and people inside, and letters written by participants and facilitators of established prison writing and education programs. These letters make visible the range of moves available to individual writers within circumstances of restriction and surveillance, as well as the flexibility of the epistolary genre itself. While the resulting partial listening remains a challenge when engaging texts from inside, we argue that ignoring these fragmented communications risks losing a rich source of insight about how identities and communities build and move between prison walls and the free world. We utilize community-centered listening as a means for identifying listening relationships within the letters we observe as well as navigating our relationships to these letters, particularly given the fact that we were not their original recipients, and so, therefore, must imagine our way into the listening relationships articulated within them. To practice ethical rhetorical engagement, we examine connections between epistolary literacy practices within the U.S. incarceration system and seek to make visible the ways that these letter exchanges and interactions deepen our approaches to active, community-centered listening. The featured letters underscore the need for social, affective—and often material—support for people experiencing mass incarceration, and challenge educators and researchers to think through the nuances of how and when people write toward social change. The emergent rhetorical and material resilience demonstrated in these and other letters encourages scholars to consider the collective and relational possibilities of extending the work of active community-centered listening through situationally-relevant genres like letter writing.

## LETTER WRITING AS COMMUNITY-CENTERED LISTENING BEHIND BARS

In her study of letter exchanges between people incarcerated on death row and penpals on the outside, Janet Maybin demonstrates the key role that letters and letter-based relationships can often have in helping incarcerated people establish and maintain a range of social identities and relationships beyond those assigned by the prison. As one incarcerated person included in Maybin's study wrote about their penpal relationships, "I've found myself being an adviser, counsellor, marriage consultant, religious instructor, brother, friend, lover, editor, writer, poet" (159). For many incarcerated correspondents, letters provide a means for reforming or reimagining existing identities and relationships, as well as creating or imagining new identities and relationships. We cannot measure the "success" of such acts of resistance, or know anything about the specific experiences of the writers we look at besides the fragments they leave on the page. However, what we can see is how the writers make space—or listen for—community through the connections they make as well as the absences they leave on the page. More broadly, in the context of prison, letters contribute to the construction of communities committed to both making visible lived experiences of incarceration, and to creating key connections that can temporarily breach walls traditionally meant to confirm colonizing power relationships.

Many writers to LGBT Books to Prisoners use their requests as an opportunity to seek out community and affirm their identity through their letters, and replace negative responses to identity (officers, fellow prisoners, family/friends outside) with validation of self-identification, mirrored emotions, and social interactions. The following two authors illustrate:

> Please tell us more about the types of books you want:

> I'm not really sure, just something that is similar to my current situation, not being out but feeling sexy about how I feel on the inside, confused but FAB!! (official form letter)

> I'm a bi-sexual prisoner in the hate filled California prison system. . . . There are only two of us LGBT prisoners on the building as far as I know and we are several cell's [sic] away so we don't get to help one-another much. So any help you can share with me, I'd be very grateful and would gladly pass on to him also.

The writers take seriously the invitation to engage with the LGBT Books to Prisoners process by choosing to locate themselves as part of the LGBTQ+ community and as interested recipients of future books, materials, and correspondence. They model both an interest in listening and confirm a will to be seen/heard as part of a larger community.

As literacy artifacts composed within highly regulated environments and for specific purposes, letters often work to represent the conditions and challenges faced by incarcerated people in general, as well as the ways that literacy is accessed and circulated behind bars. As these two writers attest, both communication and books are highly valued as both escape and social capital, allowing, as Megan Sweeney has argued, those inside to "revision and rescript their lives" (3):

> Opportunity presents this occasion to one again reach out to you with best wishes in thought for everyone of you there being a blessing to those of us whom are reaching out for the aid you provide to the LGBT community of incarcerated people. It's been some time since my last communication to you and I am in need of some other reading materials to embrace a mental reprieve from the madness of prison life.

Listening In

> Thank you for being there for all of us. You are the only Books
> to Prisoners supplier that will send gay novels. Which are loved
> by all of us! I pass them around to others that don't get many
> books from the outside. By the time all of us have read them
> the covers are falling off. I donate them to the library but they
> don't show up on the shelves. I don't know if it's staff or the
> inmate orderlies that stops them from being used.

Notes like these make visible the conditions of incarceration and extend the
work of the LGBT Books to Prisoners beyond one-on-one correspondence and
exchange, invoking a community that builds upon the initial gifting of books by
validating the needs of people inside and allowing them to continue the act of
circulation and community-building.

Others write to "LGBT family" or otherwise reference family or kinship in
their opening lines, invoking the capacious understanding of family that characterizes relationships in the LGBTQ+ community. For example,

> Thank you for all you are doing for all the LGBT Familys
> [sic] in and out of prison. All the work you "all" do is truly
> amazing and a true blessing to us men and women behind
> these prison walls. "It makes us feel not so alone." Thank you
> and I hope you all have a safe, happy and fun Thanksgiving
> and Christmas.

We can see the multiple meanings that "family" serves in examples such as these,
reinforcing kinship/allyship relations between incarcerated writers, the allies
receiving their requests, and the community of LGBTQ+ readers and writers
served by the organization. Applying a community-centered listening approach
means listening to the ways in which the letter-writers form community with
the organization and with other LGBT people through the kinship and relationships they invoke in their letters. Working with archives featuring writing from
prison offers researchers windows into carceral contexts and creates a direct call
for more active involvement in prison literacy work for those committed to a
community listening centered on contexts of racism and repression.

Despite these moves to revise and rescript, the institutional specter of the
prison remains a constant presence in letters, as writers demonstrate keen awareness of the institutional limitations on their literacy practices. One writer offers
a solution to limited computer access by creating a semi-form letter to counter
the material constraints he faces (e.g., "only eight (8) envelopes per month" and
"valuable time that we are given on a word processor"). Moreover, he demonstrates a keen rhetorical awareness of the potential pitfalls of this choice: readers

141

may already be reluctant to respond to prisoners, particularly when communication comes through a form letter. "As a person incarcerated, many places do not like to respond to inquiries from inmates," he writes. "Therefore, please forgive me if this letter sounds like a form letter. It is easier to make one letter to send out than to draft several different letters." The writer names this and calls for human compassion and kindness, and notes the power of second chances. His ultimate request supports this philosophical stance: he asks for a wedding planner to help those inside marry and materials to tutor inside since the prison does not provide any.

Other writers are compelled (for many reasons) into action and use letters to name and update others on their advocacy efforts inside, offering accounts intended to parallel the outside activist work of LGBT Books to Prisoners. With each package of books that goes inside the facility, a short, personalized note accompanies the delivery. Letters reveal how writers often draw strength and motivation from correspondence with book senders who recognize their identification beyond a cisgender status quo behind bars:

> I have past [sic] the last books you have sent me to other
> struggle LGBTQ people and we are all grateful [sic] for all
> you do for us. It personally means the world to me that peo-
> ple like you all are more than willing to help our community
> and for that I thank you. I would also like to say thank you to
> Emma as well for the beautiful note that was wrote to me. I
> am here and your commitment has made me start a group to
> stand up for our rights. I have had it approved for my name
> change and also for transgenders to get there private shower. I
> would like to make a donation for the cause if you would let
> me know who to make the check out to. I believe hole [sic]
> heartedly that it is deserved.

While many writers mention and applaud personal correspondence with outside volunteers, others make visible the power exercised by the system when even a brief note halts delivery from a prison mailroom, interrupting relationships that depend on both institutional compliance and the ability to hear and be heard in ways that make malleable the institutional structures intended to box people, their stories, and their community connections in. As the writer below indicates, the ability of an institution to stall or even paralyze book delivery makes way for a new rhetorical challenge, one in which writers must both cede to regulations and convince a sender that it is worth trying again, that he (and all the other inmates at that institution) are worth the "inconvenience" of resending the books:

> "The only problem was there was a handwritten note, even though it was not a letter. . . . My Captain said that I should write to you and ask if you could resend the books without a note or letter in the package with the books. I apologize for the inconvenience. I also hope this does not hinder you sending books to me or other inmates. Again I would like to apologize to you for this inconvenience. I also want to thank you for your time."

As these texts illustrate, the letters received and sent from carceral contexts are rich examples of the complex power and communication dynamics that people writing to and from prisons face. They connect place and time through writing by constituting listening roles for writers and readers as both authors and audiences. Letter-writing moves readers and writers toward relational resilience as they listen to, learn from, and move toward self-identifications and affirmations beyond those inscribed upon them by carceral spaces and expectations. In such spaces, community-centered listening means listening for and with the communities invoked in the letters as well as the listening practices of the letter-writers. In other words, letter-writers are always already writing from and to communities; here, the letter embodies the process of rejecting a socially predetermined identity (e.g., criminal) by invoking alternative identities through the communication and anticipated (positive) reception. In the case of incarcerated people, who are in an institution focused on isolation, normativity, and individual responsibility, letter-writing is a particularly important means for maintaining identity and promoting connection. For scholars and activists outside, letters gathered in archives such as this invite a critical listening, a community-centered listening that calls for action toward social change, the need for which is concentrated in spaces like prisons where dominant narratives of identity often afford little space for diversity or equity.

When thinking about letter writing as an act of community listening, response is essential in building a deep sense of community that supports people through their time in prison by forming lifelines to the outside. Numerous letters describe the real impact notes from LGBT Books to Prisoners volunteers have, demonstrating how they also provide a sense of connection and community, inviting a strengthened rhetorical resilience as writers navigate the dehumanizing realities and capricious conditions of imprisonment:

> The thing that made the difference was a simple sheet of paper with three words . . . "You are important." It actually brought me to tears. It totally hit the spot. . . . Your choice of words was perfect for fixing a wounded soul.

Such individual responses are designed to counteract the dehumanization people experience in prisons as they are stripped of their identities and individuality. Many organizations that seek to reach in, as the above writer notes, do so out of a sense of charity, not solidarity (cf. Hubrig). The image of the wounded soul as a descriptor for the impact of prison on millions of U.S. citizens is pervasive and speaks to the impact of mass incarceration. The writer's words demonstrate response as an essential component of community listening through letters in carceral facilities to create connection and community that sustains people in these institutions that are not designed to be sustaining.

Response serves another important function in these facilities for queer and trans people: in addition to the creation of community and life-sustaining affirmation, letters can serve as an important means of protection. Across the United States, queer and trans people are subjected to particularly high levels of violence and mistreatment. The very presence of letters, according to Maya Shenwar, can alert the administration that the person receiving mail has a support network of advocates and allies outside of the prison. This is illustrated by the open letter, a form made visible by well-known public figures who have experienced incarceration, such as Martin Luther King Jr. and Angela Davis. Designed to reach multiple recipients and be read by a wide public, the open letter is employed behind bars to fight conditions of isolation and provide support that transcends literal and metaphorical walls. It is also a way to confront the ever-present mediation of institutions, since open letters invite a wide and informed readership, pressing readers to face the material and affective conditions of U.S. incarceration that remain potentially less visible in transactional letter exchanges (e.g., book request letters). Open letters demand a public hearing, and invite public discomfort with the realities of incarceration as social issues requiring social investment rather than individual challenges that might be overcome through the delivery of books or other interventions focused on individuals rather than clarifying a larger social responsibility.

In an open letter printed in *Out Magazine* in 2013, Kate Bornstein writes to Chelsea Manning during her incarceration at the Leavenworth Federal Prison. A note at the top of this piece acknowledges several of the conditions that Manning faces: this letter will have to be mailed to her since she has no internet access, and it will have to arrive under Manning's dead name. This note highlights the material impact of institutional mediation, communicating to wider audiences not only a refusal to allow Manning her preferred name, but also making visible the treatment she endures at the prison: she is a woman incarcerated in a men's facility, she has been placed in extreme solitary confinement for long periods of time, and she lacks access to hormones, to name just a few. The bulk of the letter, however, offers Manning support, community, and affirmation. Similar to letters received by the LGBT Books to Prisoners program, she invokes the language of family, an important metaphor in the queer community, to tell Manning that she is not alone: "There are already folks out here who proudly call themselves your sisters, and brothers. You've got uncles, and you've got aunties, like me." And, like any auntie entrusted with the care of a niece in a bad position, Bornstein entreats Manning to stay alive and make herself as safe as possible. Beyond that, Bornstein asks Manning to embrace her in-between state as a survival strategy behind prison walls. She says, "Experience as much ecstasy as you can, with the girl/boy body you've got right now. You are occupying an in-between stage of transition, and most cultures consider that place pretty darned magical and powerful." She acknowledges the limitations of her situation and brings in this advice to help Manning survive and, as far as possible, thrive. This letter is a lifeline that connects Manning to the outside world, to a wider community of support and listening. It also has a dual audience in mind: the addressee specifically, of course, but also a wider readership. Writing and publicizing this genre of letter writing in prisons functions as a way to engage a wider public in prison issues, as much as a lifeline to a specific incarcerated individual.

When Chelsea Manning was preparing to leave prison, she published an open letter in *The Guardian* addressed to her fellow incarcerated people she left behind. Like many open letters, she emphasizes connection beyond the barriers that separate them: "I know that we are now physically separated," she writes, "but we will never be apart and we are not alone." She also addresses the community that she and others created while incarcerated, and all that she learned from them: "The most important thing that you taught me was how to write and how to speak in my own voice. I used to only know how to write memos. Now, I write like a human being, with dreams, desires and connections. I could not have done it without you. . . . And to anyone who finds themselves feeling alone behind bars, know that there is a network of us who are thinking of you. You will never be forgotten." Both open letters address the specific difficulties that trans women experience in prison. Trans people are subjected to higher rates of incarceration and violence once behind bars. Letters—in this case, open letters—seek to call attention to these conditions and offer a lifeline to keep incarcerated people afloat, working, as Marion Vannier argues, to "illuminate the continuities and discontinuities of penal power over time" (252). Response to letters fulfills an important material purpose in sustaining the literal community-centered listening that activates writers and their familial and community networks, as well as the communities formed through the partial listening (always institutionally-mediated) of readers who may have the ability to pursue material and systemic change.

## ACTIVATING ETHICAL COMMUNITY-CENTERED LETTER/LISTENING AS PANDEMIC RESPONSE

Ethical community listening in carceral facilities (one that keeps the idea of risk and vulnerability central to the communications) is vital to understanding how literacy practices like letter writing might play a role in disrupting a carceral system weighted down heavily by centuries of abuse, racism, and inequity. Our reading of these archived documents, as well as our own interactions with writers inside during the COVID-19 pandemic, heightens our awareness of the need for a community-centered listening that accounts for the particular material conditions inside carceral facilities. Like so many other social inequalities, the pandemic brought the importance and precariousness of letter-writing for incarcerated people into new light. As programming and visitations in jails and prisons were put on hold across the country, letters became one of the only ways for incarcerated people to communicate with friends and family on the outside and thus became a way to enact listening through letter-writing practices. Early in the pandemic, ProPublica published excerpts from letters written by people incarcerated in the Harris County Jail in Houston to tell the story of COVID-19's spread in the facility (MacDougall). In response to loss of access to recording equipment, etc., the podcast *Uncuffed*, which is produced by people behind bars in California prisons, pivoted to recording letters from friends and family on the outside, who read the letters they wrote to their loved ones stuck on the inside of California prisons during the pandemic. Critical Resistance Portland, a branch of the well-known Critical Resistance abolitionist organization, launched a letter-writing campaign aimed at encouraging the wider public to "write a letter to all 14,000 people caged in Oregon's state prisons" as part of a coordinated effort to bring awareness to the impact of COVID on incarcerated people. These direct actions tug wide-ranging publics toward the silences they may not have previously heard; writing letters to incarcerated people in state prisons makes space for listening in to both the wider complexities of mass incarceration and toward the stories and circumstances of individuals, hauntings, and audiences invoked.

Such efforts were mirrored by the programs we are involved with when the facilities we worked with closed their doors to outsiders as the virus spread. Alexandra's prison courses were temporarily suspended before pivoting online, reducing incarcerated students to a single Zoom screen. The SpeakOut! literacy program that Tobi directs in northern Colorado worked to recognize the pragmatic and affective disruptions experienced by both inside writers and facilitators when writing workshops were abruptly truncated and communication nearly silenced. The program tried to pivot by sending collaborative letters of support inside—and publishing them in the spring journal alongside participants' work to maintain the affective connections that these programs embrace:

> We can now understand your apprehension about the suspension of the SpeakOut! Writing workshop due to the outbreak of the corona virus. But, let me assure you that we are working hard to continue with our writing workshop remotely and to have your work published. What matters to us is to support you write and make your voice heard. Even though we will not meet in person, we will be able to feel your hope and happiness that usually radiate at the writing workshop in your responses to the prompts that we will send. Don't let this situation quench your passion for SpeakOut! writing—keep writing, keep your voice being heard! I hope it will be refreshing for you to know that we are still receiving writings for publication, especially writings on color, light and darkness. (129–130) Jail Volunteer, *SpeakOut! Journal*, Spring 2020

> I miss you all so much and hope you and all of your loved ones are doing well in these unprecedented times. I know that we are all feeling so many different emotions; shock, grief, fear, anger, uncertainty, uneasiness. I hope that you have used writing as an outlet during these past few weeks. I wanted to let you know that you have all been on our minds and we have not forgotten about you! We have been in close communication and are brainstorming new ways to keep our community strong. I know that there are days we don't always feel up to writing, but I feel that for many of us, the urge to write has grown (considering much of our time has opened up), and let's be honest—writing keeps us sane. (131) Community Corrections volunteer, *SpeakOut! Journal*, Spring 2020

These sample letters from SpeakOut! facilitators express concern for incarcerated people by offering statements of support that recognize and articulate the particularly difficult times that writers would be facing behind bars and encouragement for continuing to use writing to deal with the difficulties in the months ahead. Here the facilitators write into the unknown—not knowing what the pandemic would bring for them—and affirm community through their shared knowledge of prison writing. The physical absences we would all soon experience became emblematic of the larger, historically entrenched fragmentation that writers working within carceral spaces experience, always partial, always fragmented.

This one program's attempt to adapt was shared and replicated elsewhere as writers worked to share stories of pandemic survival and loss from inside. Such projects call on audiences to listen to experiences of the pandemic as it unfolded inside prison, as well as to understand the experience of watching a pandemic take hold from within prison. The 2020 Prison Writing Awards anthology published annually by PEN America included a thirty-two-page collection of "pandemic letters" from award winners; the eighteen letters document the heightened restrictions and isolations experienced by people in prison, including a sense of helplessness to participate in the global response, as writer Nick Browning attests: "The real world has come to resemble the incarcerated one in ways I wouldn't have thought likely" (288). Another collection, *Hear Us: Writing from the Inside During the Time of Covid,* created by Exchange for Change and Disorder Press, opens with an image of a submission letter from Bob R. Williams Jr., whose essay "In Memoriam: 2020's Covid-19 Losses to the Death Row Community," describes how San Quentin has "become a sort of home" for him, and how "COVID-19 came into my home and left with a few of my friends and associates" (64). For Williams and others, letters, poems, and other written and visual forms provide a way to write their experiences into our memories of the pandemic, creating a record of listening that counters narratives that privilege dominant discourse and risk erasing the experiences of people in prison.

For many incarcerated writers, the pandemic has also provided a new way of communicating the systemic injustice and broken conditions that have long characterized the prison system. Eduardo Martinez argues that society views "inmates as viruses" and describes the common COVID-19 symptom of losing smell and taste as "not a bad thing if you've ever eaten prison food or have been confined and clustered with over 82 men in a Florida prison dormitory with no A.C. or proper ventilation" (18). Many writers in the collection also reference the murder of George Floyd, both as a means of showing solidarity with the Movement for Black Lives and the protests against police violence held around the world in 2020, and to reinforce the systemic connections between police violence and mass incarceration. Israel (Izzy) Martinez takes up the language of COVID-19 as well as the Movement for Black Lives and the murder of George Floyd in his declaration that "I haven't breathed properly in almost a decade" (111).

While we hope the conditions created by COVID-19 are temporary, the responses to those conditions demonstrate the powerful potential of letter writing behind bars as a means of enacting deep listening practices within confining institutions and beyond as letters circulate into communities physically outside of the prison walls.

# TOWARD LETTER WRITING AS RHETORICALLY RESILIENT COMMUNITY-CENTERED LISTENING

> [R]esilience is not a state of being but a process of rhetorically engaging with material circumstances and situational exigences. . . . Resilience does not necessarily return an individual life to equilibrium but entails an ongoing responsiveness, never complete nor predetermined.
>
> – Elizabeth Flynn, Patricia Sotirin, and Ann Brady, *Feminist Rhetorical Resilience*, p. 7

Although many of us have spent significant time thinking through the implications of isolation and resilience (or lack thereof) of our physical, social, and mental systems of support in recent years, incarcerated people have long experienced a more deeply entrenched pandemic, one that perpetuates racial bias, violence against non-cisgender and non-heterosexual people, class discrimination, and withholding educational resources. The letters we listen to in this essay exemplify these inequities and suggest ways that scholar educators committed to community-centered listening might participate in active social change efforts behind bars. Elizabeth Hawes' letter, featured in the 2020 PEN America award winners essay collection, exemplifies the kind of rhetorical resilience that can emerge and sustain writers inside:

> Hey COVID—
> You've been reaching out to prisoners, so I'm dropping you a line.
>
> I'll be the first to admit I've cried over someone or something every day since mid-March. Your march of destruction, along with the mark for global justice, have made for a rainy spring. But with sorrow comes new ways of viewing the world, an opening to new possibilities, potential & reform. This is a year of expression & turn around.
>
> It's true you have worn us down, but here's the higher truth: You can't break us. You can't break the warriors of prison. We get up every day—always isolated without family, with no internet connection, or pets, or reasonably-priced phone access. We get up every day from this mattresses to cheap food & substandard medical care—unable to vote & barely paid at our jobs—and unable to care for our loved ones the way we would hope to. And yet, we get up every day.
>
> Last week, you killed two men who lived at the Fairbault prison. You might not remember their names, but we do. We

Cavallaro, Hinshaw, and Jacobi

are a powerful piece of resistance. We live by codes. We lean on each other, we check on each other, we take care of those who need care.

We ache for reform, and it is coming. You will not break us.

Yeah, I'll wear a mask. I'll wash my hands. I'll pray for the healing of all people. Every damn day.

Hey COVID, do you hear me? You got nothing.

(Letter from Elizabeth Hawes, PEN AMERICA)

As teachers, scholars, and active citizens committed to community writing and listening, we recognize the compelling approaches to rhetorical resilience that writers like Hawes and the others cited in this chapter embody through their words and actions. We call upon our like-minded peers to extend the community-centered listening tactics modeled by writers behind bars and featured here to other contexts where suppressed people need support in reaching equitable opportunities and life experiences. Academic models of listening and scholarship often fall short of the kinds of active and reciprocal community engagement that we see as a vital component of community-centered listening. We turn to contemporary work being done by transdisciplinary/community-engaged groups like the Alliance for Higher Education in Prison and activist groups like Critical Resistance for Action as exemplars that prioritize community needs and voices. We reach toward organizing and policy work that deploys storytelling and literacy work to advocate for human rights through campaigns that "ban the box" or restore enfranchisement. We recognize sustainable and validating rhetorical nuances in letters from carceral spaces that compel readers to move beyond individuating authors as victims of a corrupt system, shitty circumstances, or poor life choices; rather, we hear a strong calling out of power inequalities as individual letter writers self-select into identity groups and toward collective action that includes participatory action research, co-authorship, and the co-creation of listening opportunities in spaces of extreme inequity. The powerful "we" that Elizabeth Hawes invokes cuts across hundreds of letters and reaches thousands of readers calling all of us to listen in, listen up, and take action.

## WORKS CITED

Bornstein, Kate. "Open Letter: Kate Bornstein to Chelsea Manning." *Out Magazine*, 26 Aug. 2013.

Castillo, Tessa, Michael J. Braxton, Lyle May, Terry Robinson, and George Wilkerson. *Crimson Letters: Voices from Death Row*. Black Rose Writing, 2020.

Cavallaro, Alexandra J., et al. "Inside Voices: Collaborative Writing in a Prison Environment." *Harlot: A Revealing Look at the Arts of Persuasion*, no. 15, 2016, http://harlotofthearts.org/index.php/harlot/article/view/323/188.

Fishman, Jenn and Lauren Rosenberg, editors. *Community Writing, Community Listening*, special issue of *Community Literacy Journal*, vol. 13, no. 1, 2018.

Flynn, Elizabeth, Patricia Sotirin, and Ann Brady. *Feminist Rhetorical Resilience*. Utah State UP, 2012.

Furrio, Jennifer, editor. *Letters from Prison: Voices of Women Murderers*. Algora, 2001.

García, Romeo. "Creating Presence from Absence and Sound from Silence." Fishman and Rosenberg, pp. 7–15, https://doi.org/10.25148/clj.13.1.009086.

———. "Haunt(ed/ing) Genealogies and Literacies." *Reflections*, vol. 19, no. 1, 2019, pp. 230–252.

Gramsci, Antonio. *Letters from Prison*, edited by Frank Rosengarten. Translated by Raymond Rosenthal Columbia UP, 2011.

Hawes, Elizabeth. "Letter from Elizabeth Hawes." *Breathe into the Ground*. PEN America, 2021: 273.

Hear Us: *Writing From the Inside During the Time of COVID*. Disorder Press, 2021.

Hinshaw, Wendy. "Writing to Listen: Why I Write Across Prison Walls." Fishman and Rosenberg, pp. 55–70, https://doi.org/10.25148/clj.13.1.009090.

Hubrig, Ada. "'We Move Together:' Reckoning with Disability Justice in Community Literacy Studies." *Community Literacy Journal*, vol. 14, no. 2, Spring 2020, pp. 144–153.

Kennedy, Percy. *Voices of the Fatherless: Letters from Incarcerated Dads Aimed at Breaking the Prison Pipeline*. BookBaby, 2021.

Lebow, Lori. "Woman of Letters: Narrative Episodes in the Letters of Emily Dickinson." *The Emily Dickinson Journal*, vol. 8, no. 1, 1999, pp. 73–96.

MacDougall, Ian. "Letters From the Houston Jail." *ProPublica*, 1 May 2020. https://tinyurl.com/47sc3ejj.

Manning, Chelsea. "Open Letter." *The Guardian*, 13 Feb. 2017.

Maybin, Janet. "Death Row Penfriends: Some Effects of Letter Writing on Identity and Relationships." *Letter Writing as a Social Practice*, edited by David Barton and Nigel Name Hall, John Benjamins Publishing Company, 2000, pp. 151–78.

———. "Death Row Penfriends: Configuring Time, Space, and Selves" *Auto/Biography Studies*, vol. 21, no. 1, 2014, pp. 58–69.

Milne, Ester. "Email and Epistolary Technologies: Presence, Intimacy, Disembodiment." *The Fibreculture Journal*, no. 2, 2003, https://tinyurl.com/mm7ybwwh.

PEN America. *Breathe into the Ground: 2020 Prison Writing Awards Anthology*. PEN America 2021.

Ratcliffe, Krista. *Rhetorical Listening: Identification, Gender, Whiteness*. Southern Illinois UP, 2005.

Rowan, Karen, and Alexandra J. Cavallaro. "Toward a Model for Preparatory Community Listening." Fishman and Rosenberg, pp. 23–36, https://doi.org/10.25148/clj.13.1.009088.

Shenwar, Maya. *Locked Down, Locked Out: Why Prison Doesn't Work and How We Can Do Better*. Berrett-Koehler Publishers, 2014.

Sweeney, Megan. *Reading is My Window: Books and the Art of Reading in Women's Prisons*. U of North Carolina P, 2010.

Thompson, Shawn. *Letters from Prison: Felons Writing about the Struggle for Life and Sanity Behind Bars*. Harper Collins, 2002.

"Volunteer Letters." *SpeakOut! Journal.* Spring 2020: 129–31.

Wilson, Anita. "'Absolutely Truly Brill to See from You': Visuality and Prisoners' Letters." *Letter Writing as a Social Practice*, edited by David Barton and Nigel Name Hall, John Benjamins Publishing Company, 2000, pp. 179–98.

"Writing to A Person in Prison." 10 Oct. 2021, https://www.sisterhelen.org/writing-to-someone-in-prison.

# PART 3. NEGOTIATING SELF
# AND COMMUNITY

This collection invites readers to encounter community listening praxes *in situ* not once, not twice, but three times across a decade of chapters. The opening section, Chapters 1–3, matches hauntings and possibilities—but not because they are opposites or at odds, although convention would have us see them that way. Instead, in relation to community listening, past and future are dynamic, balancing elements. They manifest in and in between explicitly demarcated spaces such as prisons; they are woven into the 1s and 0s that become activists' social media threads; they are interleaved into the ephemera that persist as permanent records through library archives and archivists. In the second section of this volume, which spans Chapters 4–6, contributors reflect on how community listening can, across media, operate as powerful bolsters or supports. Through murals, letters, and radio shows, practitioners of community listening forge and maintain the kinds of relations that help sustain disparate communities over time.

The third and final section of Community Listening casts in relief the complex dynamics of a familiar dyad: self and community. Another perceived binary, this compound term is complicated and thereby energized in Chapters 7–10 by examples of community listening that directly engage civics and politics. In one southcentral U.S. city, for example, community listening enables self-identified "red" and "blue" locals to co-construct a new and shared "community of dialogue" (Chapter 7). In the Midsouth, a multidisciplinary group of feminist scholars identifies lessons learned—about race and place and the possibility of social justice—through retrospective community listening (Chapter 8). In another southern university town, a white graduate student and transplant to the area forges "storied community listening" to reflect on her ongoing efforts to listen, really listen to the nuanced stories that comprise the place she has come to live (Chapter 9). Last, on a southeastern university campus, faculty and students gain something greater than training through their work with a community partner. Learning to take risks and be brave in new ways, they evolve and develop a community-engaged pedagogy of "daunting community listening"(Chapter 10).

Fittingly, all four chapters offer examples of community listening emplaced geographically in the southern U.S. While this extensive region contains cultural multitudes, it is home to shared legacies, hauntings, and glimmers of possibility that call for community listening. It is also fitting that contributors to the final chapters of this volume answer this call explicitly as academics—teachers, researchers, and campus administrators—as well as short- and long-term

153

Part 3

members of the communities where they work and live. As we observed at the outset of this volume, community listening is a set of relational praxes that emerge organically wherever people strive to understand one another. It is also a praxis that can be ethically studied, formally taught, and deliberately learned. The following chapters model exemplary ways of doing so.

CHAPTER 7.

# CIVIC COMMUNITY LISTENING: THE NEXUS OF STORYTELLING AND LISTENING WITHIN CIVIC COMMUNITIES

**Bailey M. Oliver-Blackburn, April Chatham-Carpenter, and Carol L. Thompson**
University of Arkansas, Little Rock

*Although research shows that listening is a key ingredient in building relationships within conflict situations, minimal research exists on how listening is used within civic communities of divergent groups. This ethnographic case study of a Braver Angels alliance, an organization that has successfully created community amid the American political divide, explores the community practices that have influenced their growth. The Braver Angels organization functions, in part, by teaching and practicing focused, empathic listening. The organization also encourages opportunities for individuals to explain how they developed their currently held views through narrative storytelling. Our study examines how such moments create greater understanding and acceptance across the political divide, in the context of community listening in civic communities. Our research holds the potential to locate practical ways individuals can build communities of dialogue across differences through storytelling and listening, which can be instituted in personal, professional, organizational, and political contexts.*

Political polarization has been growing in the United States and other democracies for some time (Carothers and O'Donahue 257), with "affective polarization" rising. This polarization has been illustrated by recent elections in the U.S., in which citizens have become more hostile to each other (Lyenger et al. 129). Citizens and organizations alike have begun to heed the call to help alleviate this polarization, including the Braver Angels organization.

As a non-profit with over 11,000 citizen members, the National Braver Angels organization attempts to provide opportunities for people to talk about

DOI: https://doi.org/10.37514/PER-B.2025.2531.2.07

and through their differences at both national and local levels. Because of the nature of this organization and its emphasis on what happens at the local level, the ensuing dialogue is typically not just about politics but also about relationships within their civic community. The founders of the non-profit and the volunteers that bring the mission to specific localities work to create place-based communities of people across political divisions, who respect and listen to each other. This chapter uses the work of one of the local chapters (termed "alliances") of this organization to demonstrate how interpersonal communication practices can be used in the public communication context when you bring divergent groups together to work and engage in thoughtful dialogue with each other. The key in these contexts is for the participants to learn to engage in "civic community listening," defined as listening that operates in a civic context in which individuals openly share their diverse perspectives and listen to others with the goal of understanding, as they work across their political differences.

Viewing the work of one local Braver Angels alliance, located in the South-Central region of the United States, we attempt to identify and illustrate specific communication practices found in civic community listening. In this chapter, we demonstrate how this type of communication can expand civic communities, by focusing on the discursive storytelling and listening practices used to build such a community.

## CASE CONTEXT

The local Braver Angels alliance of focus in this study started unofficially in August 2018, with an initial meeting of 11 people. The alliance's goals were initially to (a) establish and extend trust among their participants, (b) organize effective work to progress their mission, and (c) grow membership and impact.

In September 2018, the Braver Angels alliance hosted an initial Red-Blue workshop, one of the first workshops to be developed by Braver Angels. After that, they formed an official charter and created a leadership board for the alliance. One of the key criteria Braver Angels used for membership on the board was a balance between Red (conservative-leaning) and Blue (liberal-leaning) leaders, with approximately equal numbers of each. The Braver Angels alliance also distinguished between "voting members" and "members." "Members" are defined as anyone who has paid their $12 annual dues to the national organization. By contrast, "voting members" must have organized some type of workshop or event or contributed their time and efforts to the alliance in some other way. During the first 6–9 months of meetings, the original 11 group founders did most of the work. By 2024, the Alliance had grown to over 300 members and over 1900 subscribers, with approximately 75 members with voting privileges.

Along with regular meetings, the alliance hosts Braver Angel's standard workshops, in addition to locally-developed experiences, such as "Coffee and Conversations" and "How Ya' Doing" sessions, to keep people in touch with the alliance and each other. They also sponsor a Media Action Group, which works on creating action plans based on alliance discussions and input. The Braver Angels Alliance creates multiple structured and unstructured opportunities for community participants to build relationships across the political divide. These types of experiences allow members of the organization to have conversations in pairs, small groups, and large groups, sometimes all within the same meeting, depending on how the meeting is designed.

To gather information on this Braver Angels alliance, we, the authors of this chapter, attended and participated in various meetings and workshops offered by the alliance. In addition, we held semi-structured interviews with alliance leaders and members, following an Institutional Review Board (IRB) approved protocol,[1] and created field notes of our own experiences of participating. Across our fieldwork and interviews, our goal was to identify how community was built across the political divide within this alliance. Overall, our data consisted of seven interviews held virtually (totaling 6 hours and 47 minutes and 305 transcript pages) and field notes from nine workshops/meetings hosted by this alliance (totaling 86 pages of field notes). We then worked independently and in teams to code our data for practices that contributed to building community across the political divide and identified *empathic listening* and *narrative storytelling* as two factors that contributed to a sense of shared community across Braver Angels alliance members. Along with discussing the nature of communities, the following sections of our chapter will examine each of these in turn. Then, we highlight existing literature in these areas to demonstrate how both listening and storytelling practices can ultimately contribute to community listening taking place within politically divergent civic groups.

## FROM COMMUNITY LISTENING TO CIVIC COMMUNITY LISTENING

This study defines a community as "a group of individuals who share a mutual concern for one another's welfare" (Vogl 9). For individuals to truly feel they belong to a community, they need to feel like their voices and input are being heard. They often do this in "civic communities," or communities in which individuals work together to try and improve their communities, political institutions, and/or communication around some issue (Putnam). When a civic

---

1    IRB protocol number: # 21-020-R1

community, such as Braver Angels, fosters and encourages hearing individual voices, they can accomplish goals as a collective better. However, topics such as politics are often seen as inherently dichotomous, with the assumption that political affiliations represent a set of beliefs or values one must either support or flat-out reject. The same dichotomies can be applied to religion, lifestyle choices, or even child-rearing—the assumption is that you must either be for or against a cause or topic, and that choice will determine your community. This dichotomous assumption can make individuals wary of speaking up (avoid contributing their voice) or can foster unproductive dialogue where individuals are pitted against each other to argue who is right or wrong on a said topic (competing voices). Ultimately, this dichotomous assumption interferes with building a civic community across these differences, an obstacle the Braver Angel organization aims to overcome.

Community leaders of such groups, which include members with differing beliefs and value systems such as those found within Braver Angels alliances, are therefore tasked with figuring out how to make each individual feel heard and valued to accomplish these collective goals. One way to approach such a task is to engage in "community listening," which Jenn Fishman and Lauren Rosenberg argue involves, "deep, direct engagement with individuals and groups working to address urgent issues in everyday life, issues anchored by long histories and complicated by competing interpretations as well as clashing modes of expression" (1). Moreover, Fishman and Rosenberg argue community listening is more than simply paying attention during the listening process, and instead also includes

> awareness of, as well as responsibility for, being part of an evolving process [which] demands alertness to different inter-actions and openness to being changed by them . . . [creating] an element of risk to community listening because responding in an ethical and engaged way to others means being willing to change. (1)

The Braver Angels organization encourages community listening as their workshops and meetings place equal emphasis on individuals sharing their perspectives and listening to the viewpoints of others, to increase the likelihood of understanding each other and create change in their relational and group dynamics.

Indeed, when members of a group share stories and employ listening practices to actively engage with each other across their differences in the context of a community, they are participating in community listening. Put simply, storytelling and listening become an entrée or an invitation for others to enter their co-constructed community. As we share and listen in community, we willingly approach the community's world of hardship and pain, or accomplishment and joy. This type of communication can lead to change and to the building of what Bordone calls "conflict resilience," or "the ability to sit with and be fully present around those with whom we have fundamentally different views on critical issues" (70). Communities that encourage personal storytelling and teach listening practices are more likely to have members who feel valued and are less apprehensive to speak on controversial topics, typically viewed as dichotomous or intractable conflict issues.

Existing studies on community groups have noted the importance of incorporating structures for dialogue into communities, as members work to bridge their differences to create action and change. For example, Robert R. Stains, Jr. argues that in these types of settings, there is a "generous openness" from listeners to each other (3) and the power of such listening becomes clear as it occurs:

> Participating in a dialogue may be the first time someone has had a conversation with people of different identities that does not begin with making someone wrong because of who they are. . . . People who experience being seen more fully in terms of how they experience themselves in their identity apart from the limiting and often demeaning stereotypes attributed by others report feelings of liberation and connection. This experience opens their own curiosity to more complex stories and deeper feelings expressed by "the other." (Stains 3)

When applied in the civic community context, such as the one we studied in Braver Angels, one activity that appears to be successful for such purposes is to front-load a mini-experience that demonstrates and reinforces the power of the bridging organization's methodology and structure, before doing the organizational part of a meeting. The organization we studied aims towards having a conservative (Red)-liberal (Blue) balance in the facilitation of meetings, as well as breakout sessions, in "an attempt to get Reds and Blues talking back and forth and listening back and forth" (Participant Four; interview participants identified by assigned number only). They also detail and emphasize Braver Angel's ground rules early on in their meetings and hold people accountable for abiding by those ground rules throughout a workshop or meeting. Along with the ground rules, the meetings are also structured with a clear agenda, starting and ending times, and whole-group share-outs. There are often opportunities for smaller group discussions within breakout rooms or groups as well. Through their workshops and meetings, and the structures guiding them, the Braver Angels alliance of focus in this study utilizes storytelling and listening, as civic community listening practices, to build and sustain community across the political divide. They have found that experiencing the other (i.e., the opposing political affiliation) means that members sit with each other, amid their differences, and learn to understand each other in the context of their civic community.

## DISCURSIVE PRACTICES TO BUILD COMMUNITY

Community listening fosters the type of active engagement with and across differences to allow civic communities to be built. Discursive practices such as storytelling and listening can be used to both build and sustain such communities.

### STORYTELLING

Previous research has pointed to the benefits that emerge from storytelling, particularly regarding fostering a sense of community amongst groups (e.g., Andolina and Conklin; Lemmie et al.; Lohr and Lindenman). This research can be connected to what we observed in this civic community, in terms of its communication practices. Communication scholar Walter Fisher developed the narrative paradigm, a theory that describes how human beings use storytelling. Fisher believed storytelling was intrinsic to human nature, calling humans, *Homo Narrans,* or storytelling creatures. In the narrative paradigm, we see a "theory of symbolic actions, words and/or deeds that have sequence and meaning for those who live, create or interpret them" ("Narration" 2). For Fisher, narration is more than telling a story; it involves collective culture, history, and personal, corporate, and national stories that already exist and are already known. Telling stories thus is the way human beings co-construct our social worlds. It also becomes an optimal method for creating a civic community, one that holds oft-competing tensions of displaying care for its members while discussing political differences. This is done for the joint purpose of finding common ground across differences and building an even greater sense of community amid differences.

One research effort by scholar John Higgins illustrates themes Fisher revealed as he described the effects of disseminating stories of various groups from Cyprus in potential conflict on the island. The deeply personal stories provided an avenue that allowed workers to navigate tense situations in Cyprus by sharing personal stories of its people. Higgins described such storytelling as valuable in establishing a community (3). He devised a way for individual stories of the oppressed to be heard by other communities through media. Higgins emphasized that when people tell their stories, they become socially empowered. The story itself "encourages meaningful dialogue among participants" (3). Ultimately, Higgins determined that stories develop community by fostering interpersonal relationships, empowering the people who are telling the stories, creating understanding and empathy between those in the community, and constructing a fertile framework for deep listening that can build strong relational bonds within the civic community.

In our research, *storytelling* emerged as an optimal method for creating unity and empathy in the Braver Angels alliance, like what Kim Peters and Yoshihasa Kashima, as well as Joy Hackenbracht and Karen Gasper, found when they investigated the role of emotional self-disclosure in increasing persons' motivation for listening. Importantly, Braver Angels ground rules create a fruitful space for storytelling. The positive climate established in a Braver Angels meeting is conducive to open discussion as members are asked to listen when others are speaking, to respectfully acknowledge a contribution to the group, to probe with curiosity for more information, and to phrase their opinions in "I" messages. At one meeting, as they discussed mask-wearing amid the COVID-19 pandemic, the host explained to the group "I" messages vs. "You" messages as "explaining how you feel versus casting a wide stereotype net on others." At another point in the meeting, the host thanked a person for using "I" statements but said to focus on the current activity's emphasis on hope and asked the group to give suggestions for how to foster hope. These ground rules and their enforcement of them throughout alliance meetings/workshops foster a space more conducive to personal storytelling and the kind of empathic listening that may be invoked by such storytelling.

Indeed, Braver Angel's participants often come to organizational meetings already aware of the climate that surrounds the meeting. For example, Participant One, a Red leader in the Braver Angels alliance, said, "I think everyone who goes through those [Red-Blue workshops] has the same reaction, that it gives you a safe space to talk about how you see things and to speak about them and listen really to people with, you know, different views . . . based on the politics, you know, the political situation."

Such an environment carefully crafted by Braver Angels encourages people to participate, and to share those deeply held feelings, attitudes, and ideas, with the knowledge that what they say will be well received. Although not all participate at the same level, it was clear from our interviews and observations that some do and find relationships built to be richer as a result. One participant in a workshop sponsored by the alliance described one such moment, as she shared her own experiences that led to her views on abortion.

> An important moment for me was gaining the courage to give
> my comment on abortion, and then to hear [a Blue-leaning
> individual] say that he found the way I put it resonated with

> him. Part of me wanted to hold back, because it was the kind of statement that could alienate some viewers, especially from a Blue perspective. But, I felt drawn to say it, because it seems to me that if this project of honest civil engagement is really possible, then it should be possible for me to express my true thoughts on an issue that has primary importance to me in the realm of politics, despite it being a divisive and polarizing issue. And it was so encouraging, therefore, to see the comment well-received, and to see that it actually revealed something commonly valued. I felt a very real and good human interaction.

Allowing these types of values to be shared within the context of our experiences illustrates the need for the type of "sitting with" across our differences that Bordone calls for when noting how storytelling can help us understand each other and see each other as human beings deserving of respect (70). This type of storytelling, when accompanied by empathic listening, can lead to the building of individual relationships, as well as the trust and vulnerability needed to build a healthy civic community across political differences, prompting community participants to engage in meaningful dialogue where there had been no dialogue before.

Participant Two, a Blue Alliance member, discussed storytelling by explaining a Braver Angels podcast she heard where the moderator was interviewing two people from different sides of the political spectrum. She found it comfortable to hear the stories of why each person became "a Red" or "a Blue." She said that telling the story "is a more connecting way to know someone. I mean our human brains are designed to resonate with stories. You know, we had storytelling long before we had anything, any written word."

Typically, though, Braver Angels meetings involve thoughtful dialogue and respectful listening, which tends to create a receptive climate where people feel free to share their ideas openly, similar to what Molly W. Andolina and Hilary G. Conklin found, as well as Valerie Lemmie, Kathy Quick, and Brian N. Williams, in their work on building communities through dialogue and listening. In the community we studied in these meetings, the impetus to delve deeply into issues seemed to erupt spontaneously, at times, and other times it was unspoken. In one alliance meeting, for example, participants discussed the statewide power failure in their state during a severe winter storm. As temperatures plunged, their state power grid failed, leaving people without power, heat, cooking, appliances, and lights for several days.

This open discussion of an event directly affecting their local community eventually evolved into a structured activity later on in the meeting. That activity

# Civic Community Listening

required Reds and Blues to talk in small groups, with people from their color group, about the monumental power failure that gripped their state. In their intra-group discussions, each color group described the values each group held, their concerns about the issue, and finally, the policies that both Blues and Reds needed to address to both understand the situation and to offer suggestions to prepare for the future. The Blues reported their discussion first:

> We feel the public and private services in our state should be accountable for disasters like this, including agencies like the Railroad Commission and [a local electric reliability council]. The welfare of people should be of higher priority than profit. People's lives, wellbeing, and property were negatively affected. Fixing this will require weatherization, tracking, and using the best technology to avoid damage, and to investigate technology from other places like Canada to help us avoid freeze damage of solar and other power services.

Then the Reds summarized their discussion:

> We all want cost-effective, reliable power with a wide spectrum of sources for Energy. [Our citizens] like being independent, but being able to step in when needed. We need some regulation, but moving to excess regulation will cause problems. Yes, we are concerned about the human cost of these problems. We have to advance the perception of safety of nuclear power, winterize all electrical energy. Find storage facilities for natural gas and research new energy forms. Everyone should be accountable.

The discussion continued, both groups speaking forcefully from their particular perspectives as Reds and Blues. However, they had all collectively experienced the same power outage. Every single member of the group had suffered loss of electricity for days while the state and the responsible energy companies worked feverishly to solve the problem. In this telling and retelling of the suffering endured with biting cold, no heat, no food, no lights, a participant quietly brought up an example, that reached something decidedly human, an archetype so strong only the barest mention was enough to evoke a profound, albeit silent, response from everyone involved. It became, as theorist and philosopher Martin Buber might say, "a moment of meeting," and as Buber further emphasized, "all real living is meeting" (26). This is a moment of real living, of profound meeting where empathy was naturally present in the electricity of the moment. She said, "The cold was intense, biting, shivering cold. We ran out of food, we were

163

freezing, just, couldn't get warm." She paused, "and I heard a baby froze to death on my street."

Not much seems as devastating as a child who died because of lack of heat. Across cultures around the world, the image of the dead child is universally wrenching. In this community, in this meeting, the group fell silent for an interlude. No one spoke. Although diverse in their beliefs for how each political side should prevent a disaster like this in the future through policy, the telling of this story reminded them of their collective humanness, of how this topic extends beyond politics and can evoke silence from anyone no matter their affiliation. The moment showed how this topic was particularly important to them, their alliance and its members, and their surrounding community. In the silence, storytelling connected Reds and Blues and deepened the shared community of these participants, despite their affiliation; they were beginning to co-construct a positive sense of shared meaning. The discussion eventually resumed as the group of Reds and Blues wrestled with the immense problems of rectifying a system that had gone terribly wrong.

While Braver Angels participants often do rely on traditional forms of argument and logical reasoning, it is with the personal and rare moments of storytelling and resulting empathic listening that the group builds cohesion, continuity, understanding, and relationships. Storytelling is enhanced by Braver Angel's intentional structure for meetings and workshops, which foster a climate conducive to storytelling through established and enforced ground rules. In short, storytelling is accomplished through the organization teaching and practicing good listening skills as a hallmark of their process. In the next section, we review this key factor in storytelling as we explore how listening is encouraged and embedded in the Braver Angels alliance of focus.

## LISTENING PRACTICES

Throughout Braver Angel's workshops, the role and importance of listening are heavily emphasized, alongside storytelling, making it difficult at times to separate out the influences of listening and storytelling. We agree with the argument made by Chantal Bourgault du Coudray, that we need a more holistic approach to communication rather than just isolating listening out as a separate behavior. We found that civic community listening, as observed in the settings of this community, occurred in specific moments in workshops but also happened where there were multiple sequences of exchanges between individuals in a group, with time allotted for both parties to be listening and telling stories.

However, since there is a big emphasis placed in the training of this organization on listening, this section looks specifically at how listening was directly taught through instructions provided before and during workshop activities, as well as how listening was also emphasized indirectly to build community across political divisions as the organization encourages participants to listen to understand and listen to learn.

The Braver Angels organization makes a point to provide a clear definition for listening at the start of workshops and alliance meetings. Collectively across activities, the organization encourages participants to "listen to understand and find common ground," similar to work done by those in the democratic education world (e.g., Andolina and Conklin). This description is often provided when reminding alliance members or workshop participants of the mission of the Braver Angels organization. For example, before a mix of Reds and Blues went into breakout rooms on Zoom to discuss that week's political concerns during a weekly "Coffee and Conversations" meeting, a Braver Angels Red leader stated, "Remember we are seeking to listen to understand, not to argue . . . Our goal is not to convince the other or change opinion, but seek to find common ground." Similarly, a Red leader for a "How Ya' Doing" meeting clarified, "The mission is not to change political views, but be open to understand others and not rebut what they say or why they are wrong—to truly listen with empathy and in good faith."

Braver Angel's leaders also instruct on how to accomplish this definition of listening by providing clear ground rules for workshop activities, similar to suggestions given by others who lead community-led efforts (e.g., Lemmie et al.). For example, a Blue leader in a workshop observed instructed participants to "Put a hand in the air or wave if you feel like the other isn't giving you time to speak" and to remember that "If there are four of you in a room, you should be listening 75% of the time and talking 25%." Additionally, leaders and workshop facilitators are asked to encourage participants to listen with the intent to ask questions back for clarity, implying participants should focus not just on hearing another but being able to paraphrase their statements back to them to make sure their interpretation is accurate. Braver Angel's leaders are strategic in providing a clear definition for listening, and enacting and enforcing rules throughout activities to ensure this definition is practiced.

Such practices are at the core of this Braver Angels community's philosophy and workshop activities, as they encourage community members to engage together actively with and across their differences. In this context, like work done by Justin Lohr and Heather Lindenman, listening within their community looks like showing responsiveness and empathy towards others, with listeners trying to understand the speaker's own experiences without inserting their own biases.

When we are communicating with someone with whom we assume to have little in common, we often engage in closed listening, where we are focused on

165

our next rebuttal or defensive argument instead of attending to and actively listening to what our counterpart is saying. Listening behaviors, such as those identified by listening textbook authors Debra L. Worthington and Margaret E. Fitch-Hauser, are important to consider when identifying how to better build environments conducive to civic community listening. For example, learning the role of listening, the importance of sharing speaking time, listening to paraphrase and ask questions in return, and practicing these concepts throughout the workshop and meeting activities allows participants and alliance members to take a proactive instead of reactive stance in their communication with someone on the other side of the political divide. In short, listening to understand allows individuals to resist listening to refute, contest, or argue. Participant One, a Braver Angel's Red founder, put it simply:

> You can listen in different ways. You can listen to rebut and build up your arguments, so then when it's your time to speak, you go for it. Or you listen to really, sincerely understand or try to understand where that other person is coming from. . . . And that's what we emphasize hugely, and I think that's a distinguishing feature of what we do—listening to understand not listening to develop your counter arguments.

The Braver Angels organization not only encourages listening to understand in hopes of mitigating defensiveness and rebuttal, but their philosophy of listening, coupled with the various events and workshops, provides an opportunity to sit with others who are different from them. Many participants echoed that their fear or disgust of the other side hindered them from even reaching out to or having conversations with those who were politically different from them. For many, the Braver Angels workshops and meetings catalyzed to break this fear or lack of opportunity to talk with those of a different political affiliation. A workshop participant explained, "[The workshops] showed you could talk about serious questions or issues in a respectful listening space where people don't agree, but they respectfully share their perspective, and I think many people are really surprised that can happen." Similarly, Participant Three, a Blue alliance leader, reflected:

> [being part of this organization] has definitely given me a real understanding of how living in an insular, within-my-own-bubble way [has been] actually unhealthy and perpetuates stereotypes and makes it easy to create characterizations of people . . . I'm very Blue [and] went to [a] workshop, and was paired up with a woman who is Red and she was talking

Civic Community Listening

about being pro-life and, like, I have very strong opinions about that, but to hear her perspective about why she's pro-life, saying that it was because she's concerned about protecting the vulnerable and those who can't protect themselves . . . that just made total sense to me, you know, like it really was like an Aha moment of "like oh, she's not out to regulate a woman's body and tell them what to do, like she is really out to protect the vulnerable who don't have somebody you know working for them." I feel this way about many things too you know!

When we self-select to associate with one group versus another group, such as we do with political beliefs in the U.S., we often loathe to talk to those we consider to be on the "other side" about their opinions, afraid of entering intractable conflicts (Jenkins 38). This loathing or even fear of engaging in such discussion can hinder the conflict resilience Bordone mentioned. Bordone states:

When we sit in the presence of others with whom we may disagree strongly but with whom we can maintain civility and curiosity, we inevitably discover domains of shared interest and connection. And, even when we do not find these, we can often develop an appreciation for why our fellow citizens may hold the views they do. This "sitting with" does not solve an immediate problem; but it prevents the kind of demonization and othering that can escalate and cause new problems down the road while promoting humanization and connection. (70)

This sitting with and conversing with someone "on the other side" allows participants the opportunity to truly understand where someone with opposing views and beliefs is coming from and can have positive implications for their relationships. This outcome is impossible without understanding and encouragement, which comes from truly listening to another.

Through establishing ground rules for activities and defining listening to understand one another, participants at Braver Angel's workshops develop a working understanding of the role listening should take in dialogue related to politics or any other divisive, dichotomous, or intractable conflict topic. Moreover, members and workshop participants are provided the opportunity to practice listening throughout workshop activities and alliance meetings. As a result, participants can take this new knowledge and experience with them outside workshops to their everyday conversations with others who may be of an opposing political background or any other identifier. In essence, Braver Angels

167

participation also helps individuals grow and learn how to be better listeners as citizens. Participant Two, who identifies as a Blue, put it this way:

> These calls and Zooms give me an opportunity to practice, if nothing else, to listen [to a] different point of view. . . . I still get into polarizing behavior when I'm with my Blue friends. But I'm less comfortable with that now. And I make some effort to use some of my new tools.

In the end, participating in Braver Angels workshops and meetings allows individuals to learn (and practice) new habits and possibly break old ones. Through structured activities, grounding meetings with a clear definition for listening, and encouraging listening practices during activities, the Braver Angels organization is helping build more collaborative, less reactive communities of individuals, despite their differing political beliefs. However, it went beyond just the official meetings of the group where such civic community listening took place. It also took place in individual connections made with each other outside of the large group meetings.

## THE NEXUS OF STORYTELLING AND LISTENING WITHIN THE COMMUNITY

Combined together, an organization that encourages and allows its members to practice both storytelling and listening will likely build and sustain a strong community, with practices that are consistent with civic community listening. Charles H. Vogl identifies four features that are instrumental in building healthy communities: (a) shared values, (b) a clear membership identity, (c) moral prescriptions on how to treat others, and (d) an insider understanding of what the community is like (10). Community building is one of the goals of the Braver Angels organization nationally, as it is with the Braver Angels alliance of focus in this research. Braver Angel's work, centered around the building of relationships across differences, with the use of storytelling and listening practices, provides a good context for civic community listening to take place.

In community literacy practices, communities, such as the alliance we studied, often have to face "incredible differences in power, in perspectives, and in discourse styles" (Higgins et al. 11) when deciding how, as a community, they can work together. To understand how they do that, as Lorraine Higgins and her coauthors stated, we need to look at the "distinctive features of these discursive spaces, the discourses they circulate, and the literate practices that sustain them" (10). As we explored how the alliance did this at the local level, we found that they (a) created safe spaces for difficult conversations with the ground rules and structures they used in their meetings, (b) focused on understanding each other and finding common ground, and (c) built respectful relationships across the political divide by doing work together and building trust. These elements are discussed in turn below.

## SAFE SPACES CULTIVATED THROUGH GROUND RULES

One of the keys to the Braver Angels alliance enabling civic community listening to happen was to create safe spaces where people can talk honestly. As noted previously, this alliance does this by setting up structures within meetings and enforcing ground rules for civil discourse, both of which contribute to civic community listening and the willingness to share stories. One of the original Red co-founders of the alliance, Participant Four, said this about the ground rules: "We're here to only speak for ourselves, not represent others. Stick to the task at hand. Be respectful. Watch the nonverbal stuff." If a person violates these rules and is corrected, but is not willing to change, they will be uninvited to future meetings. As Participant Four put it, "The alliance members know we're going to enforce ground rules, and the new people see real demonstrations that we do that." Having these structures is necessary for creating safe spaces that allow people to have "difficult conversations on hard problems that are meaningful" and "minimizes emotional reactions" (Participant Four). The alliance leaders also acknowledged they must do this as well in their own conversations with people on both sides of the political aisle.

> It's to the point where when I see a Blue exhibiting what I know in my gut is bad behavior—they haven't thought through their position as well as I think that I could have, or if they are not doing a good job of listening—I just take a step back and start remembering the ground rules to talk to them. (Participant Five, Blue co-founder of alliance)

Participant Three added this about the leaders of the alliance: "They model good listening, and I think that that really helps everyone feel comfortable and understand how we're supposed to behave in that space."

## UNDERSTANDING CULTIVATED THROUGH COMMON GROUND

A second area that the interviewees noted was important for building a civic community was looking for common ground when interacting within the community of the alliance. The common ground was seen as something that could be used as "a prelude to action," according to Participant Four. Participant Four went on to acknowledge that there was a recognition that people come at things in different ways, and that "this is not a 'one side wins, and the other side loses' kind of thing; this is both sides agree that here's something, and it doesn't have to be in the middle." In the process of listening to understand and practicing "good habits of civic discourse . . . you're realizing shared values with people who will not agree on policy positions" [Participant Four]. Participant Six, a Red alliance member, explained: "I think people believe in the same thing and they see some virtue in civil discussion and working with others to reach some common ground rather than reiterating your own viewpoint over and over again." Braver Angel's members in this alliance were better posed to understand "the other side," once they were encouraged to seek and locate common ground throughout a workshop, meeting, or other organizational activities. The importance of seeking common ground was then instilled in their mindset throughout additional interactions with those within the alliance activities and beyond, further aiding in building community across the political divide.

## TRUST CULTIVATED THROUGH SHOWING RESPECT

Several interviewees also mentioned the importance of trust being built in the context of showing respect for each other in the types of safe spaces set up by the alliance as a third way of building community. Participant Four explained it this way:

> Our goal was to inspire trust, organize effective work, grow membership and impact. Up until now, I would say the work is doing workshops and other experiences that grow membership, and then by the experience of it all, we're building trust amongst the people in the community of the alliance.

This type of trust was often built by working side by side with another person in the alliance on activities. Two of the interviewees, who are on opposite sides of the political aisle, both acknowledged that they became good friends through such work. Participant Four stated:

> M and I didn't have a political discussion until after we had organized at least two Red-Blue workshops. We worked shoulder to shoulder on really difficult tasks, and we learned to trust and respect one another, and then we talked about politics.

Participant Five agreed:

> I think that's what builds the community, more than anything else is. We're not talking about politics necessarily. We're

> working to accomplish something. . . . I think that's what
> builds the trust you know, . . . it's working side by side to
> accomplish something.

Another aspect of building trust within relationships was the behaviors related to respecting one another. Participant Three said: "It is a lot about that respect, like he's always made me feel like I'm smart and I have things to offer and contribute, that I'm being heard." This interviewee, who came into the alliance later than the founding members, explained further: "The original founding members of [the alliance]—they just have so much respect for each other. They're different from each other, but because they have such mutual respect, it really helps everyone feel that same way." This type of respect and trust can lead to finding common ground with each other, across differences, as Participant Four stated:

> It's impossible to acquire enough knowledge to really be an
> expert on all these things so that you can have a true opinion
> of the right thing to do here. The only way to get to this is to
> have a variety of friends that are trusted, that come at these
> things in different ways. That will maximize the kind of com-
> mon ground, you can all agree to get something done. It's the
> trust factor that is driving this for me.

Our observations and interviews suggest that listening and storytelling play key roles in developing a positive civic community listening climate in the Braver Angels Alliance. Good listening, as we have shown, provides the foundation for the honesty and authentic communication we saw in the excerpts of storytelling that emerged in the meetings. Below we provide final thoughts about Braver Angel's success in terms of its communication practices.

## FINAL THOUGHTS

To communication scholars like us, it is no surprise that the efforts of Braver Angel's workshops work. The success of Braver Angels, though, particularly in this time when Americans are so highly divided, is noteworthy. As communication scholars, we see, in the development and execution of Braver Angels programs, an almost perfect model of an overarching theoretical perspective described by Pearce and Pearce, in the Coordinated Management of Meaning (CMM) theory. Those who designed the Braver Angels sequence of meetings probably did not consult a textbook on how to make a better social world. But still, we see in the organization an almost intuitive understanding of that process.

For example, an initial question many CMM theorists ask is, "What are we making with our communication?" Note that this question implies "making" and "creating"—we make something with our communication. The "we" implies everyone involved. This suggests that together, *we* make or co-construct something with our communication. As all of us communicate together, we are making, or co-constructing, something real. Some have called the U.S. political situation Americans have made in the last few years toxic. The call for an organization like Braver Angels came because people recoiled at a bubbling stew of dissension in political rhetoric, news commentary, and bitter arguments that pushed friends and even family apart.

The second question in the CMM sequence is "What do we want to make?" Here the originators of Braver Angels sought a world where civic community listening could take place across our political disagreements—where people could learn to sit with each other and be fully present while hearing the experiences and stories that have led them to their views on issues, where equal emphasis is placed on individuals sharing stories and listening to understand, and where relationships are built which lead to joint action.

The last question of the CMM sequence is "What kind of communication will get us to where we want to be?" This is where Braver Angels shines. The founders of the group focused on elements of something as simple and yet seemingly out of reach as good, reflective, empathic listening. They trusted that if individuals have an audience where they can tell their stories and share their opinions and thoughts about issues important to them in respectful ways across multiple venues, they may be able to effect real change. Threads of storytelling naturally erupted from the moments of authentic listening that grew in the groups and various meetings. It was storytelling, described in this chapter as defined by Walter Fisher, that provided the glue that connected one human being to another and ultimately created a community where listening became the norm rather than the exception.

The U.S. is currently experiencing an uncommon degree of political polarization. Some writers even argue that the U.S. is more divided now than it has been at any time in its history, except for the years before the Civil War. The barrage of telltale propaganda flooding the news channels, radio stations, newspaper outlets, social media platforms, and even among individuals and families, testifies to the turmoil roiling just under the surface in American politics. This makes it imperative that we discover ways to ease the barriers separating polarized groups in the U.S. The research into this Braver Angels alliance offers insight into how one local organization has used communication practices to diminish the prickly distance between political camps and create a civic context in which community listening could take place. The listening and storytelling that is taking place within this group demonstrates that civic community listening opens other conversations and opportunities for relationships, from which civic community work can take place, as members work together in their local communities. It is clear from our research that it is possible for "interpersonal dialogic communication" to be "scaled up for public communication contexts" (du Coudray 38).

The guiding principles we observed included establishing a climate of authentic listening which fostered, above all, an accepting environment for stories to be told. In this positive setting, participants were poised to listen respectfully to thoughts, attitudes, and opinions shared by alliance members and nonmembers without interruption and judgment. Authentic storytelling emerged from that openness. The leadership for each of the meetings encouraged civic community listening through the speaking and listening practices employed.

This study shows that community listening is often not accomplished within a singular event or activity, but instead is most likely cultivated across multiple interactions and activities. Many participants felt open to sharing stories and were more apt to listen actively and without judgment after they had built relationships with other members and attendees across multiple events, workshops, or meetings. These repeated interactions and events, all of which included leaders who encouraged community listening through establishing ground rules, seeking common ground, and building trust, culminating in a community that felt safe in discussing political topics that are often seen as inherently dichotomous.

As such, we note that the success of Braver Angels depends on its attention to communication skills, particularly listening and storytelling, which encompass the whole of civic community listening happening within the organization. The snippets of storytelling that emerge when people explain their feelings and ideas about events and issues put a human face on alternate ways of viewing the same reality, lending diverse opinions and individual texture and richness that calls for thoughtful attention. Plus, storytelling encourages individuals to share reasons behind their thinking through story form. The personal story has the added value of helping people to understand a worldview that is different from their own. Combining these efforts with establishing firm ground rules for respectful communication, creating "safe places," and continually seeking common ground, inch members forward toward creating true community, and they serve as examples for other communities who are attempting to bridge differences using civic community listening.

Braver Angels illustrates what communication practices can bring people together in this fraught political environment. They have an enthusiastic membership, a membership that respects the views of others, although they may not share those views. What makes this membership unique is that each person is accorded their time in the process to detail the arguments, reasoning, and personal experiences that bring unique perspectives to the group. If we could suggest anything to enhance how Braver Angels works, it would be for the organization to find ways to integrate more storytelling into workshops and meetings, as well as to include more diverse stories from people of differing backgrounds. As we have mentioned here, many benefits grow from the stories people tell, especially by putting a human face to those people whose thinking may be so different from our own, something even more important to members of marginalized groups who may be misunderstood, misinterpreted, or systemically misrepresented on a national level. In a real sense, storytelling allows us to sit with, truly listen, and embrace those who are different, which may be the point, after all.

Braver Angels proves that solid and careful attention to listening works because it enables honest talk and storytelling. Encouraging the hearing of all voices in the group, as they both teach and practice listening skills, works to build relationships. Respecting all contributions to the discourse works to build their civic community. Our study found that it is possible to create deliberative moments while engaging in politically polarized discussions in local civic communities, by participating in discursive practices such as "a reason-giving exchange marked by disagreement, stance indicators of listening and respect, and inclusive discourse" (Sprain and Black 8). These types of practices foster perspective-taking of the other side, which Muradova notes is necessary for creating understanding within citizen deliberations (648).

This study of a specific alliance of the Braver Angels organization and the practices that foster the building of community within it provides more information on how this work can be done within such an organization, where the goal is to build relationships and community. We believe that encouraging more groups with similar aims to follow these principles might begin to make some small difference in our public discourse universally, regarding politics and beyond.

## WORKS CITED

Andolina, Molly W., and Hilary G. Conklin. "Cultivating Empathic Listening in Democratic Education." *Theory & Research in Social Education*, vol. 49, no. 3, 2021, pp. 390–417.

Bordone, Robert C. "Building Conflict Resilience: It's Not Just About Problem-Solving." *Journal of Dispute Resolution,* vol. 2018, no. 1, 2018, pp. 65–74.

Buber, Martin. *I and Thou.* Scribner. 1986. (Original work published 1958).

Carothers, Thomas, and Andrew O'Donohue. "Comparative Experiences and Insights." *Democracies Divided: The Global Challenge of Political Polarization*, edited by Thomas Carothers and Andrew O'Donohue, Brookings Institution, 2019, pp. 257–286.

du Coudray, Chantal Bourgault. "Listening as a Relational and Experientialist Praxis: Insights from Gestalt Therapy." *International Journal of Listening*, vol. 36, no. 1, 2022, pp. 31–43.

Fisher, Walter A. "Narration as a Human Communication Paradigm: The Case of Public Moral Argument." *Communication Monographs*, vol. 51, no. 1, 1984, pp. 1–22, 1984.

———. *Human Communication as Narration: Toward a Philosophy of Reason, Value, and Action*. U of South Carolina P, 2018.

Fishman, Jenn, and Lauren Rosenberg. "Guest Editors' Introduction: Community Writing, Community Listening." *Community Writing, Community Listening*, special issue of *Community Literacy Journal*, vol. 13, no. 1, 2018, pp. 1–6, https://doi.org /10.25148/clj.13.1.009085.

Hackenbracht, Joy, and Karen Gasper. "I'm All Ears: The Need to Belong Motivates Listening to Emotional Disclosure." *Journal of Experimental Social Psychology*, vol. 49, no. 5, 2013, pp. 915–921.

Higgins, John, W. "Peace Building Through Listening, Digital Storytelling and Community Media in Cyprus. *Global Media Journal*, vol. 6, no. 1, 2011, pp. 1–13.

Higgins, Lorraine, Elenore Long, and Linda Flowers. "Community Literacy: A Rhetorical Model for Personal and Public Inquiry." *Community Literacy Journal*, vol. 1, no. 1, 2006, pp. 1–43.

Jenkins, Alan. "Understanding and Managing Intractable Conflicts: A Critical Assessment of the 'System Dynamics' Approach." *Négociations*, vol. 29, no. 1, 2018, pp. 39–58.

Lemmie, Valerie, Kathy Quick, and Brian N. Williams. "Community-Led Efforts to Create Safe Communities: Diversity, Dialogues, and Directions for Moving Forward." *National Civic Review*, vol. 110, no. 1, 2021, pp. 6–15.

Lohr, Justin, and Heather Lindenman. "Challenging Audiences to Listen: The Performance of Self-Disclosure in Community Writing Projects." Fishman and Rosenberg, pp. 71–86, https://doi.org/10.25148/clj.13.1.009091.

Muradova, Lala. "Seeing the Other side? Perspective-Taking and Reflective Political Judgements in Interpersonal Deliberation." *Political Studies*, vol. 1, no. 21, 2020.

Pearce, Walter, and Kim Pearce. "Extending the Theory of Coordinated Management of Meaning (CMM) through a Community Dialogue process." *Communication Theory*, vol. 10, no. 4, 2006, pp. 405–42.

Peters, Kim, and Yoshihasa Kashima. "From Social Talk to Social Action: Shaping the Social Triad with Emotion Sharing." *Journal of Personality and Social Psychology*, vol. 93, no. 5, 2007, pp. 780–797.

Putnam, Robert. *Making Democracy Work: Civic Traditions in Modern Italy*. Princeton UP, 1993.

Sprain, Leah, and Laura Black. "Deliberative Moments: Understanding Deliberation as an International Accomplishment." *Western Journal of Communication*, vol. 82, no. 3, 2017, pp. 336–355.

Stains, Robert R. Jr. "Repairing the Breach: The Power of Dialogue to Heal Relationships and Communities." *Journal of Public Deliberation*, vol. 10, no. 1, 2014, pp. 1–5.

Vogl, Charles H. *The Art of Community: Seven Principles for Belonging*. Berrett-Koehler Publications, 2016.

Worthington, Debra L., and Margaret E. Fitch-Hauser. *Listening: Processes, Functions, and Competency* (2nd ed.). Routledge, 2018.

CHAPTER 8.

# COMMUNITY LISTENING IN, WITH, AND AGAINST WHITENESS AT A PWI

**Mary P. Sheridan, Cate Fosl, Kelly Kinahan, Carrie Mott, Angela Storey, and Shelley Thomas**
University of Louisville

*In this chapter, a cross-disciplinary group of white women colleagues reflect on their experiences facilitating campus-based antiracist reading circles. They use community listening as a lens for looking both critically and compassionately at their efforts to hold themselves and their PWI accountable for addressing structural racism.*

## SETTING THE SCENE, MARY P. SHERIDAN

In 2020, just prior to the world learning Breonna Taylor's name, I joined the Anne Braden Institute (ABI) as a Faculty Research Fellow, and later that year I was named Acting Assistant Director. As a resource for racial and social justice education and action within the University of Louisville (UofL), the ABI partners with the surrounding Louisville community on a broad range of initiatives (e.g., Civil Rights, LGBTQ History, Affordable Housing). The ABI also responds to longstanding calls for white people to educate ourselves and other whites about our complicity in white supremacy (cf. Lorde; Braden) through hosting Self-Guided Tours of Louisville's Civil Rights History and co-sponsoring Showing Up for Racial Justice organizing events.

As both a Fellow and an Acting Assistant Director, I drew upon my previous research into providing more equitable educational opportunities ("What Matters") and my knowledge of community-engaged infrastructure (Mathis et al.) to identify ways the Institute could provide opportunities for colleagues at our Predominantly White Institution (PWI) to hear and redress wide-spread, normed discriminatory practices, and in turn, facilitate larger structural changes at and beyond UofL. As a feminist scholar looking around our PWI, I noted with concern that it was frequently untenured women faculty who visibly participated in and often led unpaid antiracist labor, including the ABI reading circles that each

DOI: https://doi.org/10.37514/PER-B.2025.2531.2.08        177 of the contributors to this chapter led; at a hierarchical, male-dominated Research 1 like UofL, such service is time-consuming and professionally risky.[1] Considering how I might support the people doing this antiracist work given my institutional positionality, I suggested to the women facilitating these reading circles that we write about our experiences to make this work institutionally rewarded. Although we come from different academic disciplines, campus roles, and ranks, we are all white women seeking to move our PWI in antiracist directions. By retrospectively reflecting upon,[2] and then collaboratively theorizing our antiracist practices, I thought we could bridge the gap between service and scholarship, and we could contribute a cross-disciplinary resource for others involved in similar projects.

To jump-start our thinking, I proposed community listening methodologies to guide us. To me, community listening is a practice of defamiliarization meant to expose majoritarian biases (including our own) and to foreground community knowledge. Consequently, I introduced the concept of community listening as an attempt to ethically engage in justice-oriented research by attending and attuning to community stories, stories that language our and others' experiences, most especially of marginalized people. Among community listening's growing research tradition (Concannon and Foster; Fishman and Rosenberg; García; Rowan and Cavallaro), the informing theories that I both draw upon and question are from disciplinary scholarship related to "listening," such as feminist rhetorical listening, queer rhetorical listening, and critical race methodologies, as well as disciplinary conversations about "community." Below, I more fully articulate my community listening framework that was then taken up in distinct, often transdisciplinary ways, as evident in each facilitator's reflection.

My deepest understandings of what I'm calling listening frameworks come from feminist rhetorical traditions which, like the other traditions I explore, embrace listening as a methodology for valuing the perspectives of excluded groups, often through speculative moves that attend to muted and/or ignored voices and to the power-laden logics that construct and challenge those absences (Royster). Such listening helps people imagine other hearings, validate other

---

1  For more on the "gendered biases in the visibility and value of faculty service" (85), see Lisa K. Hanasono et al. I do not know why white women, often untenured, may be taking this risk, but I imagine several reasons, which may be shared by others at PWIs. One reason is that our colleagues of color are already spread too thin engaging in what Carmen Kynard calls "the hustle," or the constant, generally uncompensated microlabor of navigating universities, such as being on too many committees or educating white peers about individual and structural racism. Another reason is a shared conviction that institutional racism perpetrated by white people should be addressed by white people. A third reason, as told to me by people in this demographic, is their belief that if they didn't do this antiracist work, it would not happen.

2  I was struck by things I missed during the reading circles themselves, an example of what Schon might describe as the benefit of reflection on action as opposed to reflection in action.

voices, and critique normed practices of exclusion (Monberg; Powell). Often linked to Krista Ratcliffe[3], feminist rhetorical listening focuses on stories to understand how people make sense of the world. That understanding includes many steps, such as being accountable for one's stories and the world these stories create, in part by standing under (and interrogating) the cultural logics that make a story meaningful in different ways for different people and groups. Despite important critiques about its unacknowledged white privilege,[4] Ratcliffe's feminist rhetorical listening has proven a foundational concept both to help people recognize dominant cultural logics and to hear alternatives.

As white women hoping to do antiracist work at a PWI, we, like Ratcliffe, encouraged the sharing of personal stories about experiences that many of us recognized in our daily lives. Such efforts helped us build rapport with one another while we prepared to stand under the cultural logic of the stories we shared in our reading circles, a move that included our attempts to be accountable for who is privileged and who is muted. Cultural logic is the often-invisible warrants that make sense of how our everyday operates, in this case how privilege becomes normed. Because this concept resonated across our disciplinary training, cultural logic became something we listened for and tried to excavate with others in the stories we heard. In this way, discussing cultural logics helped us connect seemingly disparate events, such as the way minoritized groups are silenced in a classroom, dismissed in a faculty exchange, and made to feel unwelcome in certain academic and city spaces.

While less prevalent in my theorizing, my understanding of community listening was also informed by queer rhetorical listening. Taking a stance of critical generosity towards Ratcliffe's rhetorical listening,[5] Timothy Oleksiak states

---

3    I relied most heavily on Ratcliffe's foundational work, which has deepened and evolved. For her more recent thinking, see her collaboratively authored book with Kyle Jensen, *Rhetorical Listening in Action: A Concept-Tactic Approach*, a book that came out after this chapter was drafted.

4    Two challenges to Ratcliffe's foundational work seem relevant to this article. The primary challenge is that Ratcliffe's eavesdropping can be "akin to colonial gazing" (García, 13) in that white people may believe they can step outside of their own power and privilege as they eavesdrop on, and think they understand, minoritized storytellers. This mis-identification was something facilitators discussed as a concern, and sought to counter. A second challenge is the danger of overemphasizing rhetorical listening in relation to white/Black examples (Jackson with deLaune). Because reading circle members were white, and because these reading circles emerged out of the white police killing of unarmed black people nationwide and especially in our city, the circles did privilege counterstories based in white/black relations. Even so, facilitators addressed intersectional issues, including from their own research specializations with other minoritized groups (e.g., LGBTQ histories of erasure and repression; violence against people from the Yakama nation).

5    See *Peitho's* special issue on queer listening, perhaps especially the introduction which offers more recent sources that more fully detail this concept.

that queer rhetorical listening uses the insights of queer theory to challenge the cisgender assumptions in Ratcliffe's early constructions ("Queer Rhetorical Listening"). Like feminist rhetorical listening, queer rhetorical listening examines unacknowledged legacies of privilege that may exclude minoritized voices and therefore compromise our ability to hear and, ultimately, create more just systems. In addition, queer rhetorical listening foregrounds (among other things) a more expansive intersectional frame, and a more extensive focus on the possibilities of utopic worldmaking. Invoking José Esteban Muñoz's concept of worldmaking, queer rhetorical listening calls on people to examine imagined pasts and to posit not-yet-realized futures as ways to inform our longing to create a better present (cf. Oleksiak, "A Queer Praxis"). Both imagining and longing function as catalysts for current action as people work to build those futures. That action calls us to attend to institutional power dynamics that, as Rachel Lewis describes, "underpin" how cultural logics shape interpersonal relationships (who is included and excluded), an idea ABI reading circle members took up (see below).

Queer rhetorical listening informed facilitators' reflections on the reading circles as well as how I thought about them: in both cases, we aimed to hear intersectional histories that shaped our present and to collectively imagine better, more antiracist futures within and beyond our institutional context. In our reading circles, Muñoz's idea of temporal cruising helped us listen for moments of possibilities for antiracist practices, as when a group member discussed the various forms of police interactions she witnessed based on where she lived. Her description of looking out her home's window to see a phalanx of police at what seemed a surprising spot prompted us to look more closely at Louisville's redlining histories and the institutions that supported this practice. Seeing the tight correlations between historic redlining areas and current policing practices exposed who has rights to what types of space and protection—an issue important for many groups, though in this case an issue that highlights how those working for an antiracist present must listen to the systematic, institutional legacies that anchor the present in place (see Carrie Mott's reflection) if we are to imagine a better future.

In addition to listening research, my understanding of community listening is informed by Critical Race Methodologies (CRM), specifically the concept of counterstory which exposes, denaturalizes, and challenges majoritarian stock stories that have erased or distorted the experiences of minoritized people. Like rhetorical listening, CRM privileges stories. As Carmen Kynard notes, we have plenty of evidence, data, and reporting on racism and its consequences. Instead of more data, Kynard, drawing on Black feminist traditions, calls for more radical stories to imagine alternatives committed to decolonization through action. Such stories emerge out of, validate, and make central the experiences and knowledges of people of color. This is similar to what Aja Y. Martinez calls counterstories, which "are critical to understanding racism that is often well disguised in the rhetoric of normalized structural values and practices" (3). As both methods and methodologies—the tools and the theoretical work of destabilizing and re-writing dominant narratives that warp or occlude minoritized groups' ways of knowing and being—counterstories can take many forms, but they share two core tenants: "eliminating racism, sexism, and poverty, and empowering subordinated minority groups" through the telling of stories about their/participant lived experiences against the widely circulating majoritarian narratives (Martinez 17).

Despite the importance of CRM on my thinking, collectively our reading circles were not at the point of imagining and acting on stories that could radically overthrow university and city practices. Instead, our circles, which were almost exclusively white, were engaged in what might best be described as the "work before the work" (Rowan and Cavallaro), which might subsequently lead to such action. As part of this preparatory work, reading circle facilitators encouraged members to challenge majoritarian narratives by, for example, providing non-majoritarian news coverage about daily protests for Breonna Taylor or about hate groups' activity on campus (see Cate Fosl's reflection); or, by encouraging reading circle members to use their own stories to interrogate majoritarian takes on our city's histories, present and possible futures in regard to housing and education. Such practices helped participants recognize the unacknowledged, intertwining, habituated practices that privilege whiteness and encouraged participants both to challenge dominant views and to imagine counterfactual possibilities, such as, what if black neighborhoods had not been decimated by the building of highways? Or, what might our city look like if people of color had not faced redlining?

Within my uptake of community listening frameworks, I wrestle with at least two major limits of our experience, both of which I imagine might be concerns for others seeking to foster antiracist projects at PWIs. My first concern is about whose voices are absent. The most notable missing voices come from people of color. Given that reading group facilitators were white, as were, in the end, all group members, I am reminded of Romeo García's caution: "Stories reflect the places and positionalities of storytellers, and so many academic stories are the stories white folks tell each other, stories that echo traditions of savior or progress narratives" (12). Standing under the "sticky" (Ahmed) cultural logics of white privilege, I am forced to reckon with this absence, to acknowledge how our whiteness, even if experienced differently (due to professional status, gender, sexuality, ability, economic security, etc.), is a defining characteristic of our reading circles. Another significant set of missing voices includes those from white participants who dropped out along the way. This group offered plausible reasons why they stopped coming: people were stretched too thin; the meeting

Sheridan, Fosl, Kinahan, Mott, Storey, and Thomas

time conflicted with other job responsibilities that semester; some got COVID-19. Even so, I speculate that these stories are incomplete, and believe this incompleteness is connected to the emotional toll it takes to be open enough to listen in ways that don't recycle "white stories," which "have the potential for merely reproducing hegemonic belief rather than critiquing them" (Lundstrom, qtd in Kurtyka). These concerns highlight the balance we faced in simultaneously pushing and supporting colleagues to engage in antiracist work. At times, I wonder if people left because we called too quickly for participants to recognize and own our white privilege, as well as the cultural logics and institutional power dynamics that support this privilege (cf. Lewis); perhaps we needed more preparation to support reading group members in this process (see Shelley Thomas's reflection). At other times, I wonder if some people stayed because we didn't push hard enough. Did our fear that participants would leave if we too forcefully confronted their participation in racist policies and actions, what Robin J. DiAngelo would call "white fragility," prevent us from challenging the "white stories" of the participants who stayed (see Kelly Kinahan's reflection)? While there is no one right way to interact with reading group members, the many absent voices that haunt facilitators' reflections amplify the difficulty of supporting antiracist groups, perhaps especially in PWIs, who are attempting to do the antiracist work that community listening compels us to do.

The second limitation of our experiences as viewed through community listening frameworks addresses long-standing concerns about the term community.[6] I found the ABI reading circles, and to a lesser extent, the facilitator group, to be community-ish.[7] Unlike deeply rooted identifications that endure even when local conditions change, the reading circles emerged from a workplace sponsor that provided a temporary space to process the fault lines highlighted that fraught

---

6    Beyond disciplinary concerns (cf. Bizzell; Prior), community literacy scholars from this subdiscipline's inception have questioned what community means, asking how to build reciprocal, community-based projects on university timelines and workloads (cf. Restaino and Cella) where students and faculty are prepared to listen to and engage with local communities (cf. Mathieu), in part by dislodging university privilege to hear community voices (cf. Flower). Such work challenges halcyon views of "community," noting instead the messy, tactical work—often at odds with university structures—needed to build what might be considered reciprocal, equitable communities.

7    Elsewhere I have written about what I consider a more nuanced term to get at these notions of community, what in that context I call "knot-working collaborations" or institutionally sponsored activities that gather or braid people together for a time, based on a set project. Following Yrjo Engeström, Ritva Engeström, and Tiia Vähäaho, I argue that these people come together with their own histories and agendas for a shared project. When the project is over, they disperse, bringing what they have learned to new groups ("Knot-Working Collaborations"). Given that this term is not prevalent in our field, I follow this collection's core term, community listening, but highlight this complication.

summer. This does not devalue these reading circles. Although this process felt important to participants' understandings of themselves, and although the circles had an intensity, even an intimacy at times, these circles were fleeting by design, a characteristic common for many community-ish groups. We gathered initially as ad hoc groups of people living through daily protests for racial justice that energized and polarized our city, sharing traumatic, ongoing moments of long overdue racial reckoning that turned our city and our university upside down. We identified as UofL faculty and staff, younger and older, with differing status and from different parts of campus and different parts of the city. Some of us marched regularly throughout the summer chanting Breonna Taylor's name, while some stayed home due to rising COVID-19 infection rates, the police presence, or any number of other reasons. With diverse goals and histories, we shared this time and place, bearing witness to extremes of militarized vehicles, boarded-up buildings, concrete barricades, police snipers on rooftops, and helicopter patrols alongside silent vigils, memorials with ever-expanding collections of candles, artwork, poems, and mementos; and balloon-filled birthday parties as well as communal prayer services. Polarization marked not just downtown's "Injustice Square" but conversations with friends and acquaintances, colleagues, and students. Seeking to make sense of this intensity, we supported each other and ourselves, as collectively and individually, we prepared to support UofL students, staff, and faculty reeling from the wounds that the summer protests exposed. We located ourselves within and outside of our workplace and, for a time, convened, as García might say, to imagine "friction" within the hegemonic flows of racist stories, including those in higher education. Then, we went our separate ways. This, to me, feels community-ish.

Despite these limitations, community listening methodologies retrospectively proved helpful in this community-ish context for unpacking how our PWI both helps and hinders our ability to address individual and structural racism in our workplace. On the one hand, our academic sponsor brought us together, providing institutional space and tools for us to re-hear "the set of stories we tell ourselves, the stories that tell us, the stories others tell about us" (Rohrer 189, cited in García). Examining our stories about antiracist proclamations, faculty and staff reading circles, task force recommendations, and facially neutral but discriminatory policies, we came to better understand how the stickiness of white privilege is materially expressed in individual and institutional lives. On the other hand, these stories also make clear how academic structures play a large role in who and what have been excluded by keeping whiteness the norm and supporting white supremacy logics that erase and/or reframe other cultural logics (cf. Jackson with DeLaune). Community listening frameworks helped us attend to the jumble of competing institutional logics and the lived consequences of these logics, and they challenged us to hold ourselves accountable for recalibrating our relationship with our institution, a PWI that simultaneously attempts to create spaces to eradicate racist practices within its ranks and continues deeply embedded racist practices (see reflections by Kelly Kinahan and Angela Storey).

The reading circles, I argue, used the community listening practices with uneven effectiveness to hear non-majoritarian cultural logics within individuals and institutions, cruise their histories, and imagine better futures, all with the goal of thinking about what actions participants could take now and in the future. Through retrospective, sustained reflection, facilitators used these methodologies to better understand their well-intentioned efforts to help reading circle members both think about conditions of knowing and to act on this knowledge as they engaged in antiracist action at and beyond our PWI. This fuller uptake of community listening frameworks reinforces the value of listening to our own stories, others' stories, and the hauntings these bring on individual, community, and institutional levels. Structured reflection helps us rethink experiences we had not anticipated or even fully understood at the time and offers cautions about how thoroughly unacknowledged white privilege infuses antiracist work in PWIs, as the following reflections make clear.

## REFLECTIONS

### Building on a White Antiracist Legacy, Cate Fosl

I came to this project as ABI director and biographer of Anne Braden, a Louisvillian activist-journalist who was among the most dedicated white antiracists in U.S. history. Braden's emphasis over nearly six decades of activism was always on making visible the centrality of white supremacy in U.S. society and particularly on convincing whites of our responsibility to act against racism.

Like any biographer, I believe fiercely in the power of story as a way to connect, educate, and ideally move people to act. Even before I co-founded ABI in 2006, I often recounted Braden's powerful and unconventional life story as a counter-narrative—a way to prompt more whites to recognize our complicity in keeping racism alive and well (Fosl). Urging white listeners to undertake this early (or pre-) step toward accountability has proven far easier than getting people to act on those insights, however. The result is a two-pronged tension that, while not new in my experience of white antiracist educational work, ran all through the reading circle project discussed here. First, how can we speak to, support, and recruit more whites to take action for racial justice and not simply talk about it or listen to Black, Indigenous, and people of color (BIPOC) speakers and then return to "business as usual"? Second, how can we invest in such work without, again, redirecting resources away from BIPOC initiatives and people?

Braden often said that to undo white supremacy, we don't need the support of all whites, but we do need more—what she called a critical mass. Amid the mid-2020 COVID-19/racism pandemics and our university's stated commitment to becoming an antiracist campus, working with the accelerating number of white faculty and staff confronting institutional racism seemed an obvious imperative for the ABI, if it were to remain true to its namesake.

The small-group virtual reading circles evolved in this context. Responding to Critical Race Theory's critiques of how institutional spaces reflect majoritarian views, Angela Storey and I heightened our accountability as white antiracist facilitators by planning the circles in consultation with leaders of the Black Faculty and Staff Association (BFSA). BFSA co-chairs endorsed the value of involving more whites in campus antiracist initiatives even as they emphasized that it was painful for BIPOC colleagues to have to constantly experience whites' verbal wranglings with our own racism. Consequently, our email invitation to the wider university community identified the circles as open to all but designed to "examine white supremacy and white privilege and provide a framework for taking action against them, both individually and institutionally." It was no surprise when mostly whites responded.

One lesson in accountability to an antiracist agenda that emerged from the reading circles was a fuller acknowledgment of both the preparation and move to action that are needed in this work. As Gwen Aviles and others argue in an initial piece we read, antiracist reading is not sufficient as a tool of resistance, but it may be necessary as a corrective first step to the mis-education that most whites receive, which often carries with it in an unwillingness to betray or even recognize white privilege.

Had we five facilitators been aware of the methodologies of community listening, particularly Karen Rowan and Alexandra J. Cavallaro's ideas on the "work before the work" when we planned the circles, such knowledge would have provided a useful orienting framework. That concept is precisely what the circles amounted to. They provided spaces for predominantly white members to re-examine long-playing racial soundtracks, some for the first time, and they gave us new outlets through which we could act on that awareness. Thinking of the circles as a kind of groundwork helped me to clarify their purpose, and I introduced Rowan and Cavallaro's phrase to my group as soon as I heard it.

It was frustrating that our hoped-for collective action across circles did not materialize by the time we concluded the project after the fall term. Yet small victories matter, which is another lesson in accountability exemplified in Anne Braden's "keeping on keeping on" through half a century of unbroken activism.

185

While the reading circles did require some limited resources, they did quick work, and within a relatively short time frame, they made a modest start at the project of enlisting new white antiracists. When the Patriot Front, a violent white nationalist organization, descended on the campus in January 2021, several groups (including the ABI) successfully partnered to offer a workshop— aimed at white students, staff, and faculty—on how to respond, and many from the reading circles participated. Some reading group members also became active in forming a campus chapter of Louisville Showing Up for Justice (LSURJ).[8]

Had we persisted longer than several months—thereby devoting additional resources to them—the reading circles likely would have generated more substantive action. As it was, the circles motivated about 50 employees to educate ourselves more about racism, both personally and in the structures around us. As importantly, perhaps, the project prompted us five co-facilitators to remain accountable to one another and to the process through regular debriefings and a shared online document in which we each reflected on how each session went and shared insights and resources some of us had found useful in our respective sessions. In these ways, we five moved toward greater accountability through growing an inventory of antiracist resources for future use, affirmation of our respective commitments, and new forms of collective action beyond the circles.

The reading circle project underscores that in addition to sharing stories, our own or others', collectively and individually, whites need multiple recurring and ongoing stimuli and opportunities to motivate them (us) to act in the kind of numbers that will undermine the structures of white supremacy. This is especially true, perhaps, to strengthen accountability on a PWI, where the cultural logic of whiteness is too often an easy out.

## Considering Our Spaces, Carrie Mott

Everyone experiences space in unique ways. We're all caught in the intersections of who we are and the contexts of our lived reality. I think about this a lot as a feminist geographer, especially in relation to the university. Faculty, staff, and students on any given campus all occupy different spheres of interaction, which are compounded by silos of departments, units, research clusters, and other institutional divisions. A major obstacle to becoming an antiracist university is the way that these spatial divisions become social divisions. When we occupy different physical (and virtual) spaces, our conversations are constrained by proximity. Before the coronavirus pandemic, which increased our remote interactions, most members of the "campus community" did not interact with

---

8    LSURJ is a local chapter of a national organization dedicated to mobilizing white people to join in the struggle against racism.

# Community Listening In, With, and Against Whiteness

one another onsite and so did not know how our campus was experienced by others. In the context of community listening, our reading circles offered a way to overcome some of these spatial divisions, in part because the circles brought together staff and faculty from various sectors of the university; in part because the meetings were handled virtually due to the pandemic.

The reading circle I facilitated consisted of faculty and staff from different areas of the university and averaged 4–5 members per session of 6 regular participants. Some knew each other prior to the first meeting, but most were meeting each other for the first time. Our group spanned a range of ages, from a participant who began working at UofL in the 1970s to a recent graduate in her early twenties. One participant was male and identified as white, otherwise we were predominantly a group of white women.[9] In addition, many participants were university staff, an important difference from most of the other reading circles. Taken together, our differences, including our different locations within the university, meant that we were able to talk about race and institutional racism in multifaceted ways. One participant, for example, had worked in UofL's Affirmative Action Office in the 1990s. She had insights into how that office functioned and the ways that the university addressed race during that period, a richer perspective than most people, who were more recent hires working in narrower academic siloes.

Our group met exclusively online throughout the fall semester of 2020. For some, it was the first time they'd had an intentional conversation with others about race, while others had more experience with the topics we would deal with. Beyond our group's meetings, protesters in Louisville continued to call for justice for Breonna Taylor after her murder by Louisville Metro Police officers in March 2020. While that was not the focal point of our meetings, we regularly talked about the feeling of needing to do something, including learning more about race and racism amid our larger local context. We also noted that ongoing protests, like our group, brought people together across spatial and social boundaries. The protests also presented a powerful counterstory, pushing against the dominant narratives of Louisville as a compassionate, progressive city. Through our reading group, we were able to discuss and learn from related counterstories that addressed race and racism.

In late September 2020, the Kentucky Attorney General announced that the grand jury investigation into Breonna Taylor's murder would not charge any of the responsible police officers directly, sparking fresh waves of protest actions around Louisville. Our reading group met a few days later. Our materials that week included Redlining Louisville, a digital story map that provides

---

9    Another participant was a Black woman who attended our first meeting, but then said she could not continue due to the additional time required for pandemic teaching that Fall semester.

187

visualizations of census and other data sources and allows users to compare them to the redlining map of Louisville from the 1930s (Poe). Redlining Louisville is a visual counterstory about the history of racial segregation in Louisville. It shows the degree that racist histories of residential segregation laid the foundations for today's inequalities within the city. We looked at the map together, and I asked what things people found interesting and whether anyone took note of stories that countered the dominant narrative of Louisville's racial history. One participant was struck by where her neighborhood was on the redlining map, given recent police action to suppress protests in her area. Earlier that week, a significant mobilization of riot police had taken position near her house, and she'd watched as they prevented peaceful protesters from marching down the street. We wondered together who drew the line that determined where the police set up, stopping a protest march that had already covered a considerable distance throughout the city, and we talked to each other about how powerfully the racist legacies of the past shape our present.

During that same meeting, we discussed "The Problem We All Live With," an episode of *This American Life* about failed desegregation efforts in a St. Louis area school district (Hannah-Jones). St. Louis is only about 4 hours from Louisville, and we were able to draw strong connections between events there and within our own city. Both are situated on the cusp of the U.S. Midwest and the South, and both have long histories of segregation, racism, and police violence against Black people, including contentious desegregation battles in the 1970s. One group member shared that she had moved to Louisville as a young adult at that time and remembered the protests around integrating public schools. "The Problem We All Live With" was a springboard into conversation about the farther-reaching implications of this history, the ways that the same counterstories about Louisville's racial history have played out at a national scale.

Our reading circle meetings bridged some of the usual spatial limitations of the university. While the pandemic disrupted and challenged our time together, the virtual meeting platform is also perhaps responsible for people participating who otherwise would not due to the spatial divisions and limitations of our campus. For staff working in the Human Resources building, for example, on the extreme edge of UofL's main campus, they would have to travel considerable distances to access the main library or other buildings where meetings and events are often scheduled. The listening space of the reading circle allowed us to come together as people interested in learning the counterstories that have emerged in the context of race history in the United States and to make connections to our own professional contexts at the university. Our range of locations and positions throughout the university meant that participants were able to listen to UofL community members outside of their own work environment, facilitating our

Community Listening In, With, and Against Whiteness

ability to understand the different ways that institutional racism occurs throughout the university and our city.

## CAN WHITE SPACES BE ANTIRACIST?, KELLY KINAHAN

One purpose of community listening is "to find ways to make relationships more productive and substantial with the goal of meaningful change" (Fishman and Rosenberg 3). At the end of five reading circle meetings, the predominant sentiments among the group I facilitated were gratitude for a space to connect over shared interests in antiracist work and joy at forming new personal relationships, particularly during a virtual semester where on-campus connections were limited. In other words, partially through our practice of community listening as a reading group, we came to build new relationships and identify each other as members of an on-campus community committed to antiracist work.

Yet, as I critically reflected on the overall group dynamic along with the challenges voiced by other facilitators, I considered whether my group, made up of white, female, mostly untenured faculty fits the engaged, antiracist infrastructure of my predominantly white institution. Or, I wondered, did my group, shaped by our homogeneity in race, gender, and institutional status, fall into a pattern of validating our own voices? Were we lulled into a groupthink pattern, sustained by our whiteness, and did that keep us at the surface of antiracist dialogue? As an urban planner who sees themselves as new to antiracist work, I questioned whether my facilitation struck the right balance in trying to call in other white people to antiracist work, while not allowing a retreat into the comforts of whiteness.

Exclusively white spaces raise several dilemmas, chief among them the re-centering of whiteness that elevates the challenges of allyship over the oppression of BIPOC. Rather than listening and tuning into what we had not heard, the pull of whiteness made it easy to slip into white cultural logics, including being stuck in a loop of guilt and paralysis, focusing on -isms other than race, and not sitting with the discomfort of our own complicity in racism. While the readings provided a baseline context of unexamined histories, I wondered if our group's homogeneity meant we did not hear intersectional reflections and counterstories from our own members that could have deepened our connections to the readings and perhaps pushed us to explore the benefits we accrue from systems of white supremacy. The intersecting vulnerabilities and advantages of the group members' predominant status (i.e., privileged by whiteness yet marginalized by being untenured, as well as by being women historically overburdened with faculty service) at times crowded out deeper antiracism discussions and reflected a retreat to the comforts of whiteness. Our conversations drifted to

189

other structural challenges: researching and teaching without childcare during a pandemic, creating safe spaces for students traumatized by a summer of police violence, finding time to build relationships necessary for community-engaged research amid the pressure of the tenure clock. The goal of making meaningful change is central to a practice of community listening, and reflecting on my facilitation, this framing could have been deployed to help recenter our conversations and tie together other structural oppressions that commonly intersect with antiracist work.

In a separate, unrelated campus reading group I participated in subsequently, we read Beverly Daniel Tatum's seminal *Why are All the Black Kids Sitting Together in the Cafeteria? And Other Questions About Race*. That work exposed me to the concept of white identity development, which helped me understand some of the potential benefits of the racially homogenous ABI reading circles (Helms). Tatum's articulation of how "the social pressure from friends and acquaintances to collude, to not notice racism, can be quite powerful" (194) offered some insights on my earlier group dynamic. Because there are so many overwhelmingly white spaces that operate as colorblind or where racism is not considered, this necessitates the need for spaces that are explicitly, if imperfectly, antiracist. Even if the dialogue remains at a surface level, for instance relearning historical events through an antiracist lens, that discussion can still be an important part of the unlearning processes central to white identity development (Helms) and the meaning-making central to community listening. Tatum (203) also highlights Andrea Ayvazian's point that "'allies need allies,' others who will support their efforts to swim against the tide of cultural and institutional racism." This observation resonated with an aspect of the ABI group that I found extremely meaningful and reaffirming: candid reflections from colleagues, specifically other pre-tenured white women, about their own fears, mistakes, and anxieties, in doing antiracist work. In many cases, these reflections mirrored my own, made me feel less alone with my own shortcomings, and reinforced my commitment to continue antiracist work. This reflects an important value of engaging in community listening, which creates space for better knowing other community members and the initial relationship building between members where a community is newly forming or lacks formal organization (Fishman and Rosenberg 3). Beyond functioning as safe spaces for white allies, these spaces can also minimize harm for BIPOC by limiting exposure to the initial stages of white identity development, including processing white guilt and the discomfort of unpacking white privileges (cf. Jones; DiAngelo).

The dilemma of calling in other white people to antiracist work while resisting the sanctuary of whiteness is a constant tension in all white spaces. Overall, this reading group succeeded as a space for developing individual relationships and creating a shared space for relationship-building during an intense period where group members could explore antiracist ideas, and examine their complicity in racist university practices. Stepping into a facilitation role was important for my personal antiracist developmental process, and the experience strengthened my knowledge and resolve to continue doing antiracist work. Alongside these accomplishments, my reflections keep returning to the messy complications I still want to work on. Notably, how to address the fact that even in spaces designed to be antiracist, whiteness works to pull the conversation away from racism, tuning out the dialogue and counterstories that hold us accountable both individually and as situated actors in larger institutional frameworks.

## Confronting Whiteness; Standing under Cultural Logics to Explore Internalized Messages about Whiteness, Shelley Thomas

As a white teacher educator, my philosophy of teaching draws from the work of Paulo Freire and his notion of praxis as an iterative process of critical reflection and action. Freire also holds that oppression dehumanizes the oppressor and the oppressed (1970/2018). These ideas ground my antiracist work and seem to provide a substantive foundation. However, my experiences facilitating an ABI reading circle directed me to expand on them once I asked: How can community listening inform white antiracist work? How can participants in community listening confront white resistance? Most specifically, how is praxis shaped in community listening spaces like mine when calling in (Ross) resistant white folx, particularly folx whose resistance is grounded in experiences and personal histories that parallel my own? For me, community listening raised many unresolved and complex emotions around my capacity for and efficacy with white antiracist action. Thus, I wondered how I should work through the haunting (García) of my own tensions and confusion without burdening BIPOC. Reflecting on my experience facilitating a reading circle, I wonder how these questions might enable me to think through and to sit with the cultural logics of whiteness as to be accountable and to move the work forward.

One member of my circle, S., was a woman a bit older than I am who described experiences like my own. She was a local; she grew up near the same Louisville neighborhood as my mother's family. The way she described her negative experiences with Black folx in the newly integrated school system of the 1970s reminded me of the stories my family members shared about their own experiences. Their stories were often peppered with statements of routine othering, like "they are taking over," accusations of Black folx intimidating white children, and assumptions of stereotypical personality traits such as laziness. In my family, such statements were often speckled with the N-word for good measure, and as I listened to S., I recognized how I grew up with—and remain under— the cultural logics of whiteness.

Problematic, racist exchanges between my white family members have played back in my mind from the time I was a child, and I continued to hear internalized messages as a young adult when I taught Black high school students African and African American History. In this context, I finally learned substantive counterstories that challenged the cultural logics I had learned. Previously, as a teacher educator, I had worked with others like me: young white ciswomen from a similar geographical area, and I viewed the transition to high school teaching in a new context as an opportunity for me to walk away from the racism I learned. So, for a time after I changed professions, I actively suppressed my family memories and the cultural logics of whiteness they represented. This also meant I avoided confronting how whiteness shaped my beliefs and actions, and as a result, I ignored or, really, denied my racist past.

When S. joined the circle I facilitated, I discovered how listening to her stories meant also listening to my own. At first, when her descriptions of conversations from her past sounded familiar to me, I thought I could use the common points across our backgrounds to call her in around white antiracist work. I incorrectly and problematically reasoned that if I could "emerge" from a racist upbringing and become committed to antiracism, I was just the person to "lead" her to do so. In the reading group, she asked me direct questions about how to revise her teaching to be antiracist. In response, I sent her emails with resources and spoke directly to her about "how to" promote antiracism through her teaching.

Once she began to disengage, I felt less confident in my ability to call in and engage other white women around antiracist action. Eventually, S. dropped out of the circle, which made me further question my commitment to antiracist work and my role as a discussion facilitator. I viewed her participation as parallel to my past experiences. So, I saw her decision to leave the group as a reflection of my failure to call in a fellow white woman.

Now, with some time removed from the experience and after reflecting on it, I return to think about what I learned and how community listening informs my future actions. In particular, I think about how community listening and cultural logics allow for the simultaneous acknowledgment of my racist past and expand my commitment to confronting white antiracist resistance. García's notion of "haunting" reminds me how important it is to continue interrogating the cultural logics of whiteness. Engaging in community listening while working with S. helped me recognize that, as white women, we both stand under the cultural logics of whiteness and that sitting with the long-suppressed discomfort of white racism is also a component of praxis.

## QUESTIONING INSTITUTIONAL SPACES FOR ANTIRACIST WORK, ANGELA STOREY

How do we forge specific sites of antiracist listening and acting within the university, while also attending to the structural constraints through which such convergences take place? How do existing institutional spaces constrain the "we" of antiracist work? As a cultural anthropologist, I am interested in these questions as they push us to think across multiple scales—from the specifics of interactions to the institutional and cultural frameworks in which we act.

Conversations in the circle I facilitated had varied in tenor since they began in July 2020, and by autumn we'd settled into a reliable cadence. Our discussions made apparent that each person arrived with different expectations: some hoped to talk about individual behaviors, others sought structural analysis. Some wanted reflection, and others to act. Some were newer to antiracist work, and for others it had been part of their work in the world for decades. These distinctions allowed us to move between different registers of discussion but also caused frustration and may have influenced who dropped away. Four people, I believe all white women, had stopped attending by October, leaving the group at six individuals: one woman of color, one white man, and four white women; five were faculty (tenured, pre-tenure, and term); one was staff; and all had Ph.D.'s.

That month, we met once to read three pieces, including a chapter from activist and academic Loretta Ross, who gave the annual Braden Lecture later that year. Ross's work argues that instead of "calling out," we should employ a process of "calling in" that holds individuals and groups accountable for their exclusionary actions and statements and also seeks to repair relationships and reincorporate them into movements (Ross, Baker). In our meeting, we spoke about how each reading emphasized the power of relationships to make change: relationships between peers, between people and new information, and between those Ross identifies as engaged in the work of calling in. As we pondered the role of higher education in making change, alongside the need to do the relational work of activism, we spoke about how calling-in requires a space or collectivity to be called in to. We began to ask: who are the "we" of a calling-in process within academia? This is a question perhaps especially important at a PWI and one that, for me, made clear that our work was as much about listening to each other's experiences and perceptions as members of the same community as it was about listening to stories of UofL as an institution that shaped and housed many of our shared experiences. Someone presented a situation from a faculty assembly in which they felt a racist micro-aggression had taken place, and we discussed how we could have enacted a "calling in." Another person described how they tried to make space in meetings for voices they felt were being marginalized. Although the examples were useful because they brought the group's conversation into the spaces that we inhabited for work daily, they also felt like forcing square pegs into round holes: the institutional sites didn't seem to encourage or accept the kind of work that we wanted to introduce into them. The only spaces that seemed ready to accept antiracism work were those created just for that purpose, while other sites were governed by strong norms of interaction that favored narrow topical goals over broader process or change. They were also shaped by white cultural logics that sidelined and silenced work that would challenge racialized norms and hierarchies within them (Ratcliffe).

Questions of the "we" of academic antiracism work and of the possibilities for antiracist spaces on campus animated the remainder of our October conversations and poured over to the next month. The discussion prompted me to think about what is missing within academia. The circles did not necessarily fill that absence, but they pushed me to see and question it in myriad ways. For example, through the process of crafting a foundation for our interactions, including developing rapport and feelings of mutual trust, the group combined the difficult work of managing the abstract and the concrete, work that prompted me to ask: How do people think and act against racism, and how do we think and act against racism? Where are the opportunities for listening to messages more resoundingly about ourselves as staff, faculty, and community members, and to hear them in relation to our positions within a large PWI? How do we take existing institutional spaces and groups and shift them to become spaces for the kinds of antiracist work that is so sorely needed? How, in other words, do we push back against the hegemonic white cultural logics of a PWI? How do we escape the "stickiness" (Ahmed) of their attempts to be colorblind and "polite" and thus avoid reproducing inequalities and silences?

Our practice of community listening was one in which we attended to each other's experiences and their complexities. Through that process, we became more attuned to the structural contours of the institution that shaped us and which offered openings (or not) through which to act and engage. If we are to respond to calls for real change within institutions, we can take an approach like community listening that uses a sustained, systematic examination of personal and institutional stories to acknowledge who is and is not welcome in academic spaces and, subsequently, to re-craft spaces that encourage the "we" of antiracist action.

## LOOKING FORWARD, MARY P. SHERIDAN

Nationwide, 2020 ushered in a spate of university antiracist initiatives that sought to respond to the racial reckonings sweeping across the country (Bartlett). And yet, good intentions are no assurance of good actions. Instead, informed reflection is one among many important steps for evaluating these actions since such reflection helps people understand individual and collective experiences that had previously been opaque.

As white women committed to moving our PWI in antiracist directions, we believe community listening frameworks, applied retrospectively, have strengthened our reflections in ways that will shape our future antiracist work, perhaps most notably by helping us attend to how thoroughly whiteness is baked in, in ways we had normed and therefore not fully appreciated. By introducing stories from minoritized groups and listening for hauntings in majoritarian stories, we attuned to who is valued and who is discounted in individual, collective, and institutionally habituated ways. Such practices called us to engage in varying practices of accountability, which proved tricky in many reading circles since such moves challenge us to face the occlusions of what we and others know and to own our active complicity in oppressive systems.

These reflections raise questions for us, and likely for other white facilitators of antiracist groups in PWIs, about how to educate ourselves and other whites about our complicity in white supremacy: How hard do we push and how fully do we support differentially invested white colleagues (and ourselves)? How do we foster spaces that destabilize whiteness while we call in and remain open to being called out? How do we simultaneously labor within institutional structures and challenge the logics of such structures that shape the tacitly accepted ways people and practices operate? How do we prepare ourselves for the emotional toll these measures take? While community listening proved helpful in our retrospective analysis, wrestling with these questions before embarking on antiracist work may help others address the stickiness of white privilege in their local contexts from the outset of their projects.

In addition to the above generative questions, we offer two takeaways that may inform how others engage with antiracist actions at their PWIs. One is that community listening is not a thing, an accomplishment, checklist, or inoculation that makes us certified listeners. We are never finished. Rather, such listening-with-accountability is a disposition, a way of (re)orienting to the world. Like antiracist projects broadly, community listening calls us continually to commit to listen for and amplify voices typically excluded. While this idea is not new, it nonetheless feels important to reiterate since it is disheartening when projects end, especially when there is so much more to do, as the above reflections argue. This takeaway, then, is to acknowledge we are always doing the work before the next project's work, and there is much work to do.

A second takeaway is that community listening frameworks can help us hear the diverse cultural logics that are operating simultaneously, sometimes leading, sometimes interanimating, sometimes silencing. This simultaneity happens not just in our institutions or ad hoc groups, but also within ourselves. When deeply embedded logics surface, they can throw us into turmoil, but even when we don't recognize them, they are still operating. We address the emotional toll antiracist work takes not to shirk our responsibilities or pat ourselves on the back, but rather to prepare ourselves and others for taking on this labor, and for carrying it on. Being open to unpacking and being accountable for these multiple internalized logics is challenging, but as white women attempting to move our PWI in an antiracist direction, we believe sharing our stories, our questions, and our takeaways may help others do similar work in their local setting.

## WORKS CITED

Ahmed, Sara. "A Phenomenology of Whiteness." *Feminist Theory*, vol. 8, no. 2, 2007, pp. 149–168, https://doi.org/10.1177/1464700107078139.

Aviles, Gwen. "Reading as Resistance: The Rise of the Anti-Racist Book List." *NBC News*. 5 June 2020, https://tinyurl.com/5a43dkb7.

Ayvazian, Andrea. "Interrupting the Cycle of Oppression: The Role of Allies as Agents of Change." *Fellowship*, vol. 61, no. 1–2, 2015, pp. 7–10.

Baker, Carrie N. "For Equality, Loretta Ross Argues We 'Call In,' Not 'Call out': 'There's too Much Infighting in the Feminist Movement.'" *Ms. Magazine.* 20 May 2021, https://tinyurl.com/45cupvnh.

Bartlett, Tom. "The Antiracist College: This May be a Watershed Moment in the History of Higher Education and Race." *The Chronicle of Higher Education.* 15 Feb. 2021.

Bizzell, Patricia. "Discourse Community." *Encyclopedia of English Studies and Language Arts*, vol. I, edited by Alan C. Purves. Scholastic, 1994.

Concannon, Joe, and Bob Foster. "Listening with Šəqačib: Writing Support and Community Listening." *Community Writing, Community Listening*, special issue of *Community Literacy Journal*, vol. 14, no. 2, 2020. pp. 93–109.

DiAngelo, Robin J. *White Fragility: Why It's so Hard for White People to Talk about Racism*. Beacon Press, 2018.

Engeström, Yrjo, Ritva Engeström, and Tarja Vähäaho. "When the Center Does not Hold: The Importance of Knotworking." *Activity Theory and Social Practice: Cultural-Historical Approaches*, edited by Seth Chaiklin, Mariane Hedegaard, and Uffe Juul Jensun, Aarhus UP, 1999, pp. 345–74.

Fishman, Jenn, and Lauren Rosenberg, editors. *Community Writing, Community Listening*, special issue of *Community Literacy Journal*, vol. 13, no. 1, 2018.

Fishman, Jenn, and Lauren Rosenberg. "Guest Editors' Introduction: Community Writing, Community Listening." Fishman and Rosenberg, pp. 1–6, https://doi.org/10.25148/clj.13.1.009085.

Flower, Linda. *Community Literacy and the Rhetoric of Public Engagement*. Southern Illinois UP, 2008.

Fosl, Catherine. *Subversive Southerner: Anne Braden and the Struggle for Racial Justice in the Cold War South*. UP of Kentucky, 2006.

Freire, Paulo. *Pedagogy of the Oppressed*. Bloomsbury, 2018.

García, Romeo. "Creating Presence from Absence and Sound from Silence." Fishman and Rosenberg, pp. 7–15, https://doi.org/10.25148/clj.13.1.009086.

Hanasono, Lisa K., Ellen M. Broido, Margaret M. Yacobucci, Karen V. Root, Susana Peña, and Deborah A. O'Neil. "Secret Service: Revealing Gender Biases in the Visibility and Value of Faculty Service." *Journal of Diversity in Higher Education*, vol. 17, no. 1, 2019, pp. 85–98, https://doi.org/10.1037/dhe0000081.

Hannah-Jones, Nikole. "The Problem We All Live With: Part One." *This American Life*. https://www.thisamericanlife.org/562/the-problem-we-all-live-with-part-one. Accessed 31 July 2015.

Helms, Janet E. *Black and White Racial Identity: Theory, Research, and Practice*. Greenwood Press, 1990.

Jackson, Rachel C. with Dorothy Whitehorse DeLaune. "Decolonizing Community Writing with Community Listening: Story, Transrhetorical Resistance, and Cultural Literacy Activism." Fishman and Rosenberg, pp. 37–54, https://doi.org/10.25148/clj.13.1.009089.

Jones, Kenneth, and Tema Okun. "The Characteristics of White Supremacy." *Dismantling Racism: A Workbook for Social Change Groups*. ChangeWork, 2001, https://tinyurl.com/4h9w733x.

Kurtyka, Faith. "Hitting the Limits of Feminist Rhetorical Listening in the Era of Donald Trump." *Peitho*, vol. 23, no. 3, 2021, https://tinyurl.com/2wz8p4tw.

Kynard, Carmen. "'All I Need Is One Mic': A Black Feminist Community Meditation on The Work, the Job, and the Hustle (& Why So Many of Yall Confuse This Stuff)." *Community Literacy Journal*, vol. 14, no. 2, 2020, pp. 5–24, https://doi.org/10.25148/14.2.009033.

Lewis, Rachel. "Troubling the Terms of Engagement: Queer Rhetorical Listening as Carceral Interruptions." *Peitho*, vol. 23, no. 1, 2020, https://tinyurl.com/36sepdam.

Lorde, Audre. "The Master's Tools Will Never Dismantle the Master's House." *Sister Outsider: Essays and Speeches*. 1984. Crossing Press, 2007, pp. 110–114.

Lundström, Catrin. "White Ethnography: (Un)comfortable Conveniences and Shared Privileges in Field-Work with Swedish Migrant Women." *NORA: Nordic Journal of Women's Studies,* vol. 18, no. 2, 2010, pp. 70–87.

Martinez, Aja Y. *Counterstory: The Rhetoric and Writing of Critical Race Theory*. NCTE, 2020.

Mathieu, Paula. *Tactics of Hope: The Public Turn in English Composition*. Heinemann, 2005.

Mathis Keri E., Megan Faver Hartline, Beth A. Boehm, and Mary P. Sheridan. "Building Infrastructures for Community Engagement at the University of Louisville: Graduate Models for Cultivating Stewardship." *Building Engaged Infrastructure*, special issue of *Community Literacy Journal*, vol. 11, no. 1, 2016, pp. 146–156, https://doi.org/10.25148/CLJ.11.1.009257.

Monberg, Terese Guinsatao. "Listening for Legacies or How I Began to Hear Dorothy Laigo Cordove, the Pinay behind the Podium Known as FANHS." *Representations: Doing Asian American Rhetoric*, edited by LuMing Mao and Morris Young, Utah State UP, 2008, pp. 83–105.

Muñoz, José Esteban. *Cruising Utopia. The Then and There of Queer Futurity*. New York UP, 2009.

Oleksiak, Timothy. "A Queer Praxis for Peer Review" *College Composition and Communication*, vol. 72, no. 2, 2020, pp. 306–332.

———. "Queer Rhetorical Listening: An Introduction to a Cluster Conversation." *Peitho*, vol. 23, no. 1, 2021, https://tinyurl.com/y3xth7r8.

Poe, Joshua. "Redlining Louisville: Racial Capitalism and Real Estate." *Antiracism Digital Library*, https://sacred.omeka.net/items/show/310. Accessed 23 Apr. 2021.

Powell, Malea. "Stories that Take Place: A Performance in One Act." *College on Composition and Communication*, vol. 64, no. 2, 2012, pp. 383–406.

Prior, Paul. "Community." *Keywords in Writing Studies*, edited by Paul Heilker and Peter Vandenberg, Utah State UP, 2015, pp. 26–31.

Ratcliffe, Krista. *Rhetorical Listening: Identification, Gender, Whiteness*. Southern Illinois UP, 2005.

Ratcliffe, Krista, and Kyle Jensen. *Rhetorical Listening in Action: A Concept-Tactic Approach*. Parlor Press, 2022.

Restaino, Jessica, and Laurie Cella, editors. *Unsustainable: Re-imagining Community Literacy, Public Writing, Service Learning and the University*. Lexington Books, 2012.

Rohrer, Judy. *Staking Claims: Settler Colonialism and Racialization in Hawai'i*. U of Arizona P, 2016.

Ross, Loretta. *Calling-In the Call-Out Culture: Detoxing our Movement*. Simon and Schuster, 2022.

Rowan, Karen, and Alexandra J. Cavallaro. "Toward a Model for Preparatory Community Listening." Fishman and Rosenberg, pp. 23–36, https://doi.org/10.25148/clj.13.1.009088.

Royster, Jacqueline Jones. *Traces of a Stream: Literacy and Social Change Among African American Women*. U of Pittsburgh P, 2000.

Schon, Donald A. *The Reflective Practitioner: How Practitioners Think in Action*. Basic Books, 1984.

Sheridan, Mary P. "What Matters in the Worlds We Encourage." *Making Future Matters*, edited by Rick Wysocki and Mary P. Sheridan. Computers and Composition Digital Press, 2018, https://tinyurl.com/mvppmbxy.

Sheridan, Mary P., and Megan Adams. "Knotworking Collaborations, Fostering Community Engaged Teachers and Scholars." *Composing Feminist Interventions: Activism, Engagement, Praxis*, edited by Kris Blair and Lee Nickoson. The WAC Clearinghouse/UP of Colorado, 2018, pp. 213–234, https://doi.org/10.37514/PER-B.2018.0056.2.11.

Tatum, Beverly Daniel. *Why Are All the Black Kids Sitting Together in the Cafeteria? And Other Questions about Race*. Basic Books, 2017.

CHAPTER 9.

# ON BEING IN IT

### Katie W. Powell
University of Cincinnati

*The author of this chapter developed a theory of storied community listening while participating, as a white woman and an academic transplant, in a Fayetteville, Arkansas, restorative justice project. As she explains through personal narrative, storied community listening combines iterative and critical self-reflection through story with ongoing and reciprocal community-engaged work. She identifies, through various points of tension in the group and their conclusion, the ways in which a researcher and community member might think about listening, hearing, and critically reflecting on what it means to be a white woman working toward community healing.*

One quiet summer Friday afternoon, a few of us in the office ventured to the Arkansas Country Doctor's Museum, which featured an actual iron lung, a surprising collection of salt and pepper shakers collected by doctors' wives, and a plaque sharing the story of a prominent doctor in the area, Dr. James Monroe Boone, who was purportedly murdered at the hands of the men he enslaved in 1856. I found myself thinking about the plaque after the visit and inquired about the story to my contact in special collections at the University of Arkansas, where I worked. He directed me to Mike, a local historian in our area.[1] Mike, like many white residents in Fayetteville, had grown up hearing stories about the doctor's death as well as the subsequent lynchings of the three enslaved men believed to be responsible. According to white accounts, two were lynched by a mob; one was hanged by the state. However, Mike was working with a community group, the Washington County Community Remembrance Project (WCCRP) to share an alternative narrative that was already well known to the Black community through oral histories. The goal of the WCCRP was to erect a marker in a communal location that would prioritize—and humanize—the story of Aaron, Anthony, and Randall, the men who were lynched.

When I met Mike, I was about three years into my staff position with the honors college at the university and was regularly seeking ways to be more

---

1    All names in this story (aside from the historical individuals) are pseudonyms.

DOI: https://doi.org/10.37514/PER-B.2025.2531.2.09

inclusive of all of our students. Along with working at the university, I was in my second year of doctoral studies in English. I had just begun formally creating a list of readings for my exams that focused on story and narrative, inclusive pedagogies, and public memory. Personally, I was working to confront racial justice as a white woman and as a transplant to Northwest Arkansas, but at the time, felt frozen by the guilt of it all. I was still so new to this part of my journey and, therefore, had a sense of how much grounding and experience I lacked. Mike was really interested in the ways I could contribute and encouraged me to meet with Valerie and Terri, leaders of the group, as he thought there might still be time to get involved in their efforts. In a follow-up email to our meeting, he shared that "I think the key here is that we are allies in these projects, willing to help or learn in whatever way we can" (WCCRP, "Local History Interest").

Helping or learning in whatever way we can is, indeed, the key. I knew then as I know now that the only way to confront my trepidations is to jump in, to be in it. But in this world of performative activism, of guilt, of sadness, how can we be in it? What is the answer when it comes to striving toward allyship? How do we take concrete, intentional, and meaningful steps toward racial reconciliation? These questions, this tension, had been sitting with me through my work, through my budding research, and through my tentative foray into communal racial justice.

It is this question of being in it that centers my growth and development toward storied community listening, which I define as an embedded approach to listening that involves critical reflection through story and an active, reciprocal approach to working alongside a community. And so I took the jump. I emailed the two leaders of the WCCRP and met with them. I followed up after I felt like our meeting went well to see where I could fit. I attended meetings, and I sought to be willing to help or learn in whatever way I could. In each of these moves, I tried to align my strengths with the community's needs as we all worked toward racial reconciliation.

As I critically reflect on my membership in the WCCRP, I find that my storied community listening approach grew out of a series of important conversations that I share below to help others learn how to use this approach in ways relevant to their communities. Understanding the community history we worked with, as well as the ways in which I came to know the positionality and priorities of each group member, allowed me to carefully examine my own purpose and place. Our group's first major task of finding the perfect location, a historically Black cemetery, to place the public marker that serves both to memorialize the three young men who were accused and killed, Aaron, Anthony, and Randall, and venerate their legacy taught me the critical importance of community listening as a praxis in this work. By actively using community listening as we crafted the marker for the men's memorial, I was able to identify the leading importance of story. A reciprocal and active community relationship through my own administrative role in the coalition solidified the role of community in my definition of storied community listening. This gathering of various elements of my definition, through stories, culminated in the unveiling of our project and an earnest reflection on the meaning and further applications of storied community listening. I don't think that I am inherently arguing for best practices to remember or even plan for navigating this memory in the present day, as others have done (Hosbawn and Sturken). A storied community listening approach helps me understand my role in this story and the stories I will be part of in future community spaces. I hope that my approach might help other scholars, particularly white female scholars, navigate the intrinsically personal work of racial reconciliation.

## THE STORY OF OUR STORY

In progressive white communities throughout the American South, it's commonplace to hear people brush over the past, especially local histories of slavery. In Northwest Arkansas, for example, people say, "since we were in the mountains we didn't have much" or "people here were good slaveholders" (Bonilla Silva). Even within stories that acknowledge those enslaved, the focus we hear perpetuates the dominant narrative of criminality and subservience. Valerie, Terri, and the small community team that became the Washington County Community Remembrance Project had recently visited the National Memorial for Peace and Justice and were critically listening for community histories that contributed to the criminalization and dehumanization of Black men through centuries. In listening to the story of Aaron, Anthony, and Randall's death, the community team heard a dominant narrative that focuses much more heavily on the white man's death:

> What is agreed is that on 29 May 1856, two of his former
> slaves and a slave belonging to the brother of his deceased
> wife Sophie, David Wilson Williams, came to his house late
> one evening and demanded all his money. They beat him
> senseless with three hickory clubs and left him for dead. His
> blood stained the floorboards. He died 11 June 1856. . . . The
> slave owned by his neighbor was later tried and hanged. The
> two former slaves were lynched and hung by Dr. Boone's sons.
> The motive for the brutal death has been ascribed to jealousy
> of the perceived favoritism of an ex-slave overseer by other
> ex-slaves. Another supposition is that the slaves were put up
> to the murder by the brother-in-law who coveted the farms of
> Dr. Boone. (Singleton)

This narrative, featured at the Arkansas Country Doctor's Museum, doesn't even say their names, a call we still hear today. Additionally, "what is agreed" suggests a kind of universal truth that the coalition felt was left incomplete. Storied community listening involves a critical reflection, and critically reflecting on this story reveals that this narrative works to further the dominant role of the white man and the subservient, criminal nature of the enslaved men.

The Washington County Community Remembrance Project was founded to help the Fayetteville community begin to unpack and critically reflect on this minimized past as well as the present it very much affects. As a member of the WCCRP, I describe the group's work as coalitional and describe the group as a coalition. We worked from a variety of positionalities toward our common cause, as explained in our mission statement: "expanding our community's capacity for facing difficult truths, acknowledging the reality and damage of racism, recognizing and calling out injustices . . . and working to address them in whatever way we can" (WCCRP, "Info about the WCCRP"). One clear example of our efforts is the marker project we undertook to present a fuller story of the lynching of Aaron, Anthony, and Randall.

By embedding themselves in the community, practicing what I now term storied community listening, the Washington County Community Remembrance Project heard a contested version of the story, a counterstory that "presents a contrasting description and narrative from a different perspective" (Martinez 16) and honors the oral tradition of the Black community. Tonya, one of our early coalition members, had a friend whose family had been in Fayetteville for generations. Tonya's friend had always told her that Boone, the enslaver who had the means and access to become a doctor in 1856, was "misbehavin" in the female quarters when he attempted to assault an enslaved woman, Thursday. Thursday protected herself by taking an axe to his head. Aaron, Anthony, and Randall then defended her, though they were ultimately still given the blame. Critical to our group's mission and directly in line with the goal and intention of storied community listening is prioritizing and unearthing the ways of knowing and pieces of the story that have not been prioritized or centered. In this spirit of storied community listening, the group heard the need to bring to light these competing narratives.

## THE STORY OF OUR COALITION

When I joined in 2019, the WCCRP had received formal acceptance from the Equal Justice Initiative (EJI) to be part of their national Community Remembrance Project initiative and was gaining steam on telling the community story of the lynching of the enslaved men. From Fall 2019 to Spring 2021, we met

On Being In It

once a month as a full coalition and completed the design and installation of a historical marker commemorating Aaron, Anthony, and Randall. Additionally, we held a series of related events, including hosting a high school essay contest, working with local libraries to spread the word on this story through public lectures, and forming community relationships that worked to further conversations in our town about facing difficult truths.

Even as we worked successfully through these public-facing events, we grew in our internal work together through valuable group discussions, fraught decisions, and earnest conversations. These important tensions stemmed from our differing positionalities as we earnestly worked to best tell the story of Aaron, Anthony, and Randall to our community. Acknowledging race and local affiliation of each of our coalition members plays an important reflective role in how we grew in our storied community listening. Our activities were led by Terri, a retired Black educator originally from Minnesota, who remained our steadfast leader and, I think, struggled with the tensions between the engrained dominant narrative and the Black oral history perspective. Valerie, a Black social worker and academic who has lived in the area for six years, worked to remind us of a new way to approach history. Elizabeth, Mike, Joshua, and Ruth were our most vocal white participants, all deeply connected to Fayetteville and the Northwest Arkansas region. Their local connections led them to focus on finding proof and a sense of historical accuracy that we collectively learned was often deeply biased. Diane, a Black history professor at the university, frequently offered an academic perspective on our work together, and Tonya, a Black artist and gallery owner with deep local connections, consistently maintained the importance of emphasizing the Black community and its oral traditions. Along the way, we were also joined by a local Black male resident named Terrell, a Black Journalism professor at the university, and a young white man studying for seminary working toward reparations through churches in the area.

As a white woman in her twenties, I was the newest and youngest member of the group and had only lived in Fayetteville for five years. Our team had several academics—a history professor, a genealogist, a community historian, and a social work researcher. My background in rhetoric and composition, however, primed me to listen carefully to how we told our stories and used our words. Our work began in earnest in August 2019, and about two months later, in October, I began to formulate the topic of my dissertation, a study that examined the public memory work of our group as we installed a historical marker commemorating Aaron, Anthony, and Randall alongside growing efforts to remove a Confederate statue in our town square that a local chapter of the United Daughters of the Confederacy had worked to establish. On the Institutional Review Board (IRB) form that I needed all coalition members to sign, this only meant that I

203

was asking the coalition to allow me to observe, collect, and write on our work together. Having to ask for their consent so early in our relationship made me worry about seeming disingenuous as we worked together.[2] Opening that conversation, however, allowed me to form relationships with Valerie, Elizabeth, and Terri. Elizabeth, Terri, and I maintain communication on our reflective writing, reaching out to provide reading recommendations and hold ourselves accountable in our ever-present work toward racial justice. Valerie and Terri have published on their work together in Fayetteville's Historical Society publication, and Elizabeth is working on a grant for a similar local project. Though I started my project by looking for increased knowledge on public memory, I found the necessity of developing a storied approach to community listening and reflecting on it here to situate myself and others in the work of racial reconciliation for this and all community work.

## THE STORY OF OUR PLACES

It was in our October 2019 coalition meeting, intended to make a final decision on the location of the marker, that I honed in on the "listening" component of my storied community listening approach. By this point, we had had two formal meetings and had settled into group dynamics and conversations. We had discussed a few options for places, chosen because they either had some relevance to the story (such as the former site of the homestead where Aaron, Anthony, and Randall were enslaved) or were in public (the town square) or sacred (a historically Black local cemetery) spaces. Elizabeth put together some information about each of these places and presented it at our meeting.

As I shifted into writing about our coalitional work together for my dissertation, I found myself spending most of our meetings staying silent. I listened, I carefully took notes, I respected and admired the work of the group, but I didn't actively contribute. I rooted this decision in Krista Ratcliffe's notion of eavesdropping, which is part of her larger development of rhetorical listening. Ratcliffe introduced rhetorical listening as a tool for white scholars such as herself to use when discoursing across differences. Her definition, "a code of cross-cultural conduct . . . a stance of openness that a person may choose to assume in cross cultural exchanges," (1), was developed from reflecting on "emerging threads" in questions she received after conference presentations, comments on her writing projects, discussions in her classrooms, and her own tendency toward guilt as a white woman. I began using Ratcliffe's concept of rhetorical listening in the way one might expect at this stage in my project—pulling out the definition and

---

2    IRB protocol approval number 1912234807A001.

plopping it into my work. As an active member of the community I had been eavesdropping on, however, I soon learned I needed to question, reflect on, and expand my definition and use of this concept.

To decide on the location of the marker, Terri told us that we would, one by one, vote on our first, second, and third choice for a marker location. She felt that such a method would allow us to understand each committee member's motivations and would provide a more holistic opportunity to get a sense of our group at this stage in our forming. I immediately felt a tightening in my stomach and throat. My inner monologue became a melodrama about how the method she suggested would out me as an imposter, a scholar-in-training with good intentions but not much more. I wanted to hide. I wanted to disappear, but there was nothing I could stand behind as I was called to speak. My immediate and jarring reaction when being called to speak revealed to me that perhaps I had been using "eavesdropping" as a passive and disconnected practice instead of actively interrogating the ways in which I approach the work. I needed to expand on the way I interpreted rhetorical listening to find a more embedded approach.

As community listening scholars have explored, merely listening, even with the best of intentions, can often reinforce the privilege of white people and the dominant culture instead of truly embedding oneself in the work. In a special issue of *Community Literacy Journal,* Jenn Fishman and Lauren Rosenberg define community listening as "a literacy practice that involves deep, direct engagement with individuals and groups working to address urgent issues in everyday life, issues anchored by long histories and complicated by competing interpretations as well as clashing modes of expression" (Fishman and Rosenberg 1). Differing from rhetorical listening, for me, is the direct engagement element of the work—the "being in it" that I practiced with the WCCRP. Ratcliffe acknowledges that rhetorical listening functions "as one answer to Jacqueline Jones Royster's question: how do we translate listening into language and action?" (17). Fishman and Rosenberg acknowledge, in their introduction, their own evolution to community listening in response to both Royster's question and Ratcliffe's response. Storied community listening, then, is my own approach to this response. My development of storied community listening involves an embedded approach to listening, my own blending and building off rhetorical and community listening. Practicing this definition of listening can only be accomplished by being in it, as Terri and the coalition members had shown me through a call for direct participation.

Because I was also one of the committee members who would be asked to cast a vote, I listened to the individual votes of each member much more carefully and intentionally to parse where I felt we should place the marker. Instead of merely taking notes and observing as I had been interpreting eavesdropping to be, this forced individual participation called me out of guilty complacency and allowed me to actively be part of the group. I began to understand the importance of an embedded approach to listening that involves critical reflection through story and an active, reciprocal relationship to working alongside a community. Allowing each of us to cast our vote based on our own viewpoints and stories led us to an intentional discussion about our own individual motivations. My vote for the homestead location was rooted in what felt like historical accuracy. Many of our white Fayetteville residents (Mike, Ruth, and Joshua), voted for the very public Fayetteville Square, as they felt motivated to share with their white peers our story. Valerie discussed her vote for Oaks Cemetery, a Black cemetery that is the final resting place for generations of Black citizens in Fayetteville. These differing motivations coalesced in a discussion on our collective goals, which we decided should ultimately be about venerating Aaron, Anthony, and Randall. To prioritize this goal of veneration, of remembering their story instead of placing too much of an agenda on their memory, we then collectively voted to place the marker in Oaks Cemetery. This first instance of practicing community listening, though it made me far more vulnerable, allowed me and the rest of our coalition to join the conversation instead of standing on the outside, which in turn provided me with far more investment in our final decision. Though it draws from concepts of rhetorical listening, community listening incorporates the embedded approach to listening that I see as critical to my ultimate definition of storied community listening.

Oaks Cemetery, our chosen location, is part of a historically Black church in Fayetteville, and a core group of church members serve as the caretakers. Though the process of deciding on the marker taught me the importance of leaning into community listening, it was our coalition's interactions with the caretakers that confirmed the importance of developing an active, reciprocal relationship alongside a community that I've grown to consider essential to my definition of storied community listening. As the WCCRP individually discussed locations and collectively gained consensus on Oaks Cemetery, we had excitedly planned to ask the caretakers about its placement, as one of the WCCRP members is a member of the church and a close friend of the leader of the caretakers. We were surprised, however, that the caretakers wanted to meet with our coalition to express concerns and learn more information before making a final decision. In our excitement over veneration and perhaps our eagerness to practice what I now refer to as storied community listening, we didn't extend these realizations out to the caretakers, the actual community members (and descendants) of this sacred place.

When I arrived at the church for the caretaker meeting on a cold, windy night, I navigated immediately to my coalition members. I didn't make small talk with the caretakers before the meeting, and I spent the drive home later wishing I had visited with them, at least introduced myself, before almost othering us as coalition vs. caretakers. The caretakers, approximately ten of them, various ages and all Black, had set chairs up in front of the room, putting us in a position of authority (or placing us on trial?) in the sparsely filled, sparsely attended room. Such positioning was another realization for us as a coalition that we might need to recalibrate our expectations. Throughout the conversation, ideas circulated about identifying unmarked graves in Oaks, genealogical research, and possibly finding familial links to Aaron, Anthony, and Randall at the site and in the community. Their resistance to the placement of the marker came from additional traffic, additional upkeep, and additional work. They feared that the marker would bring unwanted attention, possibly leading to a lack of veneration for their own family dead (and eventually, them) who are resting there. I also sensed a hesitation to bring up the past, the times of overt racism, and the racial violence inflicted on their ancestors. It was quickly becoming apparent that we, as a coalition, had overstepped. By charging forward excitedly with our decision to place the marker at Oaks, we had neglected the very people who are and have been the community that Oaks, the project, that Aaron, Anthony, and Randall represent. Though I, as well as our coalition, had really turned a corner by embedding ourselves in the work, in the decisions, I had not fully grasped (or considered) the actual community, the legacy of Black individuals in our town, of the three men who had been murdered. Assuming that the caretakers would purely be excited by a marker to shed light on an untold story neglected to consider the pain and trouble that such a marker might bring.

After a series of questions and considerations, namely spoken between the caretakers and our coalition leaders, the caretakers said they would need some time to think about it and vote. As we left the fellowship hall that night, the leader of the caretakers shook our hands and asked a few of us if we had been to Oaks Cemetery. "No," many of us said quietly. Though Terri and Valerie had been, several of us who just weeks before were feeling amazing about our enlightened decision to venerate by placing the marker in Oaks Cemetery, were ashamed to admit we hadn't even spent time there. "You really should," he said calmly, "it's a special place."

This story, for me, exemplifies the critical component of community in storied community listening. Here, practicing storied community listening meant not just participating in the listening, but considering the whole community, namely those who would be directly involved. And even in joining the conversation, storied community listening as I understand it today after these reflections means listening, hearing, the levels of resistance that might come with a decision that we think is the right move. Our coalition grew and learned firsthand through this tense encounter that being embedded in the community is a necessary component of storied community listening. As I reflect on my enactment of storied community listening, the community element could have been improved not through large revelations but simply steps. Going to Oaks Cemetery and immersing myself in such a "special place" after we had made our final decision. Separating myself from the people I know in a new setting and making small talk with the caretakers to get to know them. Putting down my notebook and pen in the meeting and making eye contact, asking more questions about the loved ones buried there, or even apologizing for our shortsightedness might have led to a greater community relationship in this development of storied community listening. Practicing enacting the community in storied community listening means a million tiny decisions to choose community.

## THE STORY OF OUR WORDS

The coalition's decision on where to locate the marker (which ultimately gained the unanimous approval of the caretakers) allowed us to establish the important goal of veneration and taught me much about both community and listening. Another large and complex task was to decide what would be written on our marker. Beginning in January 2020 and continuing to our marker dedication in May 2021, the coalition split into two subcommittees. One focused on drafting text for the marker; the other collaborated with local high schools and libraries to make an essay contest, sponsored by the EJI, a reality. As with our decision to place the marker in the less public location of Oaks Cemetery, our coalition charged both subcommittees with "doing things differently" as we thought through the most inclusive way to share the story of Aaron, Anthony, and Randall that honored their memory and brought truth, or as much truth as we knew, to our community. Even though I ultimately led the essay contest efforts, it was in watching and listening to the work of the marker text subcommittee that challenged me and taught me the most about my growing understanding of story in storied community listening.

In mid-July, the marker text subcommittee emailed everyone their first draft, which would be the main topic of discussion at the next meeting in August. Because of COVID-19, our meetings were now online, and I had to join this one from the road while my husband and I traveled to his best friend's wedding. The meeting began as normal, with a now-routine checking in on everyone as the pandemic continued to surge, leaving all of us uncertain, burnt out, constantly skeptical, and craving human contact. When Terri then shifted to an open discussion of the marker text, Tonya almost immediately began to speak. She was very unhappy with the language of the initial text draft. She felt that

On Being In It

the text revealed a complete disregard for the power of oral history, for genuinely allowing Black voices to come through. Additionally, she felt that the text catered to white people and merely shared facts without addressing the nuances, the totality of the lynching of these men and their lives. She stated in no uncertain terms that she was "afraid this would happen" and felt that we were allowing the white voices, the dominant narrative, to come through.

Due to our bumpy backroad driving at that point in the call, I didn't have my camera on (though others did and service was clear) and, therefore, felt quite anonymous and comfortable saying nothing. Elizabeth, who worked directly on the marker text, tried to focus the conversation on revising. Eventually, however, silence took over the call, which ended early after a few half-hearted administrative updates. One of the items was my update on the essay contest, which I concluded by awkwardly saying something like, "I really value this conversation." But I felt frozen then and during most of that meeting, and throughout the week I stayed shaken up, wondering: What should I have said? What could I have done? How was I part of Tonya's worst fears realized?

Even as I reflect on this tense moment in our coalition's time together, I am struck by the power of reflection that has become part of the praxis of storied community listening. Here, as in the previous stories I tell in this chapter, it has been through present reflection that I interpret our silence and discomfort as a moment of growth and an essential part of community work. Tonya felt that, in our initial marker language, we were defaulting to the stock stories of our past, and she was imploring us to critically reflect on the ways in which the knowledge has been shared that are outside dominant culture standards. To practice this critical reflection that is an integral part of my approach, I look to the scholars of color who have shaped my unlearning and relearning work. I feel I have tried to listen to Aja Y. Martinez in the use of counterstory, which I hear as further need to provide a supporting role in these conversations. Patricia Hill Collins taught me that the idea of bringing in new knowledge claims, uncovering ways of hearing, processing, and determining how the story gets told, are not possible without dialogue "with other members of a community" (212). And I feel empowered by Jo Hsu's method of homing or using a constellation of stories to determine where and how we belong (9), to puzzle my way through this work. The story of our words is about expanding knowledge claims, unearthing the counterstory of oral history in our community, and critically reflecting as we focus on how we tell the story of Aaron, Anthony, and Randall.

This story is also about my own growth, legitimacy, and trepidation as a storyteller and a listener—the "critical reflection through story" element of my definition of storied community listening. I entered the coalition hoping to be embedded, invested, and in the work with the best of intentions, intentions that were

Powell

continuously challenged by the complexity of our coalition's goals and the nature of our work together. Again and again, however, I wrestled with where specifically, day to day, that placed me. As a young, white student success-staff-member-by-trade, my natural gravitation is to do. It was for this reason that I volunteered to head up the high school essay contest, which meant enough administrative duties that I always had an update to hide behind when it came to hard conversations, questions, and silences. As in my administrative update in our heated meeting around the marker text, I cast such silence as a cop-out, a form of eavesdropping, or intimidation. Lately, however, I've begun to push against such silence based on Layla Saad's casting of silence as arising out of white fragility, "a fear of being incapable of talking about race without coming apart" (53).

It is in this present reflection that I attempt to recast my administrative work for the coalition. As I reflect on this tense moment with the coalition, I see that each of us, in our own ways, moved (and moves) forward by doing, by working. For Tonya, that meant calling us back to the ultimate goal of our committee. For Elizabeth, that meant scouring historical records for some sense of truth. For me, that meant doing my part, keeping the wheels moving on all the minutia of arranging a community event, to engage in storied community listening and free up emotional space for others, like Terri and Valerie, to show us how to do the work. I found my place not as the leader, nor as an eavesdropper, but as someone co-working. My attempt at a half-hearted administrative update during our emotional conversation about the marker text, then, needs to be reframed as a part of countering my own default story of guilt and moving toward a more reciprocal and critical community relationship. This sort of reflection is the praxis of storied community listening—not simply an embedded approach to listening or striving for an active reciprocal relationship with the community, but a critical reflection, through story. Such critical reflection moves me out of guilt and shame and into accountability, allowing room for new knowledge claims, such as Tonya's suggestions on our marker text or a more focused and driven emphasis on administrative projects like the essay contest, to take the forefront over the distraction of my own white fragility.

After Terri had had time to collect herself and her thoughts from our contested meeting, she emailed our committee and asked for a follow-up meeting, which included documented agenda items to discuss the marker text, the strong feelings that Tonya had expressed, and to take our pulse in terms of realigning our mission, vision, and goals. As she had done in other meetings, Terri asked each of us to go around and share our thoughts and feelings—once again, I was not able to hide behind the silence and anonymity that I had grown comfortable within our new and uncertain virtual world. I stated, simply and without the need for eloquent realizations or guilt or shame, just how much I was learning from everyone. Through the very reflection of this story, I see that a reciprocal approach to working alongside a community, in addition to an embedded approach to listening that involves critical reflection, is a necessary part of storied community listening. Leaning into and learning from white silences and reframing a sense of co-opting into learning are all part of this process, helping me learn to listen and hear in a way that makes sense for me. Storied community listening makes way for new knowledge claims, be they personal realizations or community counterstories, that I think is critical for academics as well as white people in this frayed work. I find in this story of our words my own attempt at truthfulness, the importance of reflective storying to truly process the listening that is needed to move toward a more holistic and inclusive community.

## CONCLUSION: THE STORY OF OUR UNVEILING

The COVID-19 pandemic derailed our plans to unveil the marker again and again and again. With each new setback, we pivoted and tried to do the best we could. The public killing of George Floyd at the hands of the police in May 2020 ("Killing of George Floyd") awakened Northwest Arkansas and many communities to the racial injustices that are still part of our everyday lives, and I think only deepened our coalition's sense of purpose. This modern-day version of lynching led our area to protest the Confederate statue prominently featured in a nearby town square, and it was formally removed in September 2020 ("Crews remove Confederate monument). The conversations prompted by those protests led to an interest in the new site of public memory our coalition was working toward. As we grew closer to unveiling the marker, we felt a growing hope that we might earnestly be taking a step toward racial reconciliation, while also wanting to hold the importance of veneration over education in the way in which we publicly remembered Aaron, Anthony, and Randall.

We were finally able to hold an in-person, on-site marker dedication and unveiling ceremony on May 15, 2021. I was in my last month of pregnancy and had just graduated with my Ph.D. the weekend before. The day started rainy and cold, and there was inexplicable water gushing out from underneath our kitchen sink. I arrived at our public library before 8:00 a.m. to help Tonya assemble an art installation featuring Black art outside of our event space. We rushed from there to Oaks Cemetery, where I got to see many of our coalition in person for the first time since I had really started showing. We hugged and rejoiced, and I was able to receive a few belly rubs, so grateful that my unborn daughter Lenora could be part of the celebration (and that she hadn't come too early for me to miss it). When the ceremony began, Terrell was the first speaker. Representing both the WCCRP and Oaks Cemetery, he said a prayer and a few words about the community, including his family's local legacy. Terri read aloud the marker language on one side, which can be seen below:

> On July 7, 1856, a white mob from present-day Elkins, Arkansas, kidnapped and lynched Anthony, a Black man and Aaron, a Black teenager. They were put on trial at the Washington County Courthouse in the death of a white man, James Boone, who enslaved them. Anthony was proven innocent. Aaron was released due to lack of evidence. Disregarding the rule of law, a mob led by Boone's sons reacted violently, lynching Anthony and Aaron near the jail, most likely on the estate of Archibald Yell, the deceased former governor of Arkansas. Randall, a third accused enslaved person whom an all-white jury found guilty, contested his verdict but was refused a retrial. Like lynchings, court-ordered executions—with mobs standing by—did not require reliable findings of guilt. Randall was hanged by the state on Aug. 1, 1856, likely on Gallows Hill, which is now within the Fayetteville National Cemetery next to Oaks Cemetery.
>
> During this era when enslaved Black people commonly faced violence by white enslavers, local oral history contends that, on May 29, 1856, James Boone attempted to sexually assault an enslaved Black woman who fatally assaulted him in self-defense. The Boone family then implicated Aaron, Anthony, and Randall in Boone's death. Slavery in Washington County, as elsewhere, devalued the lives of Black people resulting in violence, including sexual assault and lynchings for which hundreds of white perpetrators were never held accountable. (WCCRP, "Our Memorial Marker Photo Attached")

Hearing out loud the words we had so carefully chosen was powerful. It was even more powerful to hear those words at Oaks Cemetery, a site that taught our group so much about being and being part of a community. Terrell reminded us that "the inscription on this memorial will be here for eternity. But as you look at it, think of it, this could be the headlines for today. . . . I challenge you, as painful as it can be, don't repeat history." Even in that moment, we were reminded that such work is ongoing. Elizabeth rang a bell for a series of wishes she, Terri, Terrell and Valerie had put together on behalf of our coalition, and thunder rolled as she wished for an end to racism. The crowd of witnesses for the ceremony was small, intentional on our part, and the service, taking place in a cemetery, felt very much like a coming home ceremony.

On Being In It

We moved from the cemetery back to the library, where I got busy directing volunteers as to where to stand to manage traffic, a mad hunt for the gospel band that had agreed to join us, and last-minute scramble for access to the ice machine for the caterer. Along this journey I had become the point of contact for the Fayetteville Public Library, the manager of our coalition email, and our formal connection to the university. As I fielded phone calls from our leaders and shoved my husband and two coalition members out to the far reaches of the library to direct lost people our way, I wondered if perhaps I had found my own way to truly be in it.

The event started late, but we didn't care. A gospel band began the service, and many in the audience enthusiastically danced. I wanted to but, embarrassed, I didn't. One by one, Terri introduced each speaker—a long-time Black Fayetteville resident who spoke about the way things used to be, our two exceptional Black high school essay contest winners, and a Black psychologist who addressed the long-standing effects of racial trauma. The ceremony ended up lasting almost three hours, perhaps too long to hold the attention of the families and guests who had gathered to celebrate. Reflecting on my lack of full participation both in the dancing and in my own logistical regrets about the ceremony length, I return to this question, this idea of truly being in it. Through the reflective nature of this cumulative event and in the further reflection of writing my story as I have established the approach of storied community listening, I feel as if I have. Even in that feeling, regrets such as inhibition in a ceremony or the lack of holding my attention are part of it. There is no perfect resolution (as much as I might strive for it), but the process, the journey, are key.

Though I was deeply exhausted from the festivities of the day, the tensions and work of the past year and a half, and the growing pressure on my belly and my feet, I ended the night with a nice dinner with our team and two representatives from the EJI who had driven down to enjoy the festivities. We had one of those dinners that might be in a movie, where the narrator pans over each face laughing and talking, and soft music tells the viewer that something truly magical is coming to an end. In many ways, it reflected to me the growth we had all done as a coalition toward storied community listening. As we recounted our time together to the EJI representatives, I heard in each of us a version of storied community listening. Valerie walked through our complicated iterations of the marker language, and it was clear that all of us still wondered about those tense moments. Terri shared a growing relationship she now has with the Oaks Cemetery caretakers, and her plans to do more projects together. Ruth explicitly stated that this work and this project, led by Black women, taught her so much that she didn't know she didn't know. Each of us, including myself, had leaned into an embedded approach to listening, only discovered through critical reflection.

213

Together, we used this approach to strive for an active, reciprocal approach to working alongside our community.

As my unborn Lenora and I drove home that night, I was struck by a beautiful May sunset, and by the countless sunsets that were stolen from Aaron, Anthony, Randall, and those whose names we will never know. In my quest to more intentionally listen, to tell my story, I can't neglect to consider the community behind it all, and who I am within those spaces. Identifying my place in the coalition meant fulfilling the "duties as assigned" work of a subcommittee that, in my opinion, takes the pressure and the strain off the voices and the people who have historically been silenced for far too long. Finding my place in the coalition also meant stepping out of my comfort zone and decentering my own guilt to participate more actively. It meant taking risks and speaking up, being truly embedded in the work.

Storied community listening involves sharing the story of how I experienced these moments of conflict and ultimately practiced an approach to help me move toward racial reconciliation. In Terri calling me in to direct participation through casting my vote on our marker location, I learned the value of an embedded approach to listening. In the caretaker's questions about my physical presence at Oaks Cemetery, I starkly discovered the importance of working alongside a community. In Tonya's honest reactions to our marker text, I found a way to critically reflect through story. In the Zoom calls, answered emails, frenzied updates, tiny exasperations, and magical moments of our coalitional work together, I found a way to be in it. In writing this story out and its many iterations, evolving from a graduate student clinging to other scholars and centering her white guilt to attempting to move toward my individual voice with my own thoughts and ideas, I have learned the critical importance of story. Storied community listening, as I have come to enact it, seeks an embedded approach to listening and includes critical reflecting through story and an active, reciprocal approach to working alongside a community. I see where this project, my writing, might speak to other white women, other female scholars, and other scholars standing on the edge of academia and community. By always striving to truly be in it as we collectively leave that edge, however, I hope to tell my story from my positionality for my own reflection and growth, in the hopes that it can speak to others in whatever form they need it.

## CODA: ON BEING IN IT

My story, as I mentioned at the beginning of this chapter, has no ultimate resolution. The marker now sits stoically at the entrance to Oaks Cemetery, and the coalition has formally disbanded. Though I keep in touch with its members, our work together is complete. I've recently moved to start a new faculty position in Cincinnati, and the unborn infant who attended our unveiling is now a walking, talking, highly opinionated toddler. And, though I'm often frustrated at white scholars who tie their newfound theories, definitions, and experiences into "a pretty bow" that blends theory and praxis at the end of their academic pieces, I find myself equally frustrated that I'm not able to do just that. Instead, I hope to take my idea of storied community listening with me into my classrooms at the university, into the community spaces I hope to be part of, into my work bringing up another young white woman. And, along with approaching these roles and spaces with storied community listening, I hope to see where it falls short. To grow it, challenge it, and evolve it as I, too, involve it in my roles as faculty, scholar, mother, white person, woman, and community member.

This is just one story. But it's my story. And if nothing else, I hope it leads me to deeper listening, to more equitable community work, to more carefully listening to my role and the role of others.

## ACKNOWLEDGMENTS

First and foremost, I want to thank the beautiful leaders of the Washington County Community Remembrance Project for welcoming me into our work together. I have been challenged by you, grown with you, and am daily inspired by your work. I'd also like to extend a genuine thanks to our editors—Jenn, Lauren, and Romeo. You took the time and attention I've been needing in this work and from this field to truly guide me through the story I do have and need to share.

This project is dedicated to Aaron, Anthony, and Randall, those that they loved, and those that loved them; to all those whose names we don't know, taken too soon in a white supremacist world, who were never given a chance to say goodbye. May we do better by continuing to try to be in it. This is a hopeful step in that direction.

## WORKS CITED

@4029 News—Fort Smith and Fayetteville, Arkansas. "Crews Remove Confederate Monument." *Facebook*. 2 Sept. 2020, https://www.facebook.com/watch/live /?ref=watch_permalink&v=2081489621995281.

Collins, Patricia Hill. *Black Feminist Thought: Knowledge, Consciousness, and the Politics of Empowerment*. Routledge, 2008.

Fishman, Jenn, and Lauren Rosenberg. "Community Writing, Community Listening." *Community Writing, Community Literacy*, special issue of *Community Literacy Journal*, vol. 13, no. 1, 2018, pp. 1–6, https://doi.org/10.1353/clj.2018.0016.

Hobsbawm, Eric, editor. *The Invention of Tradition*. Cambridge UP, 2012.

Hsu, V. Jo. *Constellating Home: Trans and Queer Asian American Rhetorics*. The Ohio State UP, 2022.

Jackson, Rachel C. with Dorothy Whitehorse DeLaune. "Decolonizing Community Writing with Community Listening: Story, Transrhetorical Resistance, and Indigenous Cultural Literacy Activism." Fishman and Rosenberg, pp. 37–54, https://doi.org/10.25148/clj.13.1.009089.

"Killing of George Floyd." *Wikipedia*, 20 Dec. 2020. *Wikipedia*, https://tinyurl.com/35wpbaxb.

"March Minutes: Community Remembrance Project Coalition Meeting." Washington County Community Remembrance Project, 3 Mar. 2020. Fayetteville, Arkansas.

Martinez, Aja Y. *Counterstory: The Rhetoric and Writing of Critical Race Theory*. National Council of Teachers of English, 2020.

"Oak Cemetery: A Forgotten Place." *YouTube*, https://www.youtube.com/watch?v=V-5J4NhOgoXA. Accessed 5 June 2020.

"Oaks Cemetery." *Arkansas Heritage Preservation Program*, https://tinyurl.com/mrr765zf. Accessed 5 June 2020.

"October Minutes: Community Remembrance Project Coalition Meeting." Washington County Community Remembrance Project, 23 Oct. 2019. Fayetteville, Arkansas.

Ratcliffe, Krista. *Rhetorical Listening: Identification, Gender, Whiteness*. Southern Illinois UP, 2006.

Reed, Niketa. "Washington County Community Remembrance Project." Squarespace, 2020, https://washingtoncountyremembers.org.

Royster, Jacqueline Jones, and Gesa E. Kirsch. *Feminist Rhetorical Practices: New Horizons for Rhetoric, Composition, and Literacy Studies*. Southern Illinois UP, 2012.

Saad, Layla. *Me and White Supremacy: Combat Racism, Change the World, and Become a Good Ancestor*. Sourcebooks, 2020.

Singleton, Mitch. "Dr. James Monroe Boone." *Arkansas Country Doctor's Museum*, Sept. 2007. https://www.drmuseum.net/dr-james-monroe-boone.

Washington County Community Remembrance Project. "Information about the Washington County Community Remembrance Project." December 2019. Washington County Community Remembrance Project. Handout.

———. "Marker text to EJI 721." 3 Aug. 2020. Washington County Community Remembrance Project. Handout.

———. "Local History Interest." 17 June 2019. Email Response.

———. "Our Memorial Marker Photo Attached." Washington County Community Remembrance.

CHAPTER 10.

# DAUNTING COMMUNITY LISTENING: DESIGNING AND IMPLEMENTING A COMMUNITY LISTENING FRAMEWORK AND ACCOUNTABILITY GROUP FOR UNDERGRADUATE STUDENTS

**Keri Epps and Rowie Kirby-Straker**
**with Casey Beiswenger, Zoe Chamberlin, Hannah Hill,**
**Lauren Robertson, and Kaitlyn Taylor**
Wake Forest University

*Informed by their work with Authoring Action (A2), an arts-based orga-
nization in Winston-Salem, North Carolina, that centers teen voices, the
primary authors of this chapter discuss the short co-curricular program
they designed to train undergraduates in community listening. To facilitate this training, the authors collaborated with a student organization to
develop the Community Listening Accountability Group (CLAG) using
tenets of community listening from rhetoric and composition and listening pedagogy in communication. Throughout the process, they closely collaborated with Nathan Ross Freeman, Artistic Director and Co-Founder
of A2, who described listening in community partnerships as "daunting,"
inspiring the concept of daunting community listening (DCL). A set of
embodied communicative praxes that center the community partner's
voice, DCL is also a disposition or openness to the discomfort that listening and related learning can entail. In designing the CLAG and its
programming, and reflecting on the process with Nathan, the authors
came to understand the significance of listening-in-process and reflecting-
in-the-moment as primary components of DCL. As noted in the contributing undergraduate authors' reflections, these components were particularly helpful in the pilot course. Ultimately, the CLAG emphasizes the
need for undergraduate students to experience discomfort and risk-taking*

DOI: https://doi.org/10.37514/PER-B.2025.2531.2.10

*in community listening practice without the pressures of grades or official assessment from traditional academic courses. The authors name the long-term goals of the CLAG and practice of daunting community listening as "listening to ourselves and our histories, listening to one another, and listening to our phenomenal partners . . . who model this radical listening every day.*

*Discuss* "emanate." *Go.*

Nathan Ross Freeman, Artistic Director and Co-Founder of the nonprofit Authoring Action, opens educator training sessions with these three words. The group, known as A2, is an arts-based organization in Winston-Salem, North Carolina, that offers teen authors conceptual tools for creating authentic pieces of writing, music, and film. When Nathan founded the organization with Lynn Rhoades in 2001, they saw a need for teen voices to be amplified in the community. In particular, they wanted local politicians and community leaders to learn from young people's lived expertise on social justice issues, including gun violence, sexual assault, and racism. To that end, A2 was founded on community listening, and in over two decades, it has become a powerful community resource. Not only does A2 help teens learn to listen to themselves and to their peers, but it also helps ensure they are heard by the local community and its leadership.

To foster the teens' confidence in writing and speaking, the A2 curriculum deliberately centers the teens' voices. Their words, stories, and experiences are the only content they use—from the "First Ink Discussion" that asks them to discuss a single word like "emanate" through the final stages of the process. Nathan's method, founded on Socratic dialogue, facilitates knowledge-sharing and confidence-building as the teens listen to how each other arrived at their own understandings of the prompt. After the authors dialogue for several minutes without Nathan's intervention, Nathan finally reenters the conversation to introduce a synonym (for example, "how is 'emanate' different from 'originate?'"). His method necessarily decenters the teacher, requiring that the instructor listens intently rather than contributing, correcting, or even affirming the students' remarks. Nathan simply repeats what students have said and presses them to "tell [him] more." This approach encourages students to clarify their perspectives and demonstrate how they understand the prompt (Ballard et al. 182). Moreover, the teens are encouraged to shift their attention away from the instructor and toward one another and themselves as they negotiate possible meanings of the prompt as a group. At the end of the "First Ink Discussion," Nathan then introduces other stages of A2's writing process that takes the authors through invention exercises across three different genres (a word table, a

Daunting Community Listening

mosaic, and finally, a written piece in the author's chosen genre) to create pieces in spoken word, film, and/or music that artfully communicate the teens' stories.

Many events and relationships serendipitously led us to Authoring Action, but for the purposes of this chapter, we focus on how our group from Wake Forest University was drawn to community listening and what we could learn about it from A2. Initially, Keri, a faculty member in Writing, and five undergraduates participated in Nathan's five-hour, intensive educator training workshop. Keri arranged the session after participating in a previous A2 educator workshop, and she invited Casey, Zoe, Hannah, and Lauren, all student leaders affiliated with the student organization Wake Women Lead, to join her. Keri also reached out to Rowie Kirby-Straker, a colleague in Communication who teaches an undergraduate course on listening, and she also extended an invitation to Kaitlyn Taylor, an undergraduate researcher who led efforts to identify relevant research and scholarship on community listening in both rhetoric and composition and communication. Together, the seven of us began planning ways to incorporate community listening into campus programming, especially for undergraduate students involved in community-engaged work. Based on her experience with listening pedagogy, Rowie explained that there were limited resources for the kind of community listening instruction at the heart of Nathan's pedagogy, and we were eager to learn all we could from him. These goals informed our long-range decision to develop an extracurricular program that centered on community listening and prepares Wake Forest students to work with A2 as mentors to teen authors. In the short term, Rowie's observation led us to pilot the Community Listening Accountability Group (CLAG), which invites everyone involved in A2's training—students, faculty, and community partners—to reflect on their individual community listening praxes and to work together to formally define community listening and evolve effective ways of teaching it, as well.

Over the four semesters that CLAG has been in development, our understanding of community listening has evolved into something Nathan taught us to call "daunting community listening," or DCL. Through our work with him and others at A2, our scholarly research, and our collaboration with initial CLAG participants, we have come to know DCL as a community listening practice that is productively intimidating and transformative for all involved. We have adopted Nathan's definition to center constant reflection: not only of the listening event in isolation, but also of the relationship between the parties and the issue(s) that brought them together. This reflection calls listeners to pay layered and contextualized attention to community events and involves not only listening in the present moment and discerning traces of the issues and relations that inform that moment; it also requires regular self-reflection and genuine consideration of listeners to examine their own ideas and assumptions along

219

with their prior and possible future actions. Nathan's point is that such listening can, and even should, be daunting, especially in difficult community conversations, and we concur. From an academic perspective, as we gained experience with DCL, we came to see how it distinctively compels listeners to make tacit knowledge explicit and open to both consideration and challenge or change.

In short, according to Nathan, DCL demands uncomfortable accountability and transformation, especially the kind that comes with honest, recursive interrogation of how and why we listen—and what it means to listen at all. In designing the CLAG, we did not necessarily start with this definition of DCL, but we realized throughout the pilot that DCL was our goal as we continued to work closely with Nathan and A2 throughout the program. In the early planning stages, we found ourselves needing to go beyond traditional instructional practices for listening outlined in communication scholarship (reviewed in the next section). Similarly, we found many useful tenets of community listening in rhetoric and composition research, but we quickly realized that we needed to situate and expand on these tenets in our work with A2. In what follows, we review this literature and outline our workshop sessions and their evolution as we strengthened our own DCL practice with Nathan and other A2 members. Throughout the chapter, we describe the importance of listening-in-process and reflecting-in-the-moment as primary components of DCL that appeared particularly helpful for undergraduate students based on our group's writings and interviews.[1] We end by reflecting on the community partner's and students' insights to capture where we are now and where we are going in our efforts to prepare undergraduates (and ourselves) for the hard work of DCL.

## COMMUNITY LISTENING IN RHETORIC AND COMPOSITION

We began building the pilot in Spring 2021, just a few weeks after Keri, Casey, Zoe, Hannah, and Lauren participated in Nathan's intensive training session. When building our curriculum, we looked to listening scholarship in rhetoric and composition and communication studies to help us identify and fill gaps we saw in undergraduate listening education. We found particularly helpful theoretical support in the 2018 special issue of *Community Literacy Journal*. In the introduction, editors Jenn Fishman and Lauren Rosenberg explain community listening:

> as a literacy practice that involves a deep, direct engagement
> with individuals and groups working to address urgent issues in
> everyday life, issues anchored by long histories and complicated

---

1    The study is approved under IRB00024321.

> by competing interpretations as well as clashing modes of
> expression. When we speak of community listening, we are not
> simply talking about paying attention, though keen attention
> is vital to any deep listening practice. . . . Instead, community
> listening is an active, layered, intentional practice. (1)

Fishman and Rosenberg's attention to action and the multifaceted, evolving process of community listening is critical to how we understand the need for more focused preparatory listening training.

Building on Fishman and Rosenberg's definition of community listening in the same special issue, Karen Rowan and Alexandra J. Cavallaro introduce a preparatory listening model to help combat the deficit narratives about communities that the media creates and perpetuates, specifically in the San Bernardino community, by identifying community assets first. To do so, the authors suggest "standing under" the discourses of these communities, as Krista Ratcliffe's theory of rhetorical listening calls us to do (30). In differentiating community listening from rhetorical listening, Rachel Jackson and Kiowa Elder Dorothy Whitehorse DeLaune (in the same special *CLJ* issue) note that community listening allows for storytelling and storylistening as a form of resistance to colonial narratives of Indigenous people. In our work, we apply the spirit of their perspective to the listening preparation work of the CLAG. Preparing to listen to community voices includes an embrace of counternarratives and existing assets, especially those of the teens of Authoring Action who often have difficulty finding authentic, meaningful spaces to share their voices.

We relate our preparatory efforts to the feminist ethics that Fishman and Rosenberg discuss. In our work, it applies most to the ways that adopting a listening stance necessitates change within ourselves. This idea of welcoming self-transformation closely aligns with Lisa Blankenship's theorization of "rhetorical empathy," which she identifies as an epistemology, a place, and a stance we must assume. Blankenship concludes:

> approaching others in rhetorical engagements must begin
> with changing ourselves, with listening, with trying to under-
> stand the personal and political factors that influence the
> person who makes our blood boil. This approach to rhetoric
> is very different from one that listens to others to make a
> point and change them. It goes beyond audience analysis and
> considering our audience and instead asks that we become
> vulnerable enough to consider our own motives, our blind
> spots, and our prejudice. Adopting this stance is vital for peo-
> ple with privilege; it is no longer an option. (8–9)

In our work with A2, this theoretical framework helped move us beyond academic approaches to audience analysis to thinking more critically about our own transformations through full-body community listening.

Ultimately, we find that the common phrase "community-engaged work" tends to flatten the complex community contexts where faculty and students participate, and DCL has helped us to consider this work's complexity more fully as we prepare for our collaborations. Attention to intentional preparatory listening can be adapted to multiple settings, including an organization in the nascent stages of development or one with a decades-long history like A2. In community contexts, listening can also be adapted over time or even at a moment's notice. For us, from the start, listening meant a lot more than the process of receiving, comprehending, interpreting, evaluating, and responding described in Thompson et al. (2004). Especially early on, community listening involved preparing for and practicing engagement of our full selves with A2's organizers. These practices guided our pilot, and they helped us to prepare to listen with complete intellectual, emotional, and embodied engagement.

## LISTENING IN COMMUNICATION: GAPS IN EDUCATION

After reviewing community listening studies in rhetoric and composition, we identified communication scholarship focused on listening, highlighting how students' particular needs are addressed (Bodie, Graham, et al.; Markgraf; Janusik). Listening research and pedagogy can be traced back to the mid-twentieth century, and some have argued that it can be traced back to even earlier in that century (Beard and Bodie 210). The research on listening pedagogy helped us detect oversights in listening instruction, and we began to imagine how we might prepare students to work with A2 as well as other community partners. It was clear from the literature that although students spend a considerable portion of their time listening, their exposure to listening instruction during (and likely before) college is extremely limited (Janusik 203; Wolvin 125). Researchers and educators have highlighted the limits of listening instruction in the introductory communication course (Ford et al.; Thompson et al. 227; Wolvin 9), where students' limited exposure to listening best practices barely scratches the surface of the complex and multifaceted roles of listening in communication overall (Janusik 5; Thompson et al. 227). This means that college students engaged in community work, whether individually or through campus organizations, tend to be grossly underprepared to be community listeners.

Interestingly, however, students often have rather optimistic perspectives on their listening skills at first. In a pre/post survey of 469 students enrolled in a basic communication course, for instance, Wendy S. Zabava Ford, Andrew D.

Wolvin, and Sungeun Chung found that students perceived themselves to be better listeners at the beginning of the course than at the end in several listening contexts (9). The authors suggest these self-assessments partly result from "students' enhanced awareness of the complex set of behaviors required for effective listening" and a "heightened sensitivity to their listening inadequacies" (11). The review of the student authors' reflections included later in this chapter reveals a similar gap (i.e., a gap between perceived and actual listening competence).

As we developed the CLAG, we learned all we could from other scholars who have worked on listening curricula and pedagogical practices. With Laura Janusik, we noted that there has been steady interest in this work but little consensus on the *how* of listening instruction (194). Among available options, the Integrative Listening Model (ILM) developed by Kathy Thompson, Pamela Leintz, Barbara Nevers, and Susan Witkowski stood out to us. They recommend a four-step process to becoming a better listener:

1. preparation,
2. application of the listening process model
   (receive—comprehend—interpret—evaluate—respond),
3. assessment of listening performance, and
4. establishment of new goals. (230)

This model incorporates elements of the International Listening Association's (ILA) definition of listening, which is "the process of receiving, constructing meaning from, and responding to spoken and/or nonverbal messages" (Thompson et al. 226). Developed by faculty at Alverno College, the ILM has been successfully used to train students in listening competence (Janusik 201). Training in listening using the ILM is part of Alverno's ability-based curriculum which situates listening as an ability to be reflected on, learned, and developed, beginning with a communication placement assessment taken before students start their first semester. The assessment includes a listening activity and self-assessment that sets up students to "not only listen to learn, but also learn to listen" throughout their college experience (Thompson et al. 236). Students are then introduced to the ILM in required communication seminars and are given multiple opportunities to apply the model (236). Details of how Alverno College applies the ILM in practice are found in Thompson et al. Given that this model had been continually used to train college students to listen, we elected to adopt it in the pilot CLAG, as well.

We did not, however, simply import the ILM into the CLAG curriculum. Instead, we used it and other resources we collected to help our students get genuine and robust training in listening. We wanted the CLAG to help them do more than pay attention to what A2 members might say. We also wanted them to be ready to manage the affective, behavioral, cognitive, and relational dimensions of listening that became the most salient in their work with A2. The students in our first pilot revealed to us that even basic knowledge about the listening process, group discussion of its complexity, journaling, and critical reflection about listening behavior in community engagement contexts can facilitate listening growth at the personal and community levels. Using the aforementioned literature, we aimed to create a recursive approach to understanding community listening and accountability that allows flexibility as we negotiate what that means within ourselves, within the group, and with the community partner.

## DAUNTING COMMUNITY LISTENING (DCL): EXPERTISE FROM OUR COMMUNITY PARTNER

While the scholarship outlined above was tremendously helpful, our most important resource was the artistic director of A2, Nathan Ross Freeman. In many ways, his ideas about community listening and DCL specifically were consistent with academic perspectives. For example, in an interview with Keri, Nathan's definition of DCL echoed Thompson et al., who characterize listening in general as "[t]he dynamic, interactive process of integrating appropriate listening attitudes, knowledge, and behaviors to achieve the selected goal(s) of a listening event" (229). Furthermore, Nathan seemed to agree with the International Listening Association that listening is "the process that includes construction of meaning and response to verbal and nonverbal messages" (Thompson et al. 226). Nathan's definition similarly requires intention, preparation, attention, and reflection; notably, however, his understanding of DCL begs for more reflection on listeners' personal histories as well as their motives and goals for listening events and relationships. Rather than reflecting on listening in general or in isolation, Nathan says that we should dwell in the discomfort of interrogating ourselves about what we really want out of each collaboration. Doing so, he believes, helps us as listeners identify where biases or selfish intentions might be driving our interactions or leading us to try to change those to whom we listen rather than ourselves.

Nathan's definition of DCL also widens the Integrative Listening Model (ILM) to encompass the entire relationship between the institutional representative and community partner, going beyond one listening event or message exchanged in that event. Further, Nathan's definition requires that the institutional party continuously seeks to comprehend, interpret, evaluate, and respond to their role in the relationship and the shared goals of that relationship. Consequently, the institutional parties become more aware of their changing attitudes toward themselves, the community partner, the relationship, and their approach to the issue at hand.

Nathan also changed the way we look at the rhetorical triangle. So often, scholars call attention to the meaning-making it illustrates by focusing on the messages that people send. Nathan's sense of DCL, by contrast, centers on the listening process along with relations between interlocutors. Nathan does not think that settling a meaning is necessary; instead, he sees being committed to building and maintaining a genuine relationship as more important. This perspective is supported by Jackson with DeLaune, who suggest that community listening should "activate relationships between peoples and places through collaborative meaning making" (37). This approach to listening allows us to "listen differently, with a community rather than to a community or for a community" (42).

In the interview, Nathan talked a lot about the listener's role, attitude, and goals. While we listen for many different reasons, when Nathan talked about DCL, he emphasized the processes of self-reflection and building relationships as the real goals. Explaining this process further, Nathan likens community listening to a deposition because of the importance of witness testimony and the intentional, thoughtful work that goes into preparing for the deposition. Based on his experience taping depositions and the mentorship he received in that role, Nathan uses the analogy to demonstrate how multiple factors work together to accurately reflect the witness testimony. He explains that just as it is crucial to plan for supporting elements of a deposition—the camera's angle for taping the witness, the location where the witness sits, the time of day, the type of room, and other factors—so, too, must the listener consider multiple contextual factors that determine what is heard, seen, and felt as the witness testifies. Nathan considers this level of careful planning as a way to "create an atmosphere of intimacy" required for community listening. He states that, like a deposition, while the actual listening interaction may take a few minutes or hours, the preparation may take days or weeks. Our review of listening pedagogy scholarship made it clear that this kind of attention to the labor of community listening is lacking in undergraduate education and must extend well beyond a typical fifteen-week semester. The timeliness of the CLAG thus became even more apparent.

In the next sections, we discuss how we initially designed and implemented the pilot undergraduate accountability program and what the students gleaned from these sessions. Then, we reflect on how we are infusing DCL in our redesign to ensure that future undergraduate participants are given more time and more tools to dwell in the discomfort of listening in community partnerships.

## DESIGNING AND IMPLEMENTING THE PILOT UNDERGRADUATE COMMUNITY LISTENING ACCOUNTABILITY GROUP

Again, we were learning about DCL while the CLAG pilot was underway; even at the beginning, however, we wanted to center the reflexive and relational focus that Nathan later clarified for us. The program goals listed below are where we started, and as we worked together, we continued to refine the focus on listening-in-process and reflecting-in-the-moment:

## PROGRAM GOALS

1. Self-assess listening styles in a community-engaged setting
2. Consider the role of active empathetic listening in community-engaged settings
3. Determine best personal listening practices in community-engaged settings
4. Apply personalized listening framework in community engagement project with A2
5. Learn the community partner's interpretation of listening and align our listening behavior with their expectations.

## LONG-TERM GOALS

1. Self-reflect on listening throughout programming with A2
2. Use listening skills to adapt to changing organizational needs
3. Develop sustainable, authentic, reciprocal relationship with A2.

We designed four, ninety-minute workshops described below (and more fully in the Appendix A) to help the students meet these eight goals. The four workshops were completed over four consecutive weeks during Summer 2021.

## SESSION ONE: "INTRODUCTION TO THE COMMUNITY LISTENING INTEGRATIVE FRAMEWORK"

The first session introduced the students to a range of listening scholarship, but primarily focused on the ILM (see Appendix A). In reviewing listening scholarship, we hoped to decenter the transactional model of communication to accommodate our evolving understanding of DCL. Ultimately, the session provided space for students to discuss speaking and listening as independent processes and to reflect on their own listening processes. This session emphasized introspection as a crucial part of preparatory listening and listening-in-process.

## SESSION TWO: "LISTENING FOR COMMUNITY PARTNER NEEDS: A CONVERSATION WITH A2'S CO-FOUNDERS"

This session included a conversation with Lynn Rhoades, Executive Director and Co-Founder of A2, and Nathan Ross Freeman. Here, we wanted to learn about the organization's current needs and the listening strategies discussed in the first workshop (see Appendix A). While we prepared questions, the conversation was intentionally partner-driven and allowed us to learn more about A2's goal to expand the educator training and the organization's current writing program with mothers of gun violence victims. At the end of this session, Nathan succinctly described what needs to happen before DCL can take place: "We have to *want* to listen. We have to mutually create an atmosphere of intimacy. I always ask the authors: 'What are you doing here? I can't listen to you if I'm not real with you.'" We left this session with that question for ourselves: "What are *we* doing here?" and used it to reflect more intentionally before the next session, as DCL calls us to do.

## SESSION THREE: "RHETORICAL EMPATHY AND LISTENING ACROSS DIFFERENCE"

In the third session, we shared what we heard to be A2's described needs and reflected on how they were different from what we initially assumed. Keri then moved on to the topic of rhetorical empathy as a way of listening across difference. Specifically, Blankenship explains, "rhetorical empathy [is] both a topos and a trope, *a choice and habit of mind* that invents and invites discourse informed by deep listening and its resulting emotion, characterized by narratives based on personal experience" (5, emphasis ours). This definition gave us another tool to use as we prepared for listening, listening-in-process, and reflecting-in-the-moment.

## SESSION FOUR: "PREPARING FOR THE UNEXPECTED"

This session focused on practicing DCL as we prepared for future partnership opportunities with A2. We focused on being honest with ourselves by acknowledging our own capacities and highlighting A2's assets; this part of the preparatory listening process led us to emphasize our ethical obligation to not over-promise the organization. For instance, we felt that we had strengths in marketing and fundraising for A2's summer programming. We determined we could offer writing/mentoring support during the weekly advanced writing workshops; however, this was only a small portion of their needs, and we would need to plan to connect them to others who might have the skills and resources that we lacked. In the spirit of accountability, we ended this session by promising that we would continue to come together, even informally, and assess why/how we were showing up and evaluating our long-term vision for our relationship with A2.

## STUDENT PERSPECTIVES

We have a sense of what students learned from the CLAG and their work with A2 thanks to the reflective writing and interviews that Zoe, Lauren, Hannah, and Casey contributed. Three main themes emerged from the students' reflections: (1) acknowledgment of their shortcomings as listeners, (2) a new understanding of what community listening entails including its limitations, and (3) resolve to continue the hard work of growing as community listeners. These takeaways helped us to see what we were already doing well in preparing undergraduates for community listening and the areas that we could emphasize in the CLAG redesign with a more intentional emphasis on DCL.

## THEME 1: ACKNOWLEDGEMENT OF THEIR SHORTCOMINGS AS LISTENERS

Students highlighted that prior to the A2 training and the listening accountability group meetings, they really did not know what listening was nor how applied in a community engagement context—that they had mischaracterized it and that they were worse listeners than they originally thought. Hannah puts it this way:

> During our very first accountability group session, I quickly realized that my expertise in listening was all but a construct. When I reflected on the way that I "listened" to others both in my personal life and in my relationships with community partners, I realized that my idea of "good listening" was totally wrong. What I thought was good "listening" had really not been listening at all. . . . I realized that despite the many hours I spent completing service projects and working with community partners, I could not think of a single time where I slowed down enough to ask, "what do you need from me?" (Hannah Hill)

For Zoe, the realization that she was not as strong a listener as she thought came with the recognition that listening was indeed a process that included continuous reflection. She notes:

> Before working with Authoring Action, I thought I knew what being a good listener was, even going so far as to identify as one. Yet, I had never thought about how effective of a listener I was. The thought of being a good listener was a quality I always thought I should obtain, but I never explored where I was in terms of my development as a listener. (Zoe Chamberlin)

## THEME 2: NEW UNDERSTANDING OF WHAT COMMUNITY LISTENING ENTAILS

Each reflection details how the students have come to a much deeper and nuanced understanding of what listening is and ways to approach it in a community partnership. This understanding is evident in the personal definitions of community listening that highlight the value of preparation, open-mindedness, self-awareness, and self-reflection. Lauren's reflection demonstrates how the students became attuned to the complexity and multifaceted nature of listening. She states:

> Where I used to see listening as complete understanding, I became able to see it as a humble recognition that I can never completely understand, but I should always try. Like all worthwhile endeavors, listening is hard work. It requires patience and persistence, concentration and compassion. It is the perfect harmony of body and soul: nodding my head, focusing my eyes, positioning my body, evaluating my biases, preparing my mind, opening my heart, finding as much power in the hush of silence as the crescendo of offering a response. Listening is not just hearing, it is an internalized, all-encompassing experience in which I am intricately intertwined with the music of the moment, continuously seeking to hear and listen and learn and understand with every part of myself entirely present and intimately engaged. (Lauren Robertson)

In unpacking how the listening process functions in a community partnership, students also underscore the importance of being comfortable with uncertainty. Casey Beiswenger states, "I realized that effective listening requires a willingness to lack all the answers, as well as a radical suspension of my preconceptions," and Zoe Chamberlin opines that although empathy and nonverbal communication were essential, "the most important aspect of listening in my eyes is the willingness to be uncomfortable." The reflections also demonstrate that students are aware of both the benefits and the limitations of community listening. Casey explains this reality:

> In working with Authoring Action, this meant acknowledging that despite my desire to work with students, the organization did not need me as an educator and I could provide more impactful support in other areas. This realization marked a significant improvement in the efficacy of my listening abilities, as well as a turning point in my approach to community partnership as well as interpersonal relationships. (Casey Beiswenger)

## THEME 3: RESOLVE TO CONTINUE GROWING AS COMMUNITY LISTENERS

Although the students' reflections characterize community listening as hard work and an ongoing process, their resolve to continue to put in the effort needed for growth is evident. Lauren Robertson states, "More than anything, this experience has taught me that listening is less about being perfect, and more about actively choosing to immerse oneself in the continuous process of preparation, empathy and reflection." Hannah Hill notes, "This is not to say that my work on listening is over—in fact, it has only just begun. Listening in community spaces demands follow-through and requires flexibility and humility."

Perhaps one of the most heartwarming outcomes of the CLAG is the way it has inspired students' plans for their careers, as Lauren's reflection demonstrates:

> This experience has inspired me to pursue a Master's program centered around seeking to understand and develop similarly innovative efforts in education. Only by opening ourselves up to listen and learn from what's new and different and ground-breaking, can we maximize a better future. (Lauren Robertson)

For all of the students, the program was the first time they had ever been asked to reflect on their listening practices, and it was certainly the first time they had reflected on *community* listening. The excerpted reflections offer a few glimpses of the work that they did and, notably, show them inviting discomfort and a full-body listening experience, as DCL requires. These takeaways intersect with what we were learning from Nathan and led us to incorporate these topics more intentionally in the CLAG redesign. The students' complete written reflections are found in Appendix B so that the "listeners" of this collection might learn from them directly.

## REFLECTING ON AND EMBRACING DAUNTING COMMUNITY LISTENING IN UNDERGRADUATE EDUCATION

After reflecting more on the pilot and debriefing with Nathan, we are determined to focus more intently on the following aspects of DCL in future programming. This more radical reflective approach, we argue, is essential for an undergraduate training program that we eventually hope to offer more widely across campus.

First, we want to emphasize the time commitment even further. In the pilot, we not only realized the necessity of preparing for our community partner interactions through research, training, and pre-interaction reflection, but also the necessity of making time to debrief and discuss the interactions with each other and with the community partner more frequently. This debriefing includes giving ourselves the proverbial space to unpack our cognitions, emotions, and behaviors during the time spent with our community partner and the youth

Daunting Community Listening

with whom they collaborate. While this observation seems obvious, we recognize how easy it is for all of us—faculty and undergraduate students alike—to confine ourselves to the typical academic calendar. As we continue the CLAG and our work with A2, we want to be more mindful of our time commitment and A2's resources. Reflecting more intentionally on DCL now, we can more clearly see that we are getting more out of the relationship than we are giving, and our long-term dedication is a big part of accountability. We need for future groups of students who participate in the CLAG to reflect deeply on the time commitment and the likelihood of uneven labor as they enter listening events and consider the longevity of the community relationship.

Second, we want to highlight more clearly that community listening involves listening with our entire being and bringing our whole selves to the interaction with our partner, flaws and all. Just as we were reminded by Nathan that listening is *seeing* the other person, we are reminded that we need to *see* ourselves first and show up with every part of our being. Nathan clearly summarizes this idea here:

> the degree to which I can subvert my gender, ethnicity, height, weight, appearance—the degree [to] which I can subvert those and predicate my person. . . . Even in my educator workshop . . . I have to leave my baggage outside. What does baggage mean—anything that is going to get in the way of me being vulnerable and open. . . . When I say 'I am listening to you' what that should mean is that '*I* am listening to you.' I *am* listening to you. I am listening to you past all my biases, I am listening to you with the essential me. (Nathan Ross Freeman)

We appreciate this perspective because in listening literature, including the best practices taught in public speaking, scholars emphasize centering the audience—not acknowledging the need to work on ourselves first to prepare for an honest interaction with the audience. Relatedly, we are intrigued with Nathan's take on honesty, which he defines as "telling the truth timely." Nathan seeks such honesty in the answers to the two fundamental questions he asks everyone in the A2 educator workshop:

1. Why are you here?
2. What do you want to leave here with?

In bringing our whole selves to each interaction, we become fully present while at the same time allowing the person to whom we are listening to be fully present also. We elevate their *presence* over ours: a balancing act. To this point, Nathan highlights the fluidity of *seeing* the other person, stating that while he prepares a syllabus for his educator workshop, that syllabus is never complete "until [he] see[s] who [he is] dealing with." This viewpoint is critical for our accountability group's evolving content, as it allows us room to grow as we get to know our partner better. Furthermore, specifically for undergraduate students, this kind of dynamic listening necessitates acknowledging their (likely) temporary residence and the histories of the local community's relationship with our private liberal arts institution. Bringing the questions that Nathan poses into our programming, we hope, will encourage undergraduate students to be honest with themselves about what they want from a relationship with A2 and other potential community partners and to think about the long-term effects those goals can have on the community partner after they have graduated.

Relatedly, on the topic of performativity and full-body listening, the student collaborators in this chapter reported being conflicted by the need to pay attention to their nonverbal communication while avoiding pretense and performative listening behavior (e.g., excessive nodding). A conversation with Nathan after the CLAG's pilot made it clear that such a concern should take a backseat when one brings one's whole self to community listening. As a believer in the saying "the body can't lie," Nathan argues that in bringing one's entire being to a listening interaction, the body naturally demonstrates listening and not simply hearing. His understanding goes beyond what much of the active listening literature suggests in terms of body language best practices, such as physically leaning in, giving eye contact, nodding, and having an open posture. In contrast, Nathan deemphasizes thinking about our body language because, in his words: "when I am listening to someone, I am also talking to them, in terms of everything, because my body will form a posture that matches my attitude." While this alignment between body and attitude is ideal, he added, "it can be challenging." This challenge is one we want to address directly in the next CLAG to help undergraduate students avoid overthinking their body language and/or trying to overperform as "good students" in each listening interaction.

Lastly, reflecting on the title of our group, we have begun reevaluating what we mean by "accountability." Nathan's interpretation of DCL inextricably links with accountability and the need to be honest with oneself. Accountability relies on all of the above steps to prepare and to *show up* honestly with one's whole self in an interaction. Nathan suggests that reflecting on one's accountability involves "the degree to which I can recognize my part in something and I can share it, and I share it in such a way where there is no argument in terms of whose fault it is, what was my part in an event or a discussion or a thought." At first, we were using "accountability" loosely—mainly referring to our promise to take time to learn with one another each week and do our homework. Now, we see more clearly how accountability necessarily extends into the relationship with the community partner.

Ultimately, as we reflect on the pilot, we understand that daunting community listening is not fixed or product-oriented; instead, it is *active, embodied, context-specific, evolving, recursive,* and *ongoing*. Additionally, as Nathan noted, we have come to understand DCL as "predicat[ing our] person" and as a "deposition" that requires a full-bodied experience, immense preparation and engagement with all of our senses, and understanding of time and space in that moment. This daunting practice necessarily pushes us to see and question our comfort zone boundaries and transcend them to bring our full selves to the community partner and engage with them as honestly and ethically as possible. In a co-curricular program like the CLAG, we need to emphasize this discomfort and risk-taking, as the program gives students the opportunity to do this work without worrying about a grade or other official assessment.

As we redesign the CLAG and invite more students and faculty to participate in Authoring Action's programming, we are excited about settling into the daunting task of listening to ourselves and our histories, listening to one another, and listening to our phenomenal partners at Authoring Action who model this radical listening every day.

## ACKNOWLEDGMENTS

We are tremendously grateful for the ongoing opportunity to learn from Nathan Ross Freeman, Authoring Action Co-Founder and Artistic Director, and Lynn Rhoades, Authoring Action Co-Founder and Executive Director. We also want to thank the student organization Wake Women Lead for their collaboration and commitment to this work.

## WORKS CITED

Ballard, Parissa J., Grace Anderson, and Stephanie S. Daniel. "Youth Experiences in Authoring Action: The Impact of an Arts-Based Youth Program on Youth Development." *Journal of Adolescent Research*, vol. 38, no. 1, 2023, pp. 178–210, https://doi.org/10.1177/07435584211006787.

Beard, David, and Graham Bodie. "Listening Research in the Communication Discipline." *A Century of Communication Studies*. Routledge, 2014, pp. 219–245.

Blankenship, Lisa. *Changing the Subject: A Theory of Rhetorical Empathy*, Utah State UP, 2019. *ProQuest Ebook Central*, https://ebookcentral.proquest.com/lib/wfu/detail.action?docID=5964813.

Bodie, Graham D., Debra Worthington ,Margarete Imhof, and Lynn O. Cooper. "What Would a Unified Field of Listening Look Like? A Proposal Linking Past Perspectives and Future Endeavors." *The International Journal of Listening*, vol. 22, no. 2, 2008, pp. 103–122.

Emmert, Philip. "A ILA Definition of Listening." *Listening Post*, no. 53, 1995, pp. 1, 4–5.

Fishman, Jenn, and Lauren Rosenberg, editors. *Community Writing, Community Listening*, special issue of *Community Literacy Journal*, vol. 13, no. 1, 2018.

Fishman, Jenn, and Lauren Rosenberg. "Guest Editors' Introduction: Community Writing, Community Listening." Fishman and Rosenberg, pp. 1–6, https://doi.org/10.25148/clj.13.1.009085.

Ford, Wendy S., Andrew Wolvin, and Sungeun Chung. "Students' Self-Perceived Listening Competencies in the Basic Speech Communication Course." *International Journal of Listening*, vol. 14, no. 1, 2000, pp. 1–13.

Freeman, Nathan Ross. Interview. By Keri Epps, 6 Mar. 2022.

Jackson, Rachel C. with Dorothy Whitehorse DeLaune. "Decolonizing Community Writing with Community Listening: Story, Transrhetorical Resistance, and Indigenous Cultural Literacy Activism." Fishman and Rosenberg, pp. 37–54, https://doi.org/10.1353/clj.2018.0020.

Janusik, Laura A. "Listening Pedagogy: Where Do We Go from Here." *Listening and Human Communication in the 21st Century*, vol. 9, 2010, pp. 193–224.

———. "Teaching Listening: What Do We Do? What Should We Do?" *International Journal of Listening*, vol. 16. no. 1, 2002, pp. 5–39.

Markgraf, Bruce. "Listening Pedagogy in Teacher-Training Institutions." *Journal of Communication,* vol. 12, no. 1, 1962, pp. 33–35.

Rowan, Karen, and Alexandra J. Cavallaro. "Toward a Model for Preparatory Community Listening." Fishman and Rosenberg, pp. 23–36, https://doi.org/10.1353/clj.2018.0019.

Stone, Erica M. "The Story of Sound Off: A Community Writing/Community Listening Experiment." Fishman and Rosenberg, pp. 16–22, https://doi.org/10.1353/clj.2018.0018.

Thompson, Kathy, Pamela Leintz, Barbara Nevers, and Susan Witkowski. "The Integrative Listening Model: An Approach to Teaching and Learning Listening." *The Journal of General Education*, vol. 53, no. 3/4, 2004, pp. 225–246.

Wolvin, Andrew D. "Listening in the General Education Curriculum." *International Journal of Listening*, vol. 26, no. 2, 2012, pp. 122–128.

## APPENDIX A. SESSION DESCRIPTIONS

### SESSION ONE: INTRODUCTION TO THE COMMUNITY LISTENING INTEGRATIVE FRAMEWORK

#### Session Goals

1. Create community among group
2. Contextualize the significance of listening in community engagement
3. Introduce key principles of listening scholarship

4. Introduce self-assessment strategies to better understand listening styles
5. Establish next steps for monitoring listening in various contexts.

## Brief Session Description and Rationale

The overarching goal of this workshop was to provide some background on listening scholarship, much of it published in the International Listening Association (ILA) journal, International Journal of Listening, and complemented by best practices from ILA resources found on their website, listen.org. Rowie facilitated this workshop and emphasized the preparatory listening stage, and asked the students to reflect on their own listening processes and start a listening journal. She also asked the students to read "The Integrative Listening Model" by Kathy Thompson, Pamela Leintz, Barbara Nevers, and Susan Witkowski, among other scholarly readings (listed below). The introductory reading significantly offered a foundation of listening theory and practice, and the students referenced the theory directly and repeatedly in their interviews and written reflections. The workshop began with centering listening in the basic transactional model of the human communication process, which illustrates the relationship between speaker, audience, message, channel, feedback, and context. This transactional model of communication is commonly found in textbooks used in introductory communication courses, but as discussed in the workshop, it does not include listening, which, as previously mentioned, tends to be included in a separate chapter of the textbook as a separate process. Furthermore, we talked about the role of emotions and emotional intelligence in the listening process. We concluded with an introduction to reflective homework activities each of us would complete before meeting the following week. The session ended with a homework activity that included taking a listening self-assessment (we recommended one from mindtools.com) and starting a listening journal. Students were encouraged to identify five ways to improve their listening as goals toward which to work in the coming weeks, to make a personal listening improvement plan to help achieve that goal, and to record their progress in their listening journals.

## Additional Readings/Materials

Brounstein, Marty. "Putting Active Listening Skills to Work." *Communicating Effectively for Dummies.* Hungry Minds, 2001, pp. 57–76.

"How Good Are Your Listening Skills?" *Mind Tools,* https://www.mindtools.com/pages/article/listening-quiz.htm. Accessed 1 Jun 2022.

Thompson, Kathy, Pamela Leintz, Barbara Nevers, and Susan Witkowski. "The Integrative Listening Model: An Approach to Teaching and Learning Listening." *The Journal of General Education*, vol. 53, no. 3/4, 2004, pp. 225–246.

## Session Two: Listening for Community Partner Needs: A Conversation with A2's Co-Founders

### Session Goals

1. Apply the listening strategies discussed in the first workshop and continue to develop a sustainable, authentic, and reciprocal relationship with A2
2. Create/sustain community among group
3. Review core principles of listening scholarship
4. Discuss reflections of listening styles and experiences since the first session
5. Establish next steps for monitoring listening in various contexts.

### Brief Session Description and Rationale

The purpose of this workshop was primarily to open up space for A2 to lead the discussion and share their goals with us. As indicated by the aforementioned goals, we hoped to begin practicing some of the listening principles introduced in the previous workshop and continue reflecting on our own listening practices that we had written about in our listening journals over the past week. Some of the significant takeaways from this session included practicing giving time/space for the community partner to share without our interruptions or suggestions. We were able to ask a few important questions that we could reflect on ourselves over the next week and come back together to debrief what we heard and how we felt we could honestly and fully show up for the community partner to help them meet their needs (continued in the next workshop description).

### Session Preparation

The questions we prepared (but did not foreground during the session) included the following:

1. What is it like being someone's (namely, students' or faculty members') "community partner?" (Shah) Another way of asking might be: "what is it like to be/feel like someone's service project?"
2. What are some of the most meaningful partnerships you have had with students and/or faculty? What made those relationships so successful?
3. What are some of the most important steps to you in the beginning stages of establishing a partnership?
4. What are some of your goals for A2 in the next year? Next five years?
5. What can our group do for you? What are the processes, outcomes, etc.? How can we specifically partner with you to help you achieve the goals you just mentioned?

Daunting Community Listening

6. Follow-up or more specific question: And what are some other ways we could continue our education, etc. with you beyond the Educator Workshop?

## Additional Readings/Materials

Shah, Rachael W. *Rewriting Partnerships: Community Perspectives on Community-Based Learning.* Utah State UP, 2020.

## SESSION THREE: RHETORICAL EMPATHY AND LISTENING ACROSS DIFFERENCE

### Session Goals:

1. Create/sustain community among group
2. Reflect thoughtfully on our conversation with A2
3. Determine action items from A2 conversation
4. Discuss distinctions between "empathy" and "sympathy"
5. Determine the role of empathy in community listening
6. Establish empathetic practices to implement into community listening sessions, specifically with A2.

### Brief Session Description and Rationale:

As addressed in the chapter, a significant portion of this workshop was designated for debriefing our conversation with A2. We devoted much of this time to discussing how their described needs deviated from our vision at the start of the conversation. We determined that while we still felt we could not satisfy all of the organization's needs, at least we knew we could use our strengths and resources to meet the goals that we could and then help connect the organization with additional resources at the university. We agreed to come back to this discussion in the fourth and final workshop series so that we could give some more time to reflect on our own strengths and where those might fit with what A2 prioritized. Doing so would give us more room for the slow thinking we would need to do to show up fully and honestly in our future interactions with A2.

The session's main topic, which interplayed nicely with our debriefing, was "rhetorical empathy," as theorized by Lisa Blankenship. Keri introduced this foundational principle of community listening and briefly introduced the book (see https://shorturl.at/630dq for an overview of the content). In reflecting on rhetorical empathy, we began by answering general questions about what we think empathy is, how it differs from sympathy, and how it intersects with/might inform our community listening. Then, Keri asked a more difficult and pointed question: "can you ever truly feel *with* others whose identity positions are unlike your own?"

237

Epps and Kirby-Straker

This question led us into a deep discussion of how empathy is often performed, and we wondered about ways to activate a practice of rhetorical empathy in community listening that was more authentic, radical, and transformative for us as listeners. Lisa Blankenship offers four characteristics of rhetorical empathy that helped us envision this practice: "1. Yielding to an Other by sharing and listening to personal stories. 2. Considering motives behind speech acts and actions. 3. Engaging in reflection and self-critique. 4. Addressing difference, power, and embodiment" (20). We found this list to be particularly helpful in thinking about how our understanding of community listening aligned with Nathan's and how we could then put these principles to practice as we moved forward in the work.

Ultimately, we looked to Blankenship's components of "rhetorical empathy" to better understand how we should enact these practices in our next interactions with A2 and the teen authors they serve. Blankenship's principles reinforced how we were already attempting to adopt a community listening stance that required intensive self-reflection and attended to unlearning/unlistening to dominant narratives of difference and power that have been deeply problematic in university-community partnerships in the past. Furthermore, the first characteristic aligned with Nathan's call for us to "leave our baggage outside" and, as much as possible, strip our biases so that we could understand the goal of the relationship and listen with our full, essential selves in our interactions with the community partner. We left this workshop committed to enacting these practices and reflecting on the question of "truly listening *with* community partners" before returning for our last session.

### Additional Readings and Materials

Blankenship, Lisa. *Changing the Subject: A Theory of Rhetorical Empathy*, Utah State UP, 2019. *ProQuest Ebook Central*, https://ebookcentral.proquest.com/lib/wfu/detail .action?docID=5964813.

## Session 4: Preparing for the Unexpected

### Session Goals:

1. Create/sustain community among group
2. Reflect on key points from previous sessions and self-reflections
3. Determine plan of action for assigned tasks with A2
4. Establish accountability plan for our group beyond structured program sessions
5. Determine goals for follow-up meeting with A2.

## Brief Session Description and Rationale:

This session allowed us to return to what we heard from Lynn and Nathan as the goals and needs for A2. During this session, we outlined specific roles that individuals in our group might offer A2, while recognizing that we would not be able to provide everything they need. Identifying our limitations, we outlined a list of possible connections—including departments and other campus offices—that might have more resources than our small group could offer. We ultimately determined what they need is support for structural components that fall heavily on their three staff members: namely, grant writing and marketing. Ultimately, too, they want their trained educators to bring the A2 curriculum into schools and areas across the nation that they have been unable to reach. After completing the training and beginning these listening sessions with them, we realized we could support them in these areas, and that is where our group's energy is directed now. In other words, as Karen Rowan and Alexandra J. Cavallaro urged us to do, we listened first for the assets and later determined where we were needed to fill in the gaps that they identified.

Since this final formal session, we have met in smaller groups and plan to meet again as a whole group to continue discussing our listening work and assess our program before starting the next program. We have begun by trying to meet some of A2's needs by assigning tasks to individuals based on their strengths and reviewing our tasks in a series of follow-up meetings with A2. Some of our action items have been accomplished: Keri recently was elected to A2's board of directors (a dire need they expressed early in our conversations) and is working with teens in the Advanced Writing Workshops on Tuesdays and Thursdays as the teen authors prepare for upcoming engagements. She is also on the planning committee for upcoming fundraisers. Rowie has been instrumental in connecting A2 with other faculty, staff, and students who have different capacities and skills that we do not have in our small group. Lauren and Zoe have developed a new school partnership that we hope will incorporate A2's curriculum in their afterschool programs. Hannah, Lauren, and Casey have worked together on marketing strategies for getting more people interested in completing the educator training. Thanks to some of these efforts, we recently recruited more WFU students to participate in the educator training we hosted at Authoring Action, and we are currently designing the next CLAG as a follow-up to this invigorating training session.

# APPENDIX B. STUDENT REFLECTIONS

## ZOE CHAMBERLIN

Seeing yourself—whether it is through media, the classroom, or elsewhere—has the power to transform your life and completely shape experiences. Listening, however, has the same potential for impact. Think about the role of listening in your everyday life. When do you listen? When do you think you listen? There is a fine line between effective listening and assumed listening or hearing. This line, however, and the power of this effective listening is consistently ignored. For, if people knew the true meaning of listening and how to truly listen, most problems we have in society would dissipate. As president of Wake Women Lead, a campus organization dedicated to mentoring children in the Winston-Salem area, my experience with community engagement thus far has been incredibly soul-feeding. Throughout my experience with Wake Women Lead, we have partnered with numerous schools and organizations. First, we primarily partnered with a non-profit organization in Winston-Salem that allowed us to work with middle school girls at a local under-resourced school. We helped these girls with their literacy skills and had social events as well. However, because the power of representation is so transformative, as an organization we wanted to expand our reach and further impact the youth of Winston-Salem. Authoring Action immediately caught our attention for a potential partnership.

When I think of Authoring Action a few words come to mind: liveliness, expression, and listening. As an organization that helps Winston-Salem students, from elementary to high school, find themselves in writing, it truly blew me away. Their unconventional methods made me excited to get involved in any way I could. Authoring Action's dedication to making writing fun and showing every student they teach that they are capable of creating something meaningful is something I will eternally admire.

To work with Authoring Action, every potential volunteer must go through a training process. This training process is over four hours long and includes conversation (called the "First Ink Discussion"), participating in numerous exercises, free-writing, and most importantly, listening. One thing I specifically remember is performing an exercise where we were given a word and told to free-write. I remember my mind flowing freely as I wrote a deep account about the inner workings of my mind. However, I immediately became uneasy when Nathan noted that we would have to share our entries with the rest of the group. I heard each of my peers read their pieces, but I was not truly listening to their words until we analyzed what their words meant, finding a deeper meaning in their thoughts. Through this process, I saw things in my peers that I have never and would have never noticed before. Before working with Authoring Action, I thought I knew what being a good

Daunting Community Listening

listener was, even going so far as to identify as one. Yet, I had never thought about how effective of a listener I was. The thought of being a good listener was a quality I always thought I should obtain, but I never explored where I was in terms of my development as a listener. Therefore, because I did not prioritize this quality I took several things away from the Authoring Action training session.

First, I learned that listening is very different from hearing. The way I interpret it is, hearing is simply letting a series of sounds enter your ears but failing to keep track of the sequence of the sounds enough to retain what is said. Listening is understanding; listening involves empathy. It involves responding with more than words; expressions are involved, physical contact may even be involved. However, the most important aspect of listening in my eyes is the willingness to be uncomfortable.

When working with students with a contrasting positionality from oneself, while listening to their experiences, there will inevitably be a point where an uncomfortable topic arises from either party. To be a listener, one who is not simply hearing, we need to allow ourselves to get into uncomfortable states and discuss uncomfortable topics so that we truly understand who we are trying to assist. You may wonder, "how can I do this?" Well, with practice it becomes less complex than one would think. The most important aspect, however, is letting your guard down and allowing yourself to put yourself in the shoes of the person you are interacting with. Though my racial positionality matched those I worked with, I was still commonly in situations where I was uncomfortable. In these moments I took a deep breath, imagined I was the person before me, and listened, analyzing each word and searching for a deeper meaning just as I had done during my transformative training session. Community engagement is more than going into a soup kitchen, making a temporary impact, and never returning. It is about learning about the people with whom you are engaging. When we know exactly who we are helping we can assist them in a way that is more personalized to them, and therefore generate a greater potential impact. As I continue working with the Winston-Salem community, specifically in a new partnership with a local school, I have seen the benefit of these listening practices in terms of how I am able to connect with the children I work with. My listening skills have allowed me to create lasting bonds with the children I am around to the point where they call me their sibling—true connections. Additionally, through this work, I see how Authoring Action's practices could be beneficial in other settings. Authoring Action is a pioneer in community engagement in Winston-Salem. Aside from the unconventional methods they practice that I feel should be incorporated into every classroom, I believe what we should all take from them is the importance of listening skills and the potential impact we can have on others if we work on the development of these skills. Learn to listen, not to hear.

## Hannah Hill

Each August, just over a thousand students travel to Winston-Salem, North Carolina, to begin their college career at Wake Forest University. As they arrive, they anxiously await the chance to dive into classes, make friends, and explore new opportunities typical of the college experience. However, many of the students who have chosen Wake Forest to further their education have done so because they're ready to make an impact on the community. After all, the university motto is "Pro Humanitate," or "For Humanity," and is broadcasted widely to both prospective and current students. There is an expectation that Wake Forest students will serve the community, and many are eager to accept.

However, serving the community is typically tacked on to a laundry list of involvements for busy Wake Forest students. Many of us are all too often eager to maximize our impact while minimizing our time commitment, and it becomes second nature to view "doing service" as only something that checks off a box and adds to a resume. Looking back, it is clear that the concept of service I was familiar with had nothing to do with listening and had everything to do with my own ego and motivations.

Truthfully, when I was initially invited to participate in our group's workshop with Authoring Action and subsequent accountability group, I was less than enthusiastic. After all, I was a great listener, and had been told so all my life. I was sure that I had nothing to gain from spending many hours learning how to do something I was already an expert at.

During our very first accountability group session, I quickly realized that my expertise in listening was all but a construct. When I reflected on the way that I "listened" to others both in my personal life and in my relationships with community partners, I realized that my idea of "good listening" was totally wrong. What I thought was good "listening" had not been listening at all. Instead, I would hear what others had to say, but before they finished speaking, I had often compiled a mental list of how to solve the perceived problem regardless of whether the speaker requested it. My "listening" was almost entirely focused on "fixing," and I would often totally disregard conversation and collaboration with others for the sake of solving what I perceived to be the problem as quickly as possible. It was almost an impulse—I couldn't help wanting to dive right in and get to work in whatever way I thought was best.

As we continued to meet as a group over several weeks, I found my ideas and perceptions about what listening was being continually unraveled and challenged. I learned that there are major differences between true listening and "listening for action," or what my concept of listening seemed to be before. Before I participated in the Community Listening Accountability Group, I felt as though I had fully committed to the "Pro Humanitate" spirit of the university. I was confident that I was doing what was expected of me: making an impact on Winston-Salem. Yet when I reflected on the ways in which I listened during our group meetings, I realized that despite the many hours I spent completing service projects and working with community partners, I could not think of a single time where I slowed down enough to ask, "what do you need from me?"

As busy students who are eager to make an impact, this is all too common of a mindset. We often enter into spaces of community partnership with an action plan before even speaking with those who are directly involved. We are eager to create solutions and massive change for the sake of showing others that we can, while completely ignoring the actual needs of the community. Service becomes something that is glamorized and allows us to pat ourselves and each other on the back, instead of being something done selflessly for the needs of others. Listening is an afterthought, not a first step—a fatal flaw that dooms the best of intentions before service even begins.

When we enter into community partnerships with a listen-first mindset, our action plan changes. Instead of focusing on our perceptions of what they "need" and jumping into action, we instead approach the relationship with a willingness to slow down, reflect, and collaborate. When asking community partners what their needs are, instead of assuming, we set the foundation for long-lasting relationships that have the potential to change the community. Am I listening to "fix," or am I truly focused on what the other individual has to say? By establishing a listen-first mindset, I know that I can be more helpful, supportive, and compassionate to others. I can create positive change, rather than a meaningless, or at least temporary, fix.

This is not to say that my work on listening is over—in fact, it has only just begun. Listening in community spaces demands follow-through and requires flexibility and humility. When I approach community partnerships with the goal of intentional listening, I must learn to be okay with being wrong, and must be willing to change my own ideas and plans entirely if needed. Listening is a continual process that is not bound by a set of processes or rules, but something that requires me to prepare, reflect, and grow in a way that is tailored to each situation and partnership.

The phrase "Pro Humanitate" has taken on an entirely new meaning for me. It is no longer a phrase that is simply characterized by the idea of "doing service" or checking off a box. Rather, the phrase represents intentional listening, deep empathy, candid humility, and above all, a willingness to keep learning. After all, to be for humanity, we must first listen to what humanity has to say.

## Casey Beiswenger

Prior to participating in the Community Listening Accountability Group, I believed that good listening only required the ability to sit silently, not interrupt, and allow the speaker to talk as long as they liked. In my early years of school, "listen to me" and "be quiet" were often used synonymously by adults, and, thus, following instructions or memorizing information were the only actions that accompanied listening. From this experience, I considered myself a mediocre listener and miscategorized individuals as great listeners simply because they demonstrated those passive qualities.

The listening research shared in the Community Listening Accountability Group prompted me to approach listening differently. Our discussion of listening frameworks and existing listening processes allowed me to craft a new definition of good listening. I came to define "effective listening" as "active listening," not a passive activity, including skills I had considered in relation to classroom learning, like speaking intentionally, preparation, and a present mind. Additionally, Hannah, another student in the CLA Group, concluded that sometimes we predetermine the purpose of a listening situation. I realized that I must approach each situation with an open mind and recognize the correct purpose of my listening. From these observations, I started to approach listening as I would a learning opportunity.

In redefining my listening, I gained a repertoire of listening tactics that led to a deeper understanding of the people around me and stronger grasp of the content I was listening to. One listening skill profoundly affected the way I listen: the ability to "echo" rather than to "project." Asking clarifying questions and repeating what I was taking away from the speaker allowed the conversation to advance. This echoing skill was not one I naturally possessed, but it dramatically improved the quality of my conversations. A new depth and nuance of the conversations followed qualities that my passive listening never allowed me to achieve. In times of active listening, I found myself responding more thoughtfully, connecting more with my younger sister while I was home for the summer, as well performing better and learning more during my technology internship. I also felt my relationship with Authoring Action become more collaborative. I saw how intentional engagement, guided by my preparation, self-reflection, and open-mindedness, was necessary to connect with the speaker, as it reaffirmed my interest and allowed for a correct understanding of their words.

When applying this idea to a conversation with Authoring Action, I realized that effective listening requires a willingness to lack all the answers, as well as a radical suspension of my preconceptions. The suspension of my preconceptions required of effective volunteers extends far beyond what any bias training has ever provided me with. I began community literacy work as a sixteen-year-old, driven by a desire to help younger students develop a skill I was so grateful to possess. My sense of gratitude for my exceptional educational opportunities ignited sympathy for others who, only by circumstance of the ovarian lottery, had not received the same opportunity. I previously worked as a reading comprehension tutor in my hometown of Cleveland, Ohio, and continued to serve as an academic mentor with Wake Women LEAD upon my freshman year at Wake Forest University. But no pre-program training had ever prepared me to be an empathetic mentor as opposed to a sympathetic mentor. Authoring Action's educator training helped me better understand the social and academic realities of the students involved. For example, working with a student's limited understanding of the parts of speech requires an empathic understanding that I had yet to fully grasp. Continuing to connect with the organization while redeveloping my listening abilities allowed me to gain an understanding of the mission that went beyond reading about it online.

Experience taught me some abilities required of an effective mentor, but throughout my participation in the CLA group, I began to understand the stark contrast between my perspective as a sympathetic listener and an empathic one. As a sympathetic listener, I approached situations saying, "I want to help," immediately offering my own solutions. As an empathic listener, I ask, "do you need help?" I focus more on partnership and collaboration than I do on a clear cut, predetermined solution. This empathic mindset can be gained from experience with community organizations, or more quickly and effectively, I believe it can be gained through focused listening training.

The CLA Group's conversation with Authoring Action was about determining what the organization truly needed, not necessarily how I could be involved, as I had originally anticipated. Eliminating my presumptions resulted in greater mutual benefit. By accepting that my personal role was relatively insignificant, I gained an understanding of the organization beyond its written mission statement. Rather than assuming I can help in a predetermined way, I surrender the mic to the experts, allowing them to lead the conversation. In working with Authoring Action, this meant acknowledging that despite my desire to work with students, the organization did not need me as an educator, and I could provide more impactful support in other areas. This realization marked a significant improvement in the efficacy of my listening abilities, as well as a turning point in my approach to community partnership as well as interpersonal relationships. Now, rather than looking to volunteer as an educator with Authoring Action, I'm looking to help them connect with organizations outside of Winston-Salem and spread their pedagogy, something they expressed greater need for than additional teachers. I'm also interested in helping the organization connect with students and other partners through social media, as marketing was a topic of importance during our meeting.

Now, I approach listening opportunities as a learning experience. I have found myself responding in a more adaptive manner, speaking more intentionally, seeking to understand an issue rather than to solve it, and connecting more deeply with those I converse with. This is a continuous process which requires effort and self-reflection, yet I feel markedly more qualified as a "good listener."

## LAUREN ROBERTSON

I remember the first moment I ever consciously thought about the art of listening. It was two weeks into the Community Listening Accountability Group, at the end of an eight-hour workday at my eye-opening yet exhausting summer job, and I was aching to escape the blistering hot sun and relieve myself of the twenty rambunctious eight-year-olds in the class I was teaching.

When, suddenly, I saw her. The genial and gentle, sweet and soft-spoken student in my class, usually so peaceful and personable and positive, suddenly sulking on the tire swing with tears streaming down her face. I pulled her aside to talk yet was quickly stunned into silence as she began unveiling deeply personal and profound struggles, strained by her parent's messy divorce and feeling unloved by her own father, a weight that no eight-year-old should ever have to bear. I was at a loss for words. How could I respond to give her some sense of comfort? How could I even fathom what comfort looks like for her? I could not relate to her experiences—I had no desire to relate to her experiences. I could not make any promises or guarantees that her concerns would resolve, or her situation would improve. I could not fill the void of her pain no matter what I'd say or do.

In that moment, it was my participation in the Community Listening Accountability Group that, like a lighthouse, guided me, not to understanding every detail or offering the perfect solution, but to work intentionally to show her I am here; I am listening; and I care. Where I used to see listening as a definitive product, I became able to see it as a never-ending process. Where I used to see listening as complete understanding, I became able to see it as a humble recognition that I can never completely understand, but I should always try. Like all worthwhile endeavors, listening is hard work. It requires patience and persistence, concentration and compassion. It is the perfect harmony of body and soul: nodding my head, focusing my eyes, positioning my body, evaluating my biases, preparing my mind, opening my heart, finding as much power in the hush of silence as the crescendo of offering a response. Listening is not just hearing, it is an internalized, all-encompassing experience in which I am intricately intertwined with the music of the moment, continuously seeking to hear and listen and learn and understand with every part of myself entirely present and intimately engaged.

As an aspiring elementary school teacher, I know how important listening is in the classroom setting. Listening is not always easy, especially with limited time, ongoing distractions, and having your own things to say. But, in education as well as life, the consequences of not listening, especially for children in critical developmental stages, can leave a noticeable and enduring strain on the ways in which people view their worth within and beyond individual interactions. Furthermore, when people do feel listened to and loved, they open up in magical ways, sharing experiences that add immense value to both classroom communities and society at large. Children, like all people, are connected by their aching eagerness to know that others care, to know that someone values their voice. As educators, the greatest impact we can have on students is not what we teach them, but how we make them feel; and at the heart of feeling loved is feeling listened to. We listen to show we care.

Beyond working with individual students, listening also allows opportunities for larger scale innovative transformations in education. Working with Authoring Action, for one, has opened my eyes to a trailblazing pedagogical approach—predicated on listening—of integrating the arts with literacy. While this approach drastically differs from the more traditional, textbook-driven methods that I encountered during my own career as a student, taking the time to absorb the wonder of the unfamiliar in their work has allowed me to better appreciate all that this non-profit has to offer. This experience has inspired me to pursue a Masters program centered around seeking to understand and develop similarly innovative efforts in education. Only by opening ourselves up to listen and learn from what's new and different and ground-breaking, can we maximize a better future.

After participating in the Community Listening Accountability Group, I find myself asking more questions, attempting to push aside outside distractions, and aiming to fully absorb the magnitude of people's words instead of putting pressure on myself to emit an immediate response. I am also exponentially aware of moments when I did not really listen and have realized that, far from being able to call myself a "good listener," this work has only just begun. But, more than anything, this experience has taught me that listening is less about being perfect, and more about actively choosing to immerse oneself in the continuous process of preparation, empathy and reflection.

# CONTRIBUTORS

**Sally F. Benson** is an independent scholar and full-time prison and community educator in Santa Fe, New Mexico. She earned her Ph.D. in Rhetoric, Composition, and the Teaching of English at the University of Arizona. Her research focuses on prison education, historical prison journalism, and self-advocacy for individuals impacted by incarceration She received the 2022 Gilberto Espinosa prize for best article in the *New Mexico Historical Review* for her piece, "The Penitentiary Community College of Santa Fe: A Cautionary History of Prison Higher Education."

**Casey Beiswenger** is a Wake Forest University alumna who studied political science and statistics. At WFU, she served as Assistant Vice President of Philanthropy for Delta Zeta Sorority and as a youth literacy tutor. Casey is committed to youth literacy and creative writing and is passionate about providing students access to literacy enrichment opportunities.

**Kyle Boggs** (he/him) is Associate Professor of Rhetoric and Community Engagement in the Department of Humanities and Cultural Studies at Boise State University. His research attempts to uncover how place-based belongings are constituted differently by our evolving relationships to land and the discourses that produce and are produced by it. As such he is interested in settler colonial theory, environmental studies, affect theory, queer and feminist theory, advocacy, and community writing. His book, *Recreational Colonialism and the Rhetorical Landscapes of The Outdoors*, will be released in 2025 through Ohio State University Press.

**Alexandra J. Cavallaro** is Associate Professor of English at California State University, San Bernardino, where she serves as the Director of the Center for the Study of Correctional Education (CSCE). In her work with the CSCE, she coordinates the Inside-Out Prison Exchange Program, a prison education model that brings together incarcerated and non-incarcerated students to take classes together inside of correctional facilities. Her essays have appeared in *Literacy and Composition Studies, Community Literacy Journal,* and *enculturation: A Journal of Rhetoric, Writing, and Culture.*

**Mitzi Ceballos** is a Ph.D. student at the University of Utah. She is a former McNair Scholar and a 2023–2024 American Association of Hispanics in Higher Education Graduate Fellow. Her academic interests include archival rhetorics, decolonial theory, and white supremacy.

**Zoe Chamberlin** is a Wake Forest University alumna who studied computer science, entrepreneurship, and writing. Zoe was President of Wake

249

Women Lead, an organization designed to support youth literacy development in Winston-Salem, and received the Junior Service Excellence Award from Wake Forest University's Office of Civic and Community Engagement. Zoe remains committed to bringing together her passions for social justice, writing, and computer science.

**April Chatham-Carpenter** is Professor of Applied Communication at the University of Arkansas at Little Rock, where she serves as Department Chair of the Department of Applied Communication and teaches classes in listening and civil dialogue, as well as research methods. She researches issues such as the use of communication to manage difficult dialogues and transformations in online teaching. Her research has appeared in the *Journal of Applied Communication*, *Atlantic Journal of Communication*, *Communication Education*, *Public Integrity*, *Journal of Educators Online*, *Innovative Higher Education*, *Journal of Research Practice*, and others. She serves as a workshop moderator and national leader for the national Braver Angels non-profit organization, and is a co-host of the Arkansas Braver Angels *On the Other Hand* podcast.

**Keri Epps** is Associate Teaching Professor in the Writing Program at Wake Forest University. Her research, teaching, and practice lie at the intersection of rhetorical genre theory, media studies, and community-engaged research. As an Academic and Community Engaged (ACE) fellow, she developed community-engaged teaching and research practices and has since applied this training while working with the local arts-based nonprofit Authoring Action to study and promote their signature creative writing curriculum for teen authors.

**Jenn Fishman** pursues teaching, research, and leadership across three areas of academic work: undergraduate research, longitudinal research, and community listening. A recipient of the Braddock Award and PI of several grant-supported projects, her publications include *The Naylor Report on Undergraduate Research in Writing Studies* (Parlor Press), *Telling Stories: Perspectives on Longitudinal Research in Writing Studies* (Utah State University Press) and special issues of *CCC Online*, *Community Literacy Journal*, and *Peitho* as well as numerous articles and book chapters. Currently, she is Associate Professor of English and Co-Director of the Ott Memorial Writing Center at Marquette University.

**Romeo García** is Assistant Professor of Writing and Rhetoric Studies at the University of Utah. His interdisciplinary research appears in *College Composition and Communication*, *Rhetoric Society Quarterly*, *Across the Disciplines*, and *Rhetoric, Politics, and Culture*. García is co-editor of *Rhetorics Elsewhere and Otherwise* (with Damián Baca, Studies in Writing and Rhetoric Series), *Unsettling Archival Research* (with Gesa E. Kirsch, Caitlin Burns Allen, and Walker P. Smith, Southern Illinois University Press), and *Pluriversal Literacies* (with Ellen Cushman and Damián Baca, University of Pittsburgh Press).

**Hannah Hill** is a Wake Forest University alumna who studied communication and health policy and administration. Hannah served as Vice President of Community Service for Kappa Delta Sorority and has dedicated herself to service and leadership. Hannah worked with Wake Forest's Office of Civic and Community Engagement to create effective strategies for local engagement and remains committed to providing grant and scholarship opportunities for teachers and students in North Carolina public schools.

**Wendy Hinshaw** is Associate Professor of English and Director of Writing Programs at Florida Atlantic University. Her scholarship includes articles on prison writing and prison-university partnerships in *Community Literacy Journal*, *Reflections: A Journal of Community-Engaged Writing and Rhetoric*, *Feminist Formations*, and edited collections on prison literacy and activism. She is a founding board member of Exchange for Change, a Miami-based nonprofit that provides educational and communication skills-building courses to students who are incarcerated to amplify and bring their voices to the outside.

**Ada Hubrig** (they/them) is an autistic, genderqueer, disabled caretaker of cats. They live in Huntsville, Texas, where they labor as Assistant Professor and Co-Director of Composition at Sam Houston State University as their day job. Their scholarship centers disability and queer/trans communities, and is featured in *College Composition and Communication*, *Community Literacy Journal*, and *The Journal of Multimodal Rhetorics* among others, and their words have also found homes in *Brevity* and *Disability Visibility*. Ada is managing editor of *Journal of Multimodal Rhetorics*.

**Tobi Jacobi** is Professor of English at Colorado State University, where she serves as the Director of the Community Literacy Center and teaches writing and rhetoric courses. Her scholarship includes an edited collection, *Women, Writing, and Prison: Activists, Scholars, and Writers Speak Out*, and essays in *Community Literacy Journal*, *Reflections: A Journal of Community-Engaged Writing and Rhetoric*, *Feminist Formations*, and *Feminist Teacher*, as well as edited collections featuring the work of writing and research behind bars. She is currently completing a book project on narrative representations of girls held at the New York State Training School for Girls in the early 20th Century and the possibilities of contemporary narrative repair with Laura Rogers.

**Kelly Kinahan** is Associate Professor in the Department of Urban and Regional Planning at Florida State University and was previously an Assistant Professor in the Department of Urban & Public Affairs at the University of Louisville. Her research examines how policies governing the built environment shape neighborhood-level inequalities and affect marginalized populations. She has published in journals such as the *Journal of the American Planning Association*, *Urban Studies*, and *Housing Policy Debate*.

251

Contributors

**Rowie Kirby-Straker** is Assistant Professor in the Department of Communication at Wake Forest University. She has directed speaking centers at two academic institutions. Building on training as an Academic and Community Engaged (ACE) fellow, she provides opportunities for cross-cultural engagement between students and local communities through storytelling and listening. Her teaching, research, and scholarly creative interests include speaking and listening competence, environmental risk perception and communication, environmental storytelling, and environmental justice.

**Carrie Mott** is Assistant Professor in the Department of Geographic and Environmental Sciences at the University of Louisville. Her work has been published in top Geography journals such as the *Annals of the American Association of Geographers*, *Antipode*, and *Dialogues in Human Geography*. Her recent paper, "Antiracist Pedagogy through Historical Archives: A Geographic Approach," is available through the *Journal of Geography*.

**Bailey M. Oliver-Blackburn** is Associate Professor of Applied Communication at the University of Arkansas at Little Rock, where she serves as the graduate coordinator for the MA in Applied Communication and the Conflict Management Graduate Certificate programs. She is a published researcher and author in the field of communication and conflict management and is a certified group facilitator and mediator for couples, families, and organizations. She has received multiple awards for her research and teaching, including the Rising Faculty Award for Excellence at her university and the coveted Sandra Petronio Dissertation excellence award from the National Communication Association.

**Katie W. Powell** is Assistant Professor, Educator in the Department of English at the University of Cincinnati, in the Rhetoric and Professional Writing track. Since graduating from the University of Arkansas, she has used her writing to reflect on how to listen as a white woman, scholar, and mother in community groups and in her new home in Cincinnati. These reflections can be seen in forthcoming articles in *Peitho* and *College English*, both of which examine white language and white positioning. Her teaching and writing directly reflect the ways she considers whiteness and her own positionality within these spaces. She credits the work she did with this community as foundational to both her professional and personal journey as a community member.

**Wyn Andrews Richards** is a Ph.D. candidate at Washington State University. Her research interests are rhetorics of racism and antiracist pedagogies.

**Lauren Robertson** is a Wake Forest University alumna who studied English and elementary education. She served as an Undergraduate Research and Creative Activities fellow and developed partnerships with several local public schools while student teaching and serving as a member of Wake Women Lead.

She is committed to community-engaged, intercultural English education and mentorship.

**Lauren Rosenberg** is Professor of Rhetoric and Writing Studies and Director of First-Year Composition in the Department of English at the University of Texas at El Paso. She is the author of *The Desire for Literacy: Writing in the Lives of Adult Learners* and numerous articles and book chapters on adult literacy education, longitudinal methodologies for writing research, and writing across the lifespan. In 2018, she and Jenn Fishman co-edited the special issue of *Community Literacy Journal* (13.1) that introduced the idea of community listening and eventually led to this book.

**Mary P. Sheridan** is Professor of English and Director of the Commonwealth Center for Humanities and Society at the University of Louisville. Her teaching and research explore questions at the nexus of community engagement and feminist methodologies. She has published in *College Composition and Communication, Community Literacy, Composition Studies, Feminist Teacher, JAC, Journal of Basic Writing, Kairos,* and *Written Communication* and is co-recipient of *Computer and Composition*'s Michelle Kendrick Outstanding Digital Production/Scholarship Award for "Remediating the Canon." Her books include *Writing Studies Research in Practice; Design Literacies;* and *Girls, Feminism, and Grassroots Literacies,* which earned the Winifred Bryan Horner Outstanding Book Award from Coalition of Feminist Scholars in the History of Rhetoric and Composition and the Civic Scholarship/Book of the Year Award from *Reflections: A Journal of Writing, Service-Learning, and Community Literacy.*

**Angela Storey** is Associate Professor in the Department of Anthropology at the University of Louisville and, in 2024, became Director of the Anne Braden Institute for Social Justice Research. Her research explores the politics of urban environments, with long-term ethnographic projects in Cape Town, South Africa, and Louisville focusing on collaborative research and engaged scholarship. She is co-editor of *The Everyday Life of Urban Inequality: Ethnographic Case Studies of Global Cities.*

**Kaitlyn Taylor** is a Wake Forest University alumna who studied finance and writing. Kaitlyn worked as a Resident Assistant and writing tutor, and she frequently partnered with WFU's Office of Civic and Community Engagement. Kaitlyn is committed to educating others on income inequality and financial literacy, specifically in marginalized communities.

**Karen Tellez-Trujillo** is an assistant professor of English at Cal Poly Pomona, where she serves as the Writing in the Disciplines Coordinator and Chair of the University Writing Committee. Her educational background and research interests lie in border, feminist, and cultural rhetorics, as well as community writing and listening. She also serves as the advisor for Rhetoric and

Composition Graduate Assistants and mentors undergraduate students in The Research through Inclusive Opportunities (RIO) program. Her essays have been published in the interdisciplinary journal *Writers, Craft, and Context* (2023), as well as in the edited collection, *Revising Moves: Writing Stories of (Re)Making* (2024). Karen is also the recipient of the 2022–2023 NCTE Early Career Educator of Color Leadership Award.

Professor of Applied Communication at the University of Arkansas at Little Rock, **Carol L. Thompson** is a former Fulbright Scholar and winner of several teaching awards, including the Southern States Award for Excellence in Teaching, the John I. Sisco Award, and the University-Wide Award for Excellence in Teaching at her institution. Carol teaches Communication Ethics, Gender Communication, Communication and Differences, and Conflict Management, among others. She has also published numerous articles about teaching and communication, winning a Southern States Communication award for her co-written article on Doctor-Patient Communication and Medical Terminology.

**Shelley Thomas** is Associate Professor in the Department of Elementary, Middle, and Secondary Teacher Education. Her research explores transdisciplinary approaches to pervasive problems in teacher education from a social justice perspective. Her recent work examines trauma-informed practices in teacher preparation. She has published in journals such as the *Review of Research in Education, Journal of Applied Instructional Design*, and *Equity and Excellence in Education.*

**Patty Wilde** is Associate Professor of English and Director of Composition at Washington State University Tri-Cities. Her work has appeared in journals such as *College Composition and Communication, Praxis: A Writing Center Journal, Rhetoric Review,* and *Teaching English in the Two-Year College* as well as in several edited collections.

# INDEX

## Symbols

#CripTheVote 17, 27, 65

## A

Aaron 213
academic contexts 14, 22, 32, 44, 60, 109, 141, 148, 152
  Alverno College 221
  University of Arkansas 212
  University of Louisville (UofL) 21, 194
  Wake Forest University 231, 245
  Washington State University (WSU) 18, 87
activism 111, 184, 191, 198
  community activism 17, 44, 148
  disability activism 17, 27, 48, 59
  hashtag activism 27, 57
advocacy 17, 33, 34, 35, 140, 148
  disability advocacy 17, 27, 50, 54, 57, 61, 64, 65
  public art as 94, 102
  self-advocacy 38, 58
Anne Braden Institute (ABI) 21, 176, 182
Anthony 213
antiracism 18, 21, 72, 82, 84, 194, 200, 210, 216
anti-Semitism 69, 82
archives 18, 20, 28, 41, 60, 87, 135, 143
Aryan Nations 18, 28, 87
Authoring Action (A2) 22, 220, 223, 226, 231, 236

## B

Beratan, Gregg 49, 53, 62, 64
Blankenship, Lisa 219, 225, 236
Borderland 15, 131
Braver Angels 21, 172
Browne, Kevin Adonis 120, 121, 126

## C

Charlie ix
Chip Thomas 18, 96, 113
  Hope + Trauma in a Poisoned Land 106
  untitled (\ 108
  untitled (Rose Hurley and grandson) 110
  What we do to the mountain we do to ourselves 104
civic community listening. *See* community listening
CLAG. *See* Community Listening Accountability Group
communication (studies) 21, 31, 158, 172, 217, 222, 233
community-centered listening. *See* community listening
community-ish 182
community listening 5, 6, 32, 44, 48, 52, 60, 61, 70, 81, 82, 87, 91, 96, 98, 118, 130, 134, 152, 156, 170, 179, 188, 190, 192, 204, 217, 219, 220, 227, 229
  as archival methodology 76, 82, 87, 143
  as critical frameworks 4, 21, 111, 179, 182, 194, 224, 233
  as evolving dialogue 97, 100, 101, 102, 110
  as feminist rhetorical practice 5, 32, 176, 219
  as integral to public art 18, 95, 98, 100, 102, 106, 113
  as non-neutral embodied methodology 10, 52, 73, 87, 118, 231
  civic community listening 15, 21, 154, 158, 162, 164, 166, 169, 172
  community-centered listening 15, 20, 137, 138, 144, 148

255

Index

daunting community listening (DCL) 15, 22, 151, 218, 223, 231
ethos of 19, 129, 130
proximate listening 15, 17, 27, 31, 33, 35, 37, 45
relational listening 19, 122, 124, 129, 130
retrospective community listening 151, 176, 182, 194
storied community listening 15, 22, 151, 200, 206, 208, 209, 213
work before the work 6, 83, 179, 183, 193, 219
Community Listening Accountability Group (CLAG) 22, 218, 222, 231, 237, 245
community literacy 11, 32, 35, 42, 48, 52, 60, 65, 166, 243
community writing 10, 42, 62, 135, 148
public art as 18, 113
Corder, Jim 32, 38, 40, 41
coronavirus. *See* COVID-19 pandemic
counterstory 21, 22, 179, 182, 186, 189, 190, 200, 207
COVID-19 pandemic 56, 57, 60, 70, 78, 80, 98, 108, 129, 135, 148, 159, 181, 183, 185, 186, 187, 207, 209
cultural logics 13, 135, 178, 179, 182, 184, 187, 190, 192, 193
Cyndy Begaye 106

**D**

daunting community listening (DCL). *See* community listening
DJ Mike (Guerrero) 19, 117, 121, 131

**E**

eavesdropping. *See* rhetorical listening
empathic listening. *See* listening
Equal Justice Initiative (EJI) 31, 200, 206, 212
ethics 5, 43, 73, 76, 78, 86, 144, 152, 156, 176, 219, 225, 231
of listening 12, 16, 18, 28, 31, 32, 35, 41, 137

**F**

feminist rhetorical listening. *See* rhetorical listening
Fishman, Jenn and Lauren Rosenberg 5, 33, 44, 48, 50, 52, 65, 78, 80, 82, 87, 118, 134, 156, 187, 203, 219
Flower, Linda 11, 14, 52, 53
Flynn, Elizabeth, Patricia Sotirin, and Ann Brady 147
Fox Jukebox, The 19, 131

**G**

García, Romeo 6, 35, 41, 43, 44, 60, 71, 76, 78, 85, 111, 113, 136, 179, 189
Glenn, Cheryl 14, 62

**H**

haunting 5, 18, 28, 32, 35, 37, 41, 43, 44, 71, 83, 136, 152, 180, 182, 189, 190, 193
Hinshaw, Wendy 6, 32, 34, 42, 86, 112, 136
hopeful listening. *See* listening

**I**

incarcerated writers 17, 20, 27, 35, 43, 91, 137, 143, 146
incarceration (mass) 32, 35, 39, 43, 49, 135, 137, 143, 146

**J**

Jackson, Rachel C. with Dorothy White-horse DeLaune 6, 32, 98, 219, 223
Jetsonorama. *See* Chip Thomas

**K**

Kee Roy John 106
Klee Benally 104, 114

**L**

LindenmanLohr_1 56
Lipari, Lisbeth 31, 33, 35, 40, 42, 44
listening 4, 9, 13, 166, 226
active listening 33

256

empathic listening 6, 7, 48, 56, 78, 85, 155, 159, 160, 162, 163, 170, 224, 243
hopeful listening 48, 51, 64
Integrative Listening Model (ILM) 222, 224
listening pedagogy 217, 222, 230, 237
respectful listening 48, 51, 61
literacy studies 11, 51
Lohr, Justin and Heather Lindenman 163
Lynn Rhoades 216, 224, 231

## M

Martinez, Aja Y. 179, 200, 207
Mathieu, Paula 62, 64
Mike, el DJ. *See* DJ Mike (Guerrero)
Mike G.. *See* DJ Mike (Guerrero)

## N

Nathan Ross Freeman 220, 225, 231, 237
Navajo Nation 18, 96, 101, 106, 108

## O

Osorio, Ruth 50, 57, 58

## P

Princess Benally 104
prison programs 20, 34
    education 17, 27, 44, 136
    LGBT Books to Prisoners 133, 135, 137, 142
promximate listening. *See* community listening
public art 18, 113, 151
Pulrang, Andrew 49, 54, 57, 64
PWI (predominantly white institution) 21, 74, 194

## Q

queer rhetorical listening. *See* rhetorical listening

## R

radio 19, 79, 131, 151
Randall 213
Ratcliffe, Krista 10, 14, 32, 44, 57, 60, 78, 83, 111, 136, 178, 203, 219
relational accountability 18, 94, 98, 113
relational listening. *See* community listening
respectful listening. *See* listening
responsibility 12, 13, 16, 18, 19, 30, 35, 73, 75, 81, 85, 87, 97, 98, 112, 141, 142, 156, 182
responsivity 12, 14, 97, 147, 163
rhetorical crip space 17, 48, 52, 56, 59, 61, 65
rhetorical empathy 219, 225, 236
rhetorical feminism 14, 62
rhetorical listening 9, 14, 32, 57, 83, 136, 203, 219
    feminist rhetorical listening 178
    queer rhetorical listening 176, 178
    rhetorical eavesdropping 9, 13, 14, 60, 136, 203, 204, 208
rhetorical resilience 19, 134, 137, 142, 148
    feminist rhetorical resilience 147
rhetoric and composition 7, 8, 11, 201, 217, 220
Rowan, Karen and Alexandra J. Cavallaro 6, 32, 83, 85, 87, 136, 179, 183, 219, 237
Royster, Jacqueline Jones 10, 13, 14, 176, 203
Royster, Jacqueline Jones and Gesa E. Kirsch 35, 73, 118

## S

settler colonialism 4, 78, 98, 112
Sins Invalid 57, 61, 64
Smilges, Logan 57, 60
SpeakOut! 42, 145
Stevenson, Bryan 30, 34, 40, 42, 43
Stone, Erica 6, 32, 86

Index

storied community listening. *See* community listening

storytelling 4, 6, 12, 14, 21, 98, 112, 148, 158, 162, 166, 170, 172, 179, 184, 208, 219

visual storytelling 96, 97, 98, 100, 112

## W

Washington County Community Remembrance Project (WCCRP) 198, 212

whiteness 12, 21, 60, 64, 74, 136, 182, 184, 189, 190, 193

white supremacy 12, 18, 65, 76, 78, 81, 83, 87, 96, 175, 181, 184, 187, 193

Wilson, Shawn 94, 97, 113

Wong, Alice 47, 49, 51, 53, 56, 59, 62, 63, 64

work before the work. *See* community listening